Tower 01: Plan
Elevation: p.9 (right)
Blank Panels: pp.94-95
Wood Grain Model: p.131
CLT Forecast: p.235

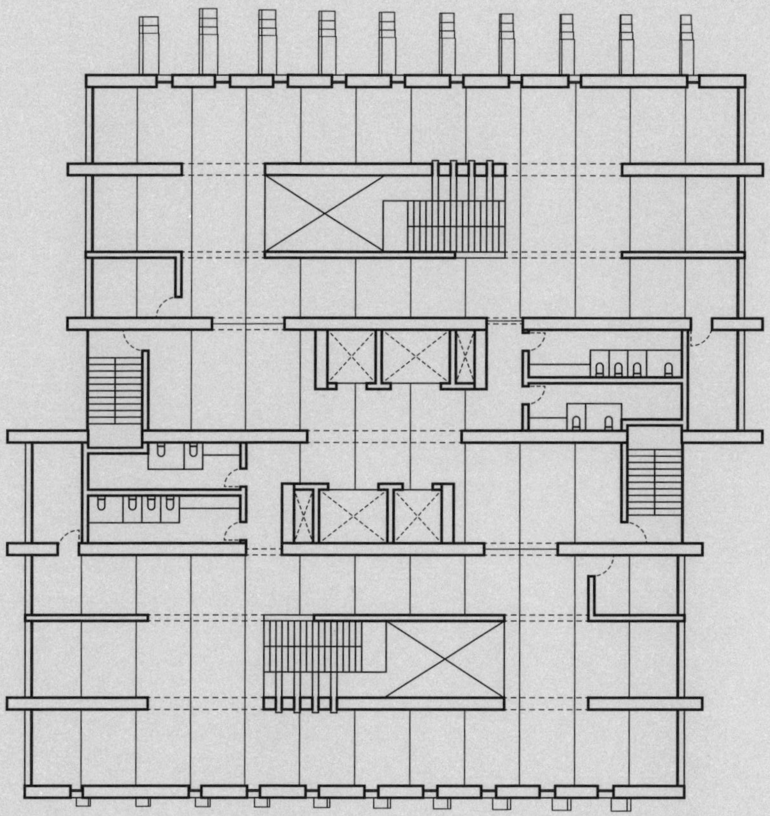

Tower 02: Plan
Elevation: p.9 (left)
Wood Grain Model: pp.132-33
Exploded Blanks: p.173
CLT Forecast: p.237

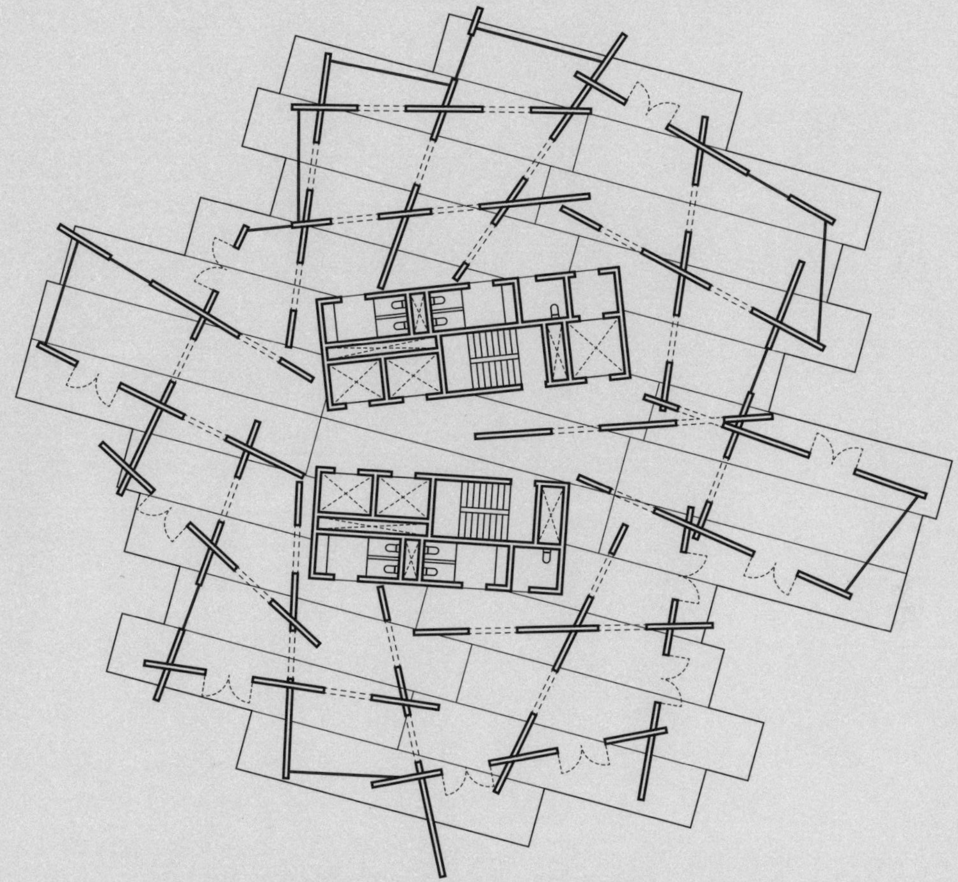

Tower 03: Plan
Elevation: p.11
Wood Grain Model: p.136
Exploded Blanks: p.176
CLT Forecast: p.236

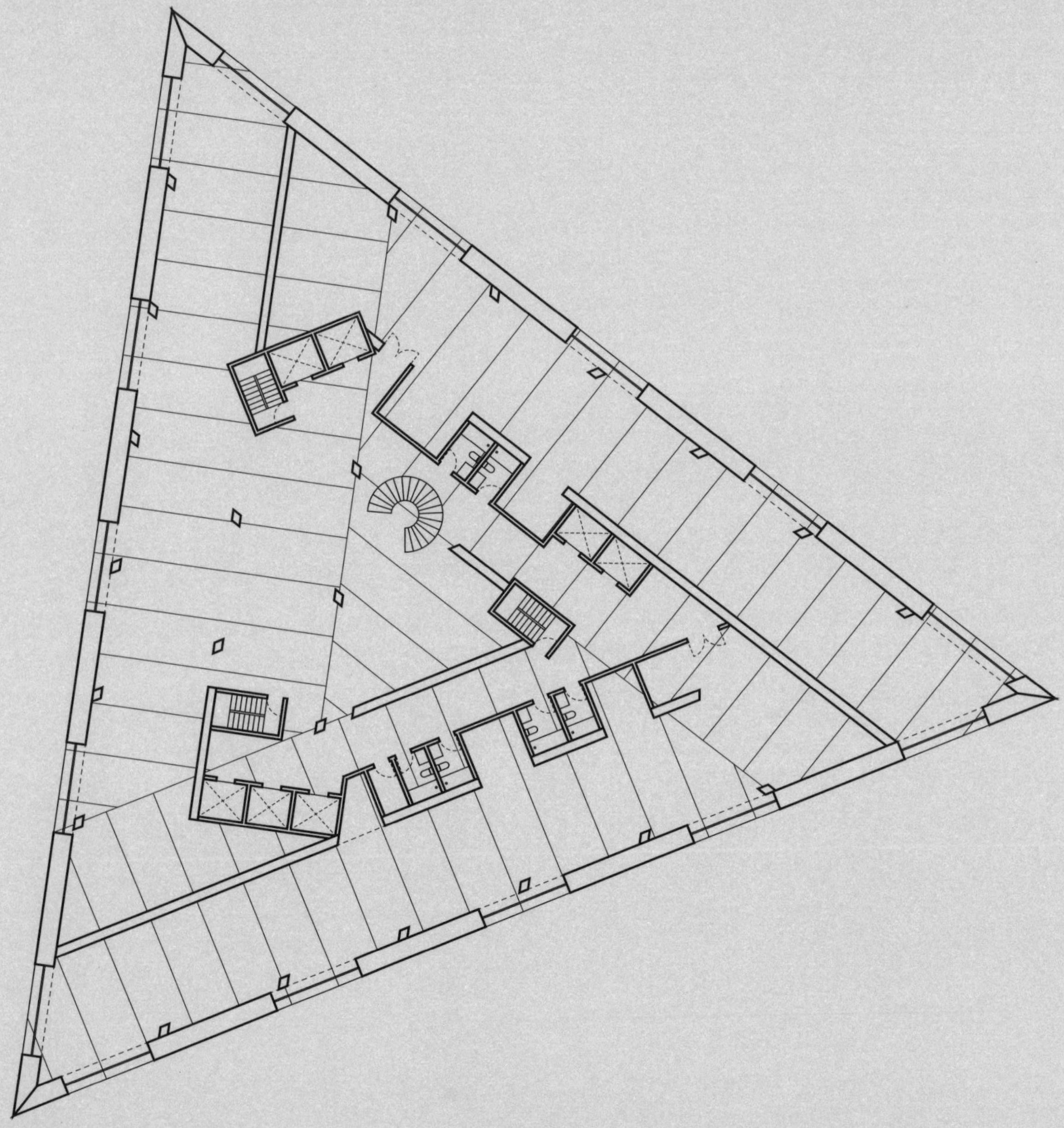

Tower 04: Plan
Elevation: p. 13 (left)
Wood Grain Model: pp. 142–43
CLT Forecast: p. 225

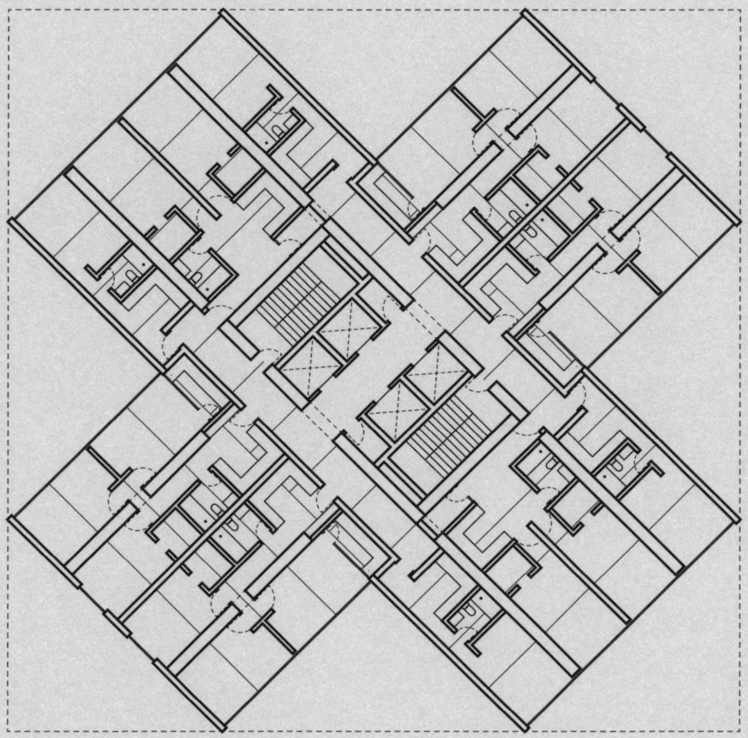

Tower 05: Plan
Elevation: p. 10 (right)
Wood Grain Model: p. 129

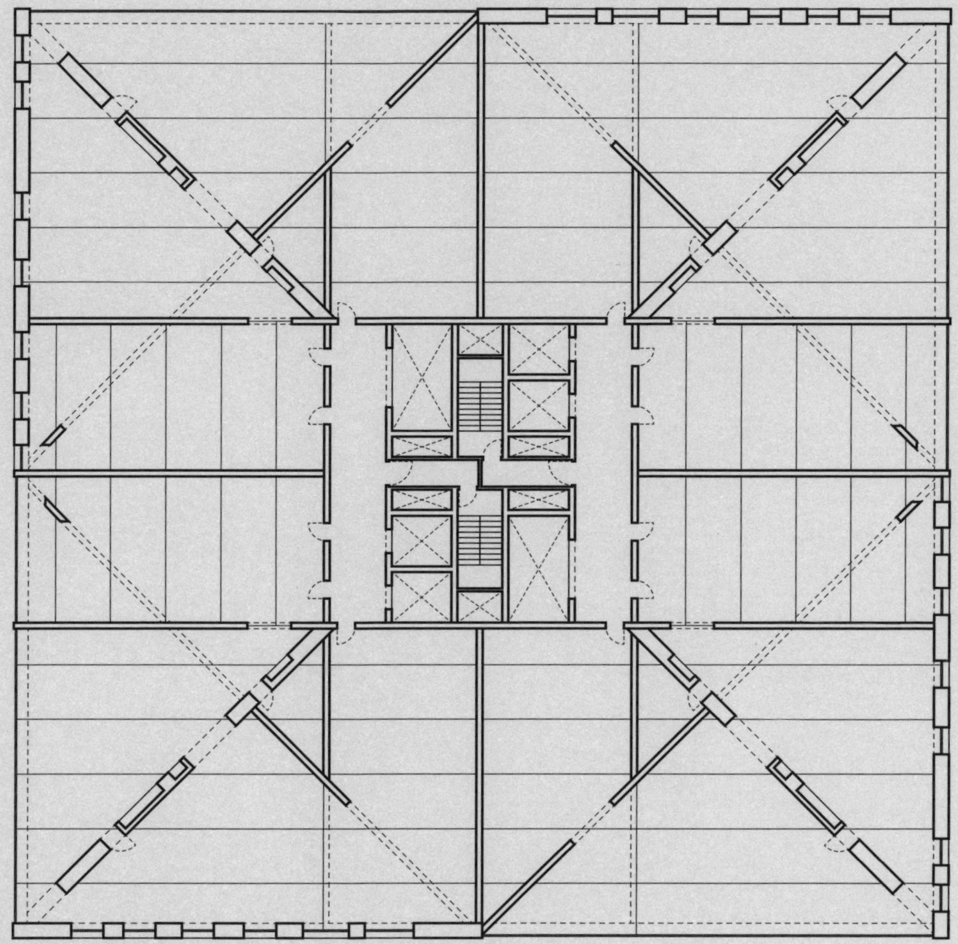

Tower 06: Plan
Elevation: p.12
Wood Grain Model: p.130
Exploded Blanks: p.175
CLT Forecast: p.226

Tower 07: Plan
Elevation: p.16 (right)
Wood Grain Model: p.144
CLT Forecast: p.231

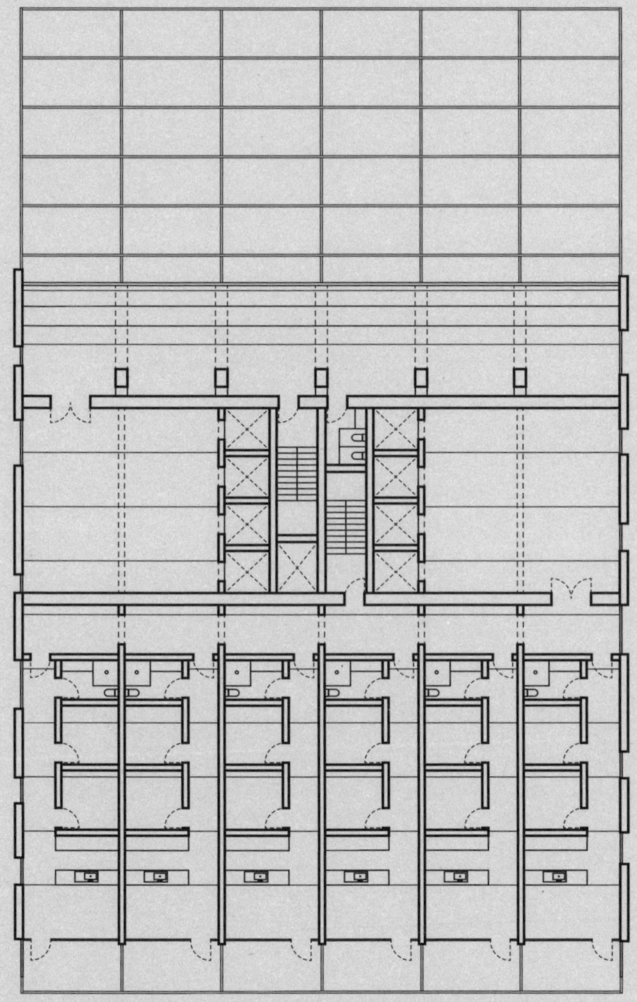

Tower 08: Plan
Elevation: p.13 (right)
Wood Grain Model: p.135
Exploded Blanks: p.174
CLT Forecast: p.227

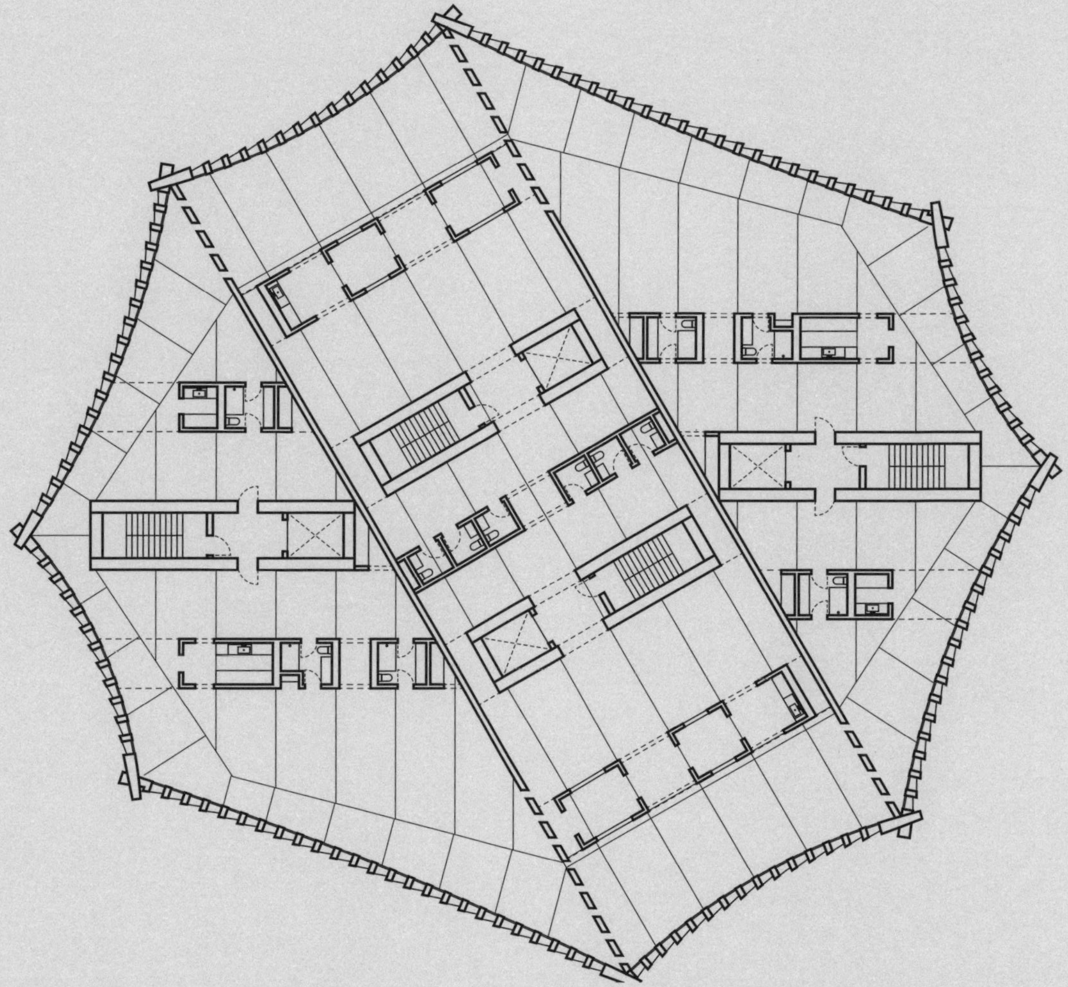

Tower 09: Plan
Elevation: p.16 (left)
Blank Panels: pp.98-99
Wood Grain Model: p.137
Structural Analysis: pp.202-5
CLT Forecast: p.233

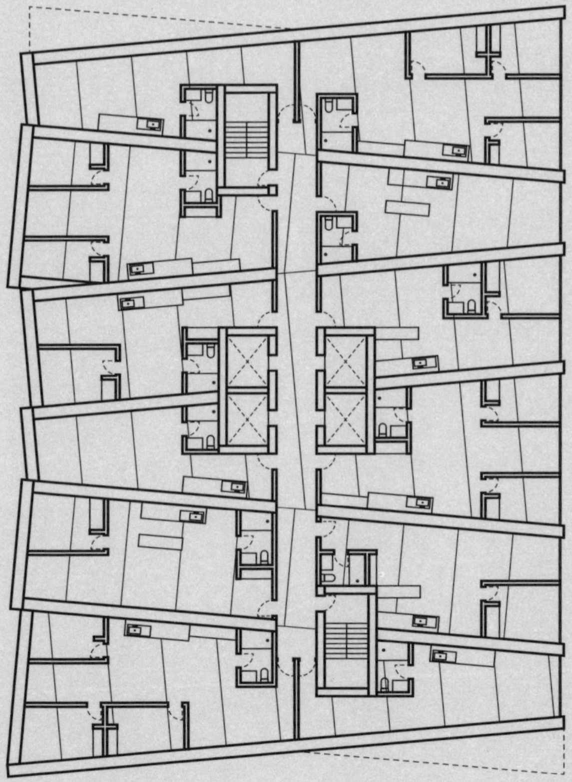

Tower 10: Plan
Elevation: p.14 (right)
Blank Panels: pp.96-97
Wood Grain Model: p.134
CLT Forecast: p.234

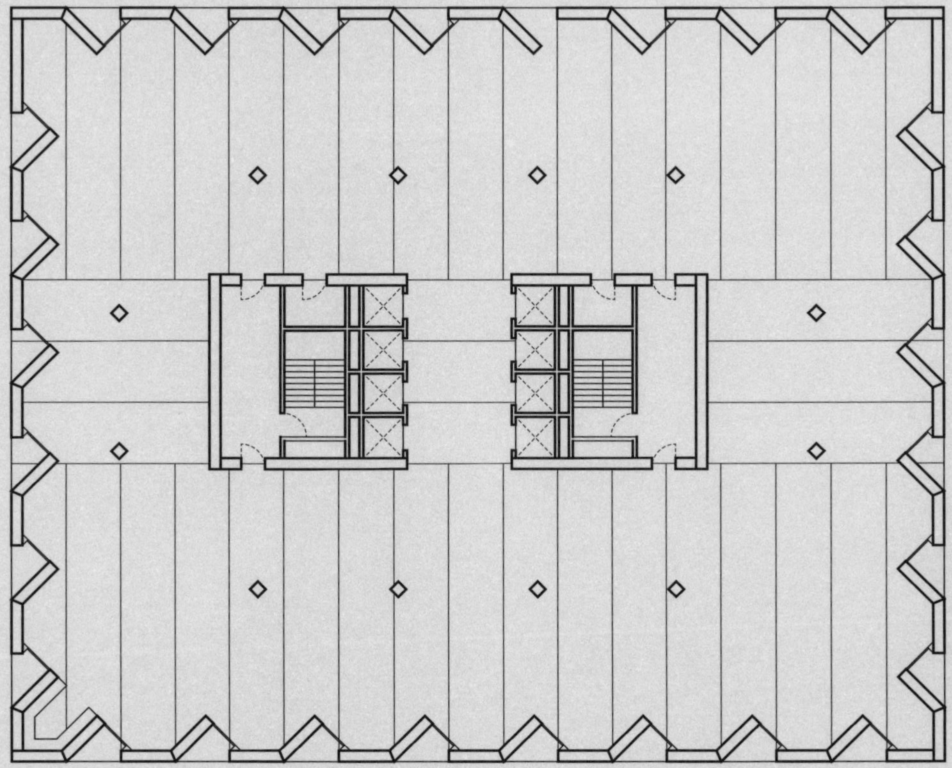

Tower 11: Plan
Elevation: p. 14 (left)
Blank Panels: pp. 92–93
Wood Grain Model: p. 140
Structural Analysis: pp. 206–9
CLT Forecast: p. 229

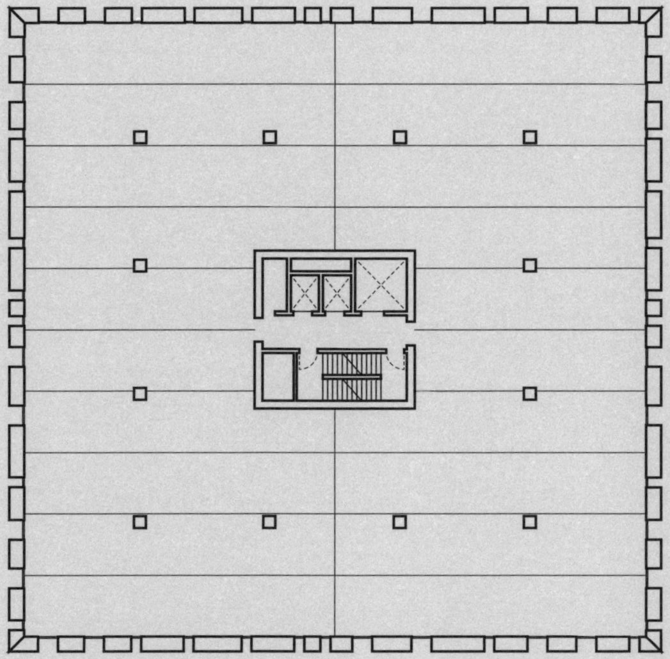

Tower 12: Plan
Elevation: p. 10 (left)
Wood Grain Model: pp. 138–39
CLT Forecast: p. 230

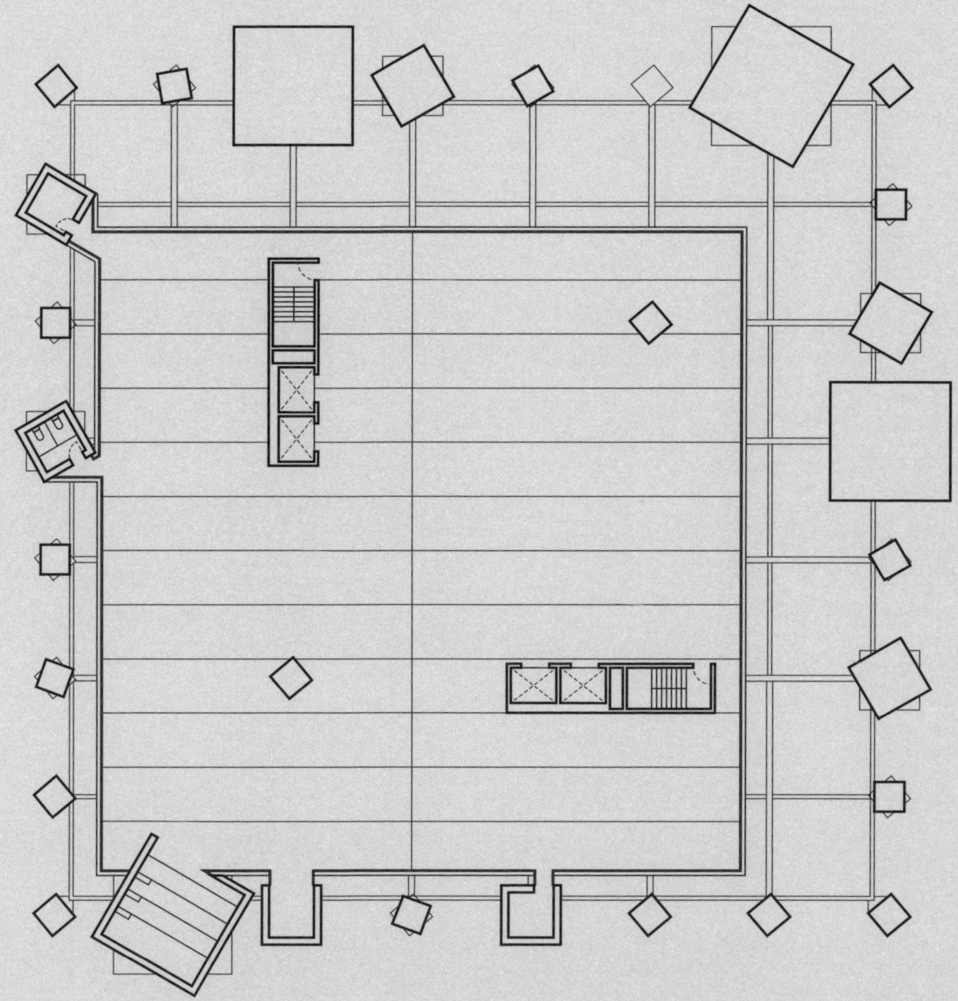

Tower 13: Plan
Elevation: p.15
Wood Grain Model: p.141
CLT Forecast: p.232

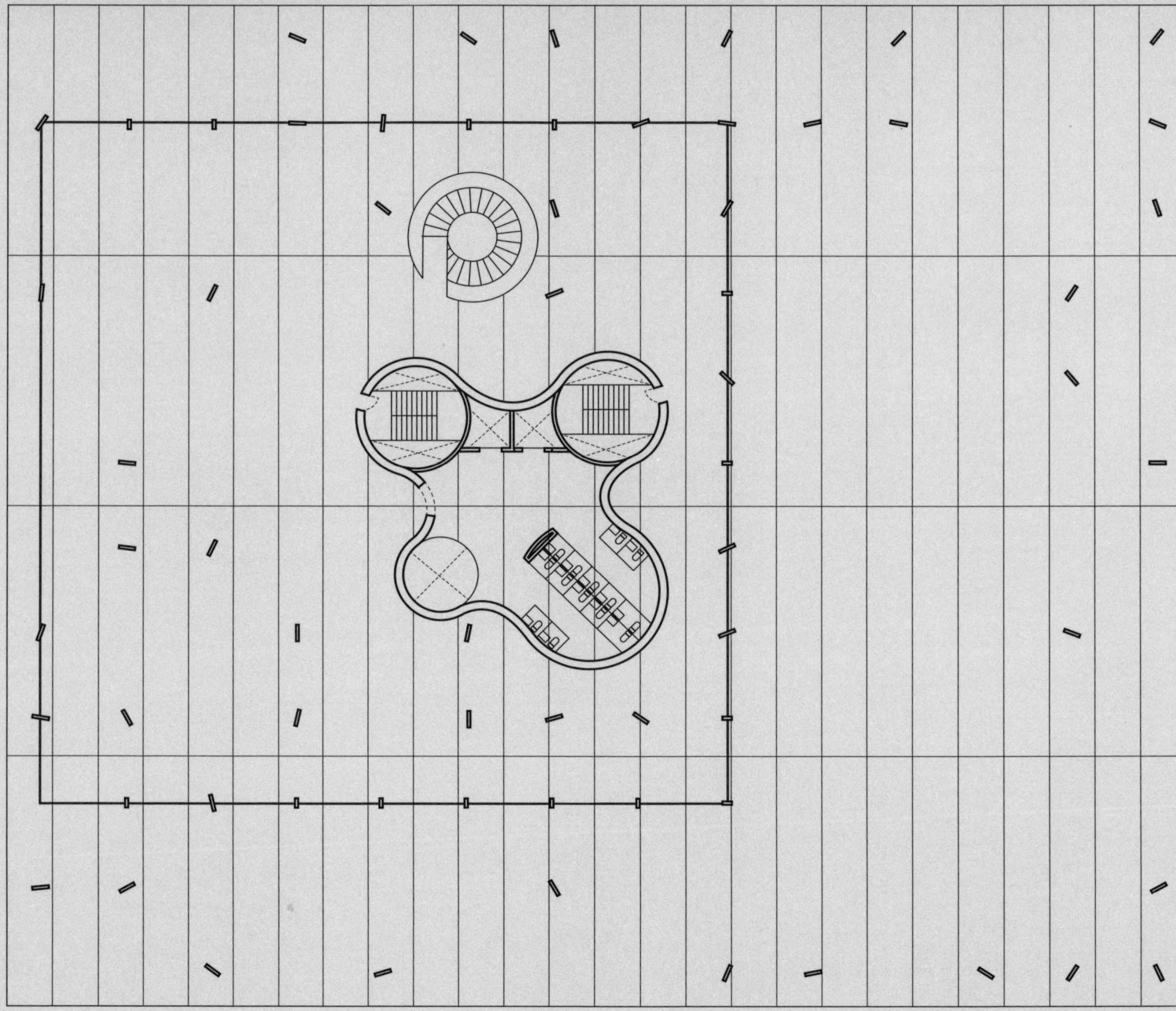

Tower 02: Elevation
Plan: p.1 (right)
Wood Grain Model: pp.132-33
Exploded Blanks: p.173
CLT Forecast: p.237

Tower 01: Elevation
Plan: p.1 (left)
Blank Panels: pp.94-95
Wood Grain Model: p.131
CLT Forecast: p.235

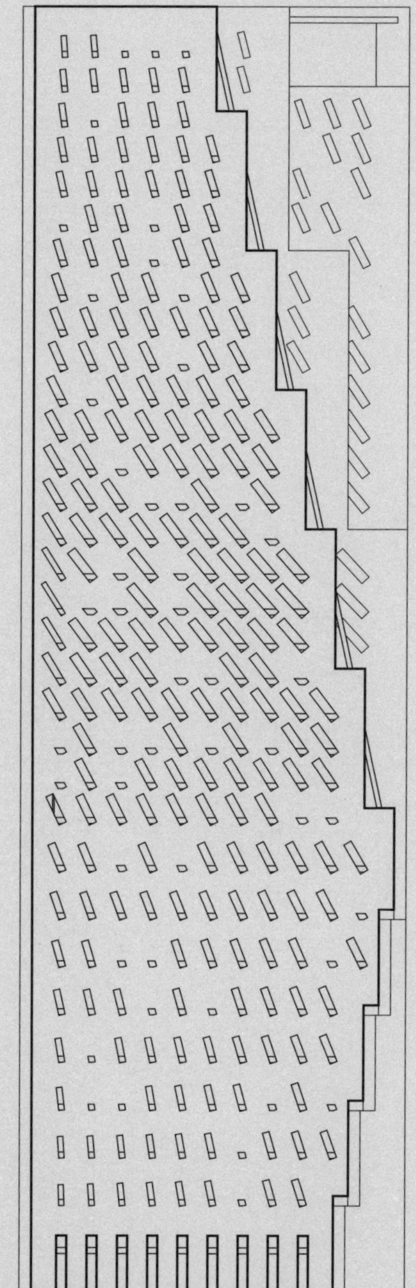

Tower 12: Elevation
Plan: p.7 (right)
Wood Grain Model: pp.138–39
CLT Forecast: p.230

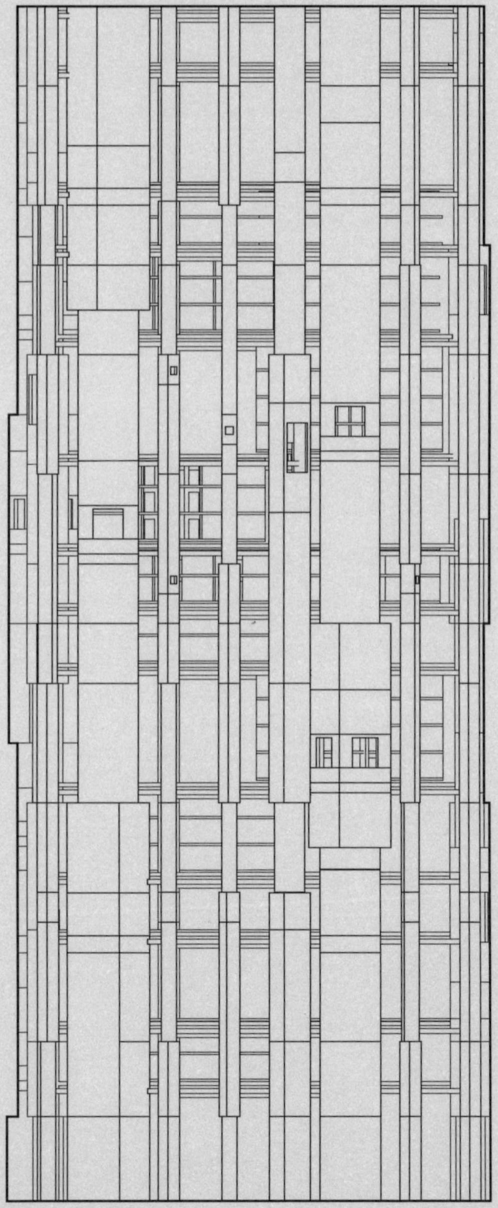

Tower 05: Elevation
Plan: p.3 (right)
Wood Grain Model: p.129

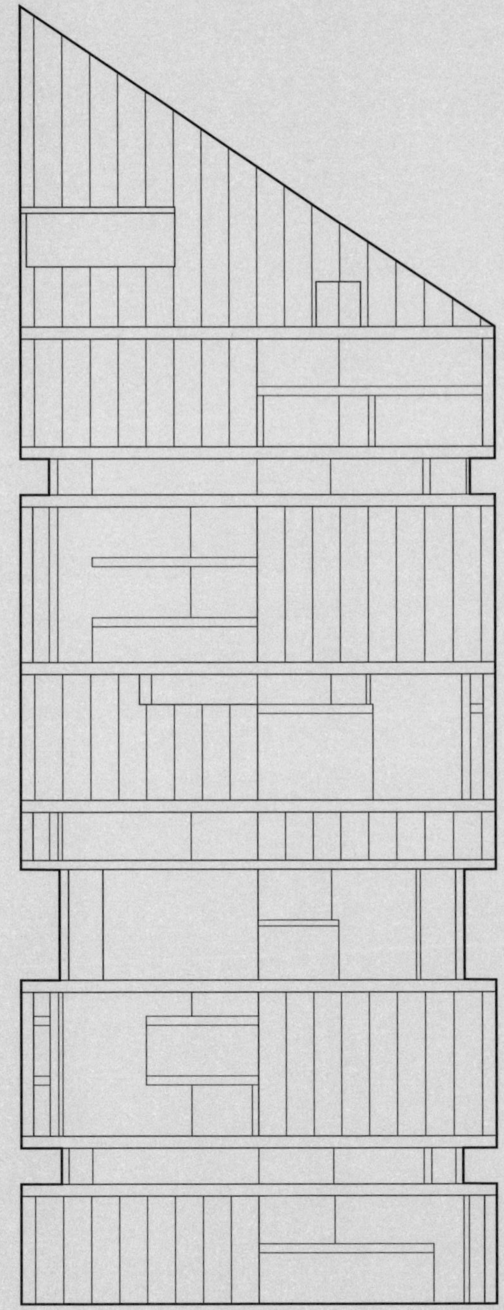

Tower 03: Elevation
Plan: p.2
Wood Grain Model: p.136
Exploded Blanks: p.176
CLT Forecast: p.236

Tower 06: Elevation
Plan: p.4 (left)
Wood Grain Model: p.130
Exploded Blanks: p.175
CLT Forecast: p.226

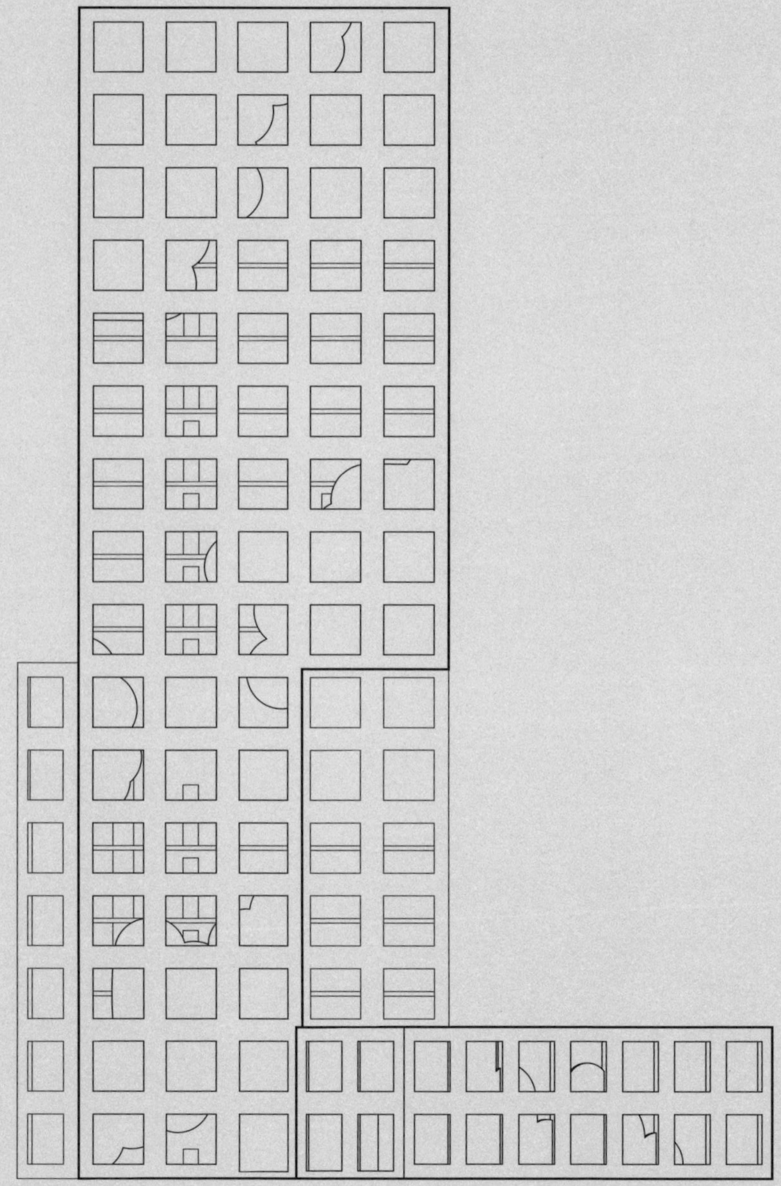

Tower 04: Elevation
Plan: p.3 (left)
Wood Grain Model: pp.142–43
CLT Forecast: p.225

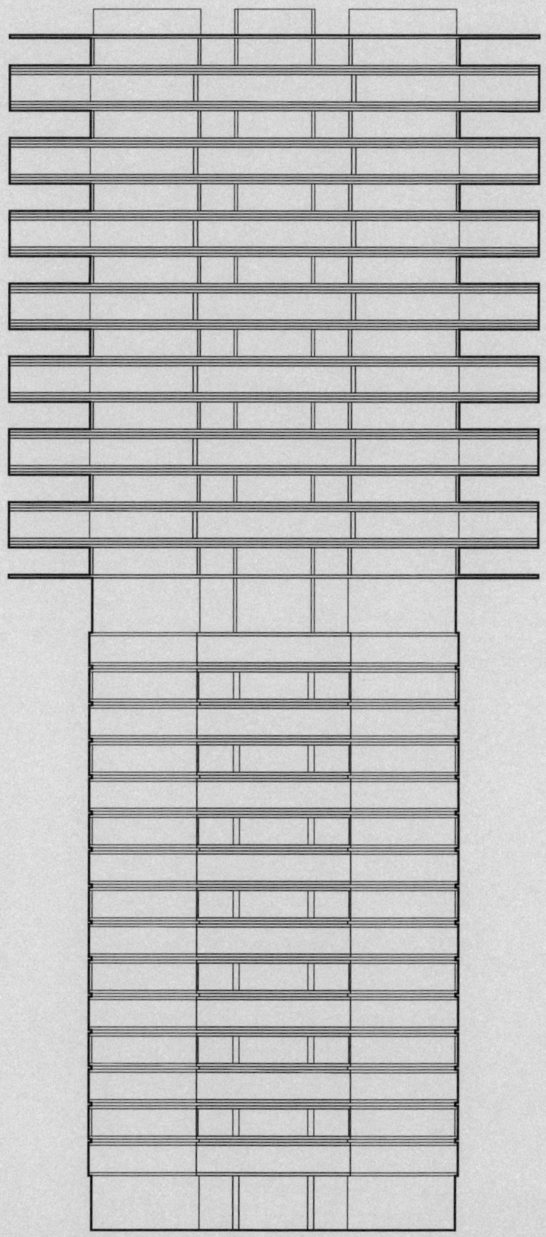

Tower 08: Elevation
Plan: p.5
Wood Grain Model: p.135
Exploded Blanks: p.174
CLT Forecast: p.227

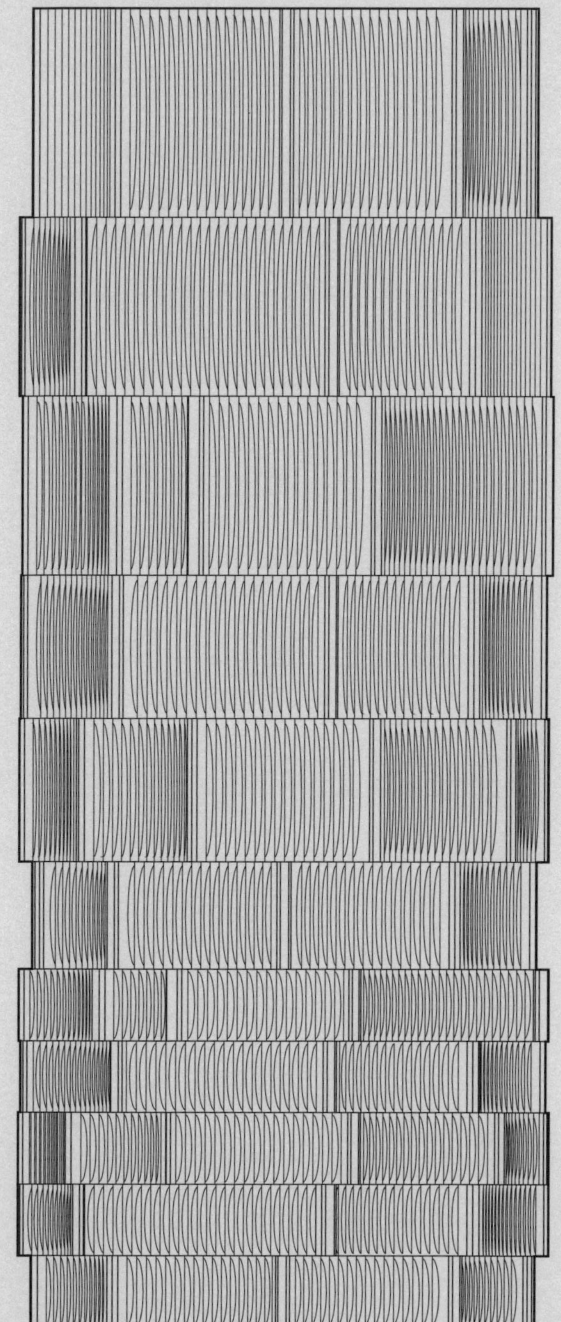

Tower 11: Elevation
Plan: p.7 (left)
Blank Panels: pp.92–93
Wood Grain Model: p.140
Structural Analysis: pp.206–9
CLT Forecast: p.229

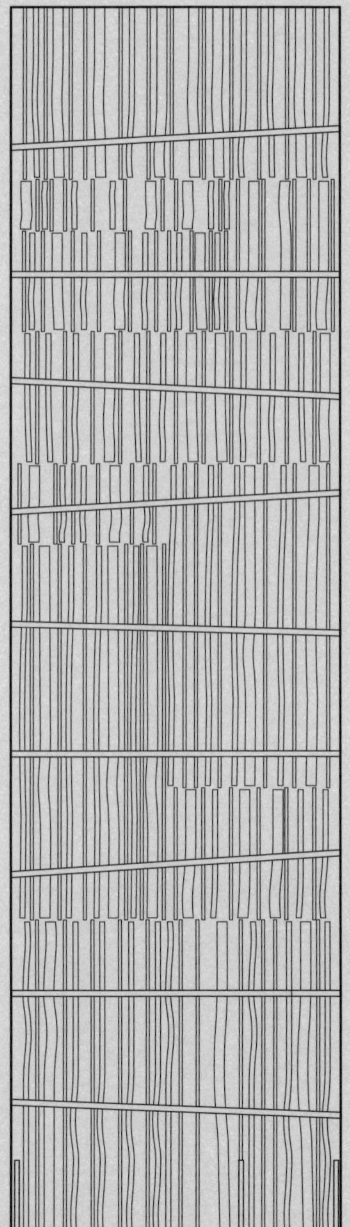

Tower 10: Elevation
Plan: p.6 (right)
Blank Panels: pp.96–97
Wood Grain Model: p.134
CLT Forecast: p.234

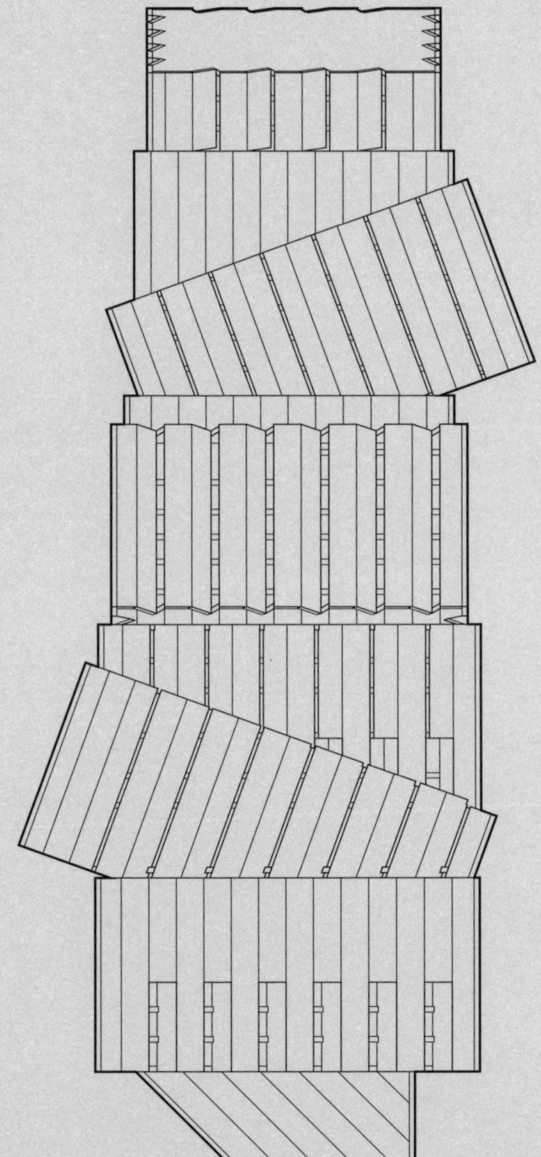

Tower 13: Elevation
Plan: p.8
Wood Grain Model: p.141
CLT Forecast: p.232

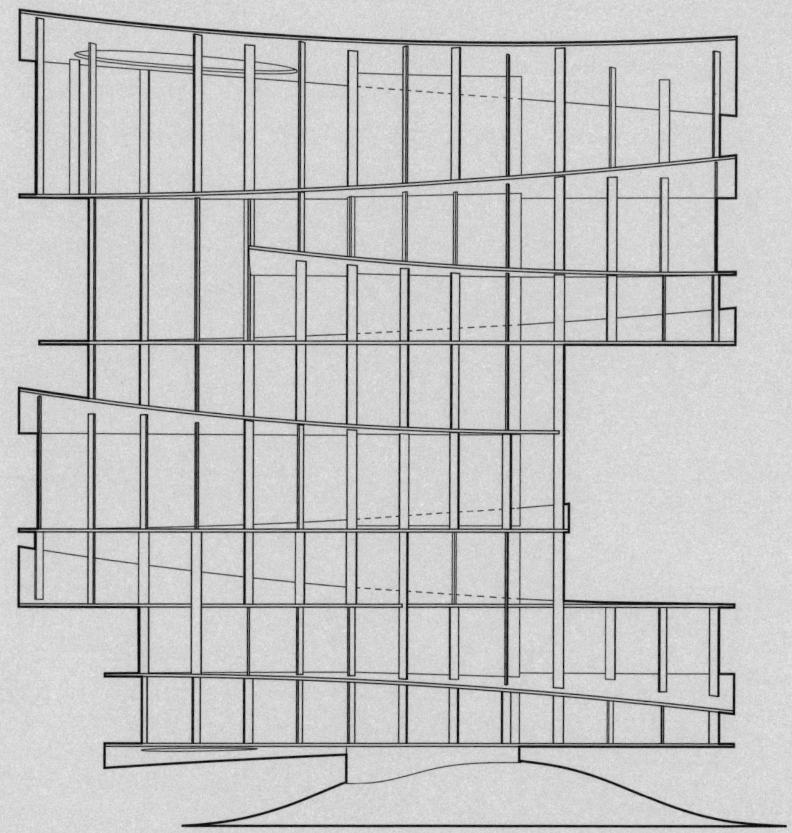

Tower 09: Elevation
Plan: p.6 (left)
Blank Panels: pp.98-99
Wood Grain Model: p.137
Structural Analysis: pp.202-5
CLT Forecast: p.233

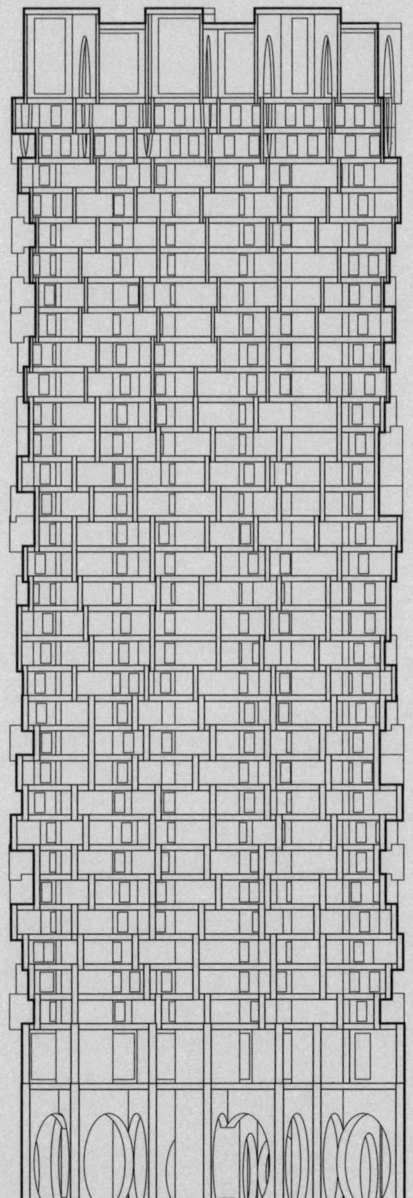

Tower 07: Elevation
Plan: p.4 (right)
Wood Grain Model: p.144
CLT Forecast: p.231

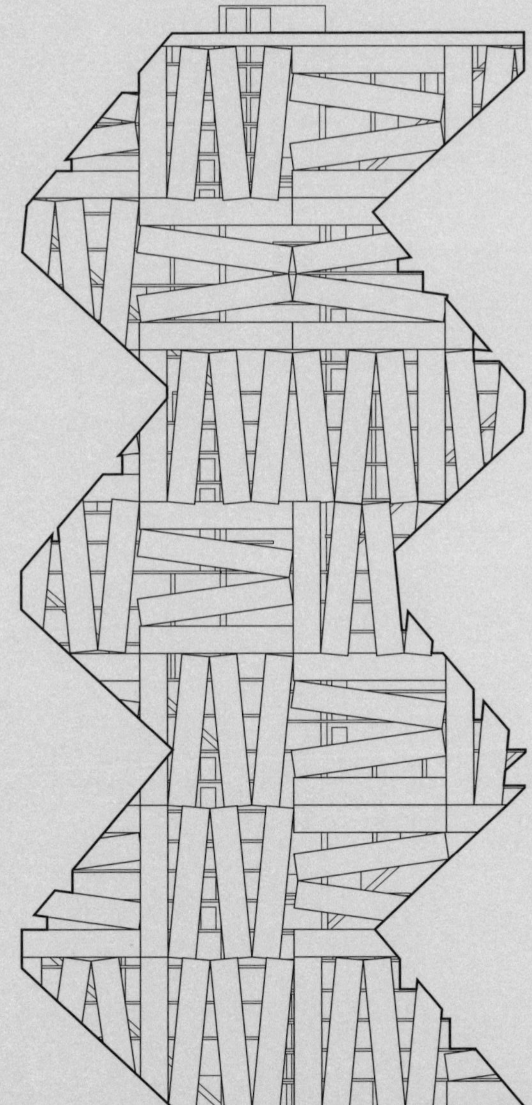

Blank:
Speculations
on CLT

Jennifer Bonner and
Hanif Kara, Editors

Published by Applied Research
and Design Publishing,
an imprint of ORO Editions.
Gordon Goff: Publisher

www.appliedresearchanddesign.com
info@appliedresearchanddesign.com

Editors
Jennifer Bonner and Hanif Kara

Associate Editor
Jayne Kelley

Research and Visualizations
Anna Goga and Edgar Rodriguez

Book Design
Neil Donnelly and Siiri Tännler

Project Manager
Jake Anderson

Project Contributors
Calvin Boyd
Benson Chien
Kyat Chin
Elif Erez
Daniel Garcia
Anna Goga
Ian Grohsgal
Edward Han Myo Oo
Anna Kaertner
Hiroshi Kaneko
Aryan Khalighy
Edgar Rodriguez
Alejandro Saldarriaga
Peeraya Suphasidh

10 9 8 7 6 5 4 3 2 First Edition

ISBN: 978-1-954081-02-4

Color Separations and Printing:
ORO Group Ltd.
Printed in China.

AR+D Publishing makes a continuous effort to minimize the overall carbon footprint of its publications. As part of this goal, AR+D, in association with Global ReLeaf, arranges to plant trees to replace those used in the manufacturing of the paper produced for its books. Global ReLeaf is an international campaign run by American Forests, one of the world's oldest nonprofit conservation organizations. Global ReLeaf is American Forests' education and action program that helps individuals, organizations, agencies, and corporations improve the local and global environment by planting and caring for trees.

Prologue: Built-in Sprezzatura

Erika Naginski

Like the ingénue, a new actor has made an entrance onto the stage shared by architecture and engineering: CLT, or cross-laminated timber, along with the blankness it proffers. The word *ingénue* seems fitting given the innocence and ingenuity in which it is etymologically inscribed; these qualities congregate as a sort of aura around CLT, which is novel and mediatic, mass-produced and environmentally sound. CLT is easy to cut and quick to span or stand upright; its manipulability, precision, impressionability, and carbon-absorptive capacities have an almost utopian cast. Hence, CLT bears the stamp of the cliché coined for the modern movement by the art critic Robert Hughes some decades ago—that is, the shock of the new.[1] Hence, too, the essays in this volume place importance on a dawning paradigm shift for which sampling, roll call, precedents, and analogies offered by high and low are necessary (art and architecture alongside popular culture). Kazimir Malevich, Henri Matisse, Le Corbusier, Agnes Martin, Mavis Pusey, Aldo Rossi, Brice Marden, Lauren Halsey, Jennifer Bolande, Big Freedia, Yeezy, Virgil Abloh, and so on: these interlocutors operate as more than a catalog of possible roles or formal and structural operations available to CLT; they lead by example, and call on CLT to enter into and have traction with a properly discursive arena, a world of critical dialogues, a purposeful entanglement with politics, society, and *res publica*—to save it from being faddish, a flash in the pan, a one-hit wonder, a thing used and abused by experts and marketers alike.

1 Robert Hughes, *The Shock of the New* (New York: Knopf, 1981).

Ornament and Structure

I evoke the shock of the new not only because of its (overused?) aesthetic currency but also because of its (inexorably!) constant refrain in explanations of technological transformations, as well as in the call for integrations of their frighteningly fast-paced temporality.[2] Yet when taking CLT's place in the discursive realms of design as a matter for serious contemplation—

2 This challenge for contemporary designers is addressed, for example, by Ajla Aksajami, *Integrating Innovation in Archi-tecture: Design,*

as the authors here do—it seems as crucial to turn to the shock of the old.[3] As I write this, I emphasize that the aim in these preliminary pages is not to offer some fulsome account of CLT's arrival to the agon of architecture and engineering—a history marked by spectacular junctures ranging from Bramante as *maestro ruinante* (pitting design acumen against engineering failures) to Enlightenment skirmishes between architects and engineers.[4] Hanif Kara is right to say that book needs to be written later. Rather, it is to leave the door ajar, momentarily, for a handful of past utterances so as to get at one or two profound contradictions CLT brings to the table (or floor or wall or roof).

Methods and Technology for Progressive Practice and Research (Chichester, UK: John Wiley & Sons, 2016).

3 I take my rhetorical lead from David Edgerton's *The Shock of the Old: Technology and Global History Since 1900* (New York: Oxford University Press, 2006).

4 See James S. Ackerman, "Notes on Bramante's Bad Reputation," in *Studi bramanteschi: Atti del Congresso internazionale* (Rome: De Luca Editore, 1974), 339–49; and Antoine Picon, *French Architects and Engineers in the Age of the Enlightenment* (French ed. 1988; Cambridge: Cambridge University Press, 1992).

Even before entering Erin Putalik's history of modern plywood, read this commentary by an eighteenth-century ébeniste: "The kind of carpentry I will treat, although less consequential than building (in other words, assemblage), nevertheless demands the most immaculate precision on the part of the Worker, or more correctly, the Artist . . . who must join to real experience of the practice, an infinity of theoretical knowledge."[5] What he goes on to describe, of course, are the skills of veneer and marquetry in which joinery, carpentry, and the manipulation of surface effects meld with wood grain, tree species, chemistry, projective geometry, and the appearance of the solid in the skin of things; this melding is highlighted in gorgeous plates whose whorls, spots, sprays, fans, strata, arrays, and wordless, rhythmic calligraphies animate the luminous glow of intricate geometries attempting to contain them (with engraving an apt metaphor for inlay). Already in this early modern enunciation of mono-medium, lamination, and a flat, planar condition, we find the need to join (*joindre*) art and science, practice and epistemology. In all this, our Artist is pointedly aware of the potential for surface and structure to collide and coalesce—musing on the chance that ornament and structure, in their seamless assemblage, might seem or even be the same thing, a tectonic surface.

5 My translation. André Jacob Roubo, *L'Art du menuisier-ébeniste* (Paris: Saillant et Nyon, 1774), 763.

Well, CLT has brought this to fore, hasn't it, in the shocking simultaneity with which it behaves as ornament and structure. It is difficult to apply the Derridean *parergon*, in which the decorative is that which is added (cosmetics) to bring out the substantive essence (cosmos) of some thing—or what the anthropologist and curator Rafael Schacter has expressed in a book on graffiti as the supplement exposing the interior, "the innate fissure within its adjunctive partner."[6] With CLT, they can be one and the same, moving beyond elegant dovetailing (of flaring tenon and mortise) to oceanic fusion (in a flat, blank entity).

6 Rafael Schacter, *Ornament and Order: Graffiti, Street Art, and the Parergon* (Burlington, VT: Ashgate, 2014), 36.

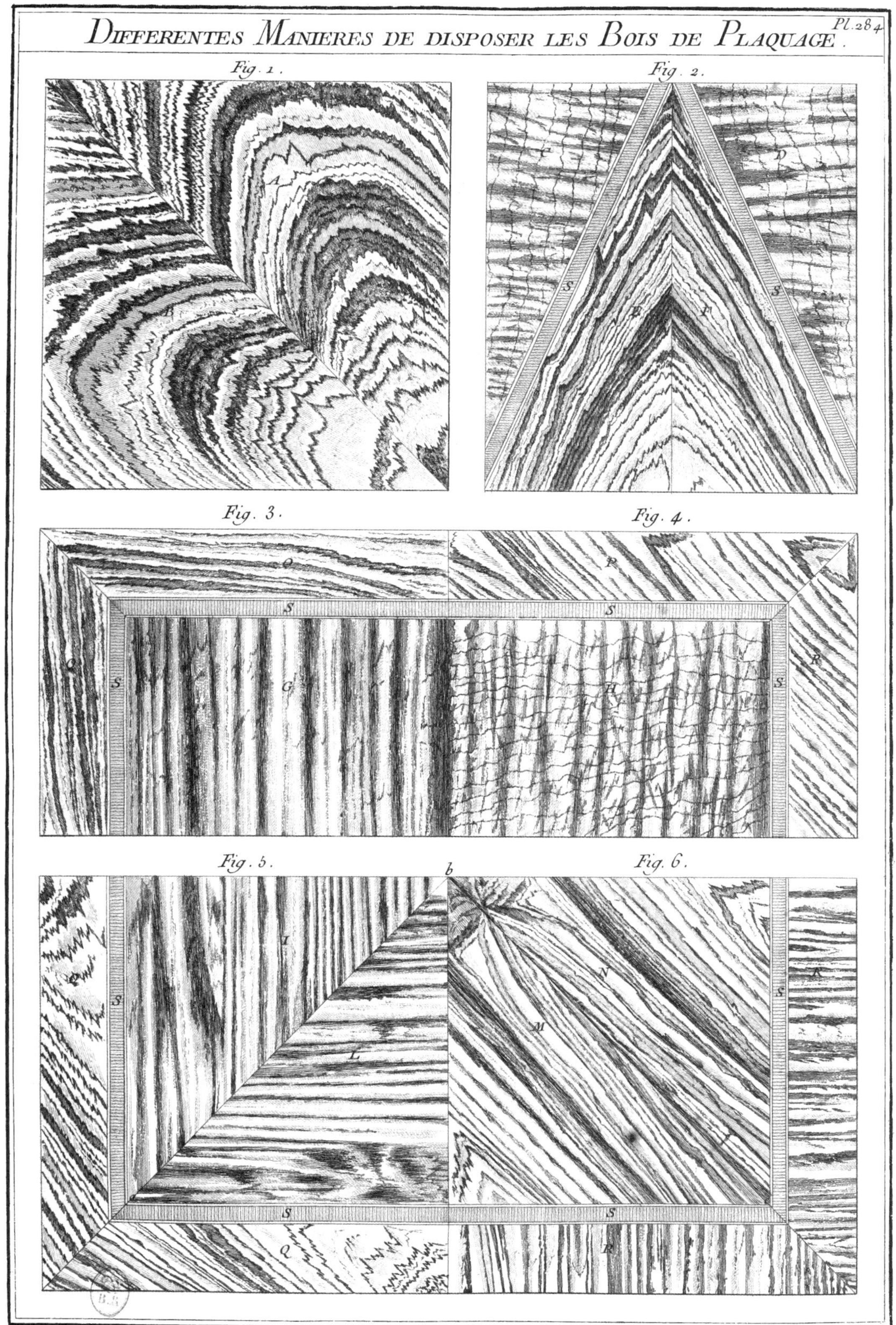

André Jacob Roubo, "Différentes Manières de disposer les Bois de Plaquage" (Different ways of arranging wood veneers), plate 284 from André Jacob Roubo, *L'Art du menuisier-ébéniste* (Paris: Saillant et Nyon, 1774).

In this sense, CLT might be understood as the destruction of the proscenium, or more rightly, its ubiquity. CLT's is quite a performance along these lines, and to elicit the early modern theatrics defined by the Italian courtier and diplomat Baldassare Castiglione in 1528, *sprezzatura*-like—a nonchalant masque of one's own careful crafting worn to project the ease, even casual effortlessness, with which one accomplishes hard tasks (even Sam Jacob alludes in his essay to the difficulty "lurking" in the slick supergraphic). With CLT, this could be serving as either stage curtain or the tower's essential frame. Simple, just like that.

In this regard, the enthralling speed of building a CLT structure—the filmic riveting on blanks swinging in the air from an on-site crane so as to transition from a horizontal pile to an upright posture or participatory element in a construction like Jennifer Bonner's Haus Gables—has precedents (think Henri Rivière riffing on Hokusai's woodblock prints to show off the mythic spectacle of labor required to erect the Eiffel Tower). Likewise, the way a full-scale CLT construction looks like a model of itself in, for example, Ultramoderne's Chicago Horizon reignites the philosophical intensity of the various liaisons translating drawings to models to buildings. But there is something new in the old here—something that takes old-world politics of revealing and concealing to the contemporary scene. Just as Instagram tempts as a means by which to depict some version of the ideal self for others to see and admire, CLT, for all it is mass-produced, functions as a space for fantasy, vogueing, appearance, and self-determination both structurally and ornamentally.

A new kind of *fort-da*? We had better not be drawing blanks with our blanks, as there is a projective cast here, to use Robin Evans's term, that has brought *sprezzatura* to the screen.

After Timber Trends, or Speculations on the Cross-Laminated Timber Blank

Jennifer Bonner and Hanif Kara

Blank

It is important to state from the very beginning of this book why we would like to direct attention away from generalities about mass timber and toward the specificity of the cross-laminated timber (CLT) blank. For decades, mass timber—structural wood in the form of large panels—has garnered robust support from architects, engineers, manufacturers, and journalists as *the* material capable of lowering the building industry's carbon footprint. The urgency of creating climate-responsive architecture has inadvertently hijacked nearly all conversations around this method of construction. And its advantages are clear: not only does wood sequester carbon, CLT is also substantially lighter and quicker to work with than steel and concrete. Mass timber, produced through sustainable forestation, allows a return to socioecological interactions that are limited by physical and biological systems, dislocating cultures of "take, make, and dispose" through a better understanding and use of resources.

But admirable and "correct" narratives around CLT's potential role in tempering the climate crisis often miscalculate, or just underestimate, what this material has to offer. As an architect and an engineer, we believe the CLT blank can and must be conceptualized *beyond* its sustainability. Ripe for interpretation by a generation of contemporary architects, historians, engineers, and critics, the CLT blank, it turns out, is not so blank after all.

What is a blank? To draw an overly simple analogy, if masonry is a construction method that uses bricks or stones, then cross-laminated timber is a construction method that uses blanks. The blank is a material unit made up of layers of wood, an anisotropic material—its strength differs across and against its grain. Individual pieces of lumber are finger-jointed and then glued together, stacked in alternating directions at right angles to one another. Pressed into three-, five-, and seven-ply composites, the laminated panels have an odd number of layers, so the grain of the outermost layers runs in the same direction. Mechanized processes of sorting, grading, planing, gluing, clamping, and chamfering allow an individual piece of softwood to become a hardened, factory-assembled blank, an industrialized object ready to be used.

Yet despite this ready-made quality, the blank is not so straightforward. It lends itself to a variety of imprecise, if still useful, descriptors: "exaggerated plywood," "oversized sheet material," "scaled-up, laminated 2-by-6s." A definition of any building material typically includes certain information, like dimensions, material properties, and weight. But even stating the regular dimensions of a blank—seemingly an easy task, just as the construction industry understands the standard dimensions of a brick[1] or the nominal versus actual sizes of lumber—quickly leaves one sorting through manufacturers' catalogs and interpreting dozens of charts. The blank is not standardized; rather, each CLT manufacturer determines the dimensions and properties of its product. Panel sizes range from 1 foot to 10 feet in width and 39 feet to 52 feet in length, while the laminate ply has varying thicknesses of 4, 7, and 11 inches, depending on the specs for each lamination. Scaled for mobility, blanks are sized to fit shipping containers and the beds of transport trucks.

A standard brick is 3 5/8 inches by 2 1/4 inches by 8 inches.

This built-in flexibility arises primarily from external conditions. But we believe the blank has even more multivalent potential for architecture—potential we argue designers and engineers should have a more active role in defining. The blank can do a lot. Given their density and thermal mass, blanks can perform well as external walls; they are easily manipulated on-site, but also allow openings to be located with much greater freedom. (Doing the same with concrete, for example, is far more complex because of the material's weight and the placement of rebar.) One structural form might require the blank as a load-bearing wall (interior or exoskeleton), but another might use the blank as a folded roof plate. In both cases, the blank is subjected to vastly different loads—axial loads, parallel or perpendicular to the grain, or bending stresses.

As it accommodates countless structural interpretations, the blank also decisively shifts architectural paradigms. For example, large spanning blanks used in the roof of a house result

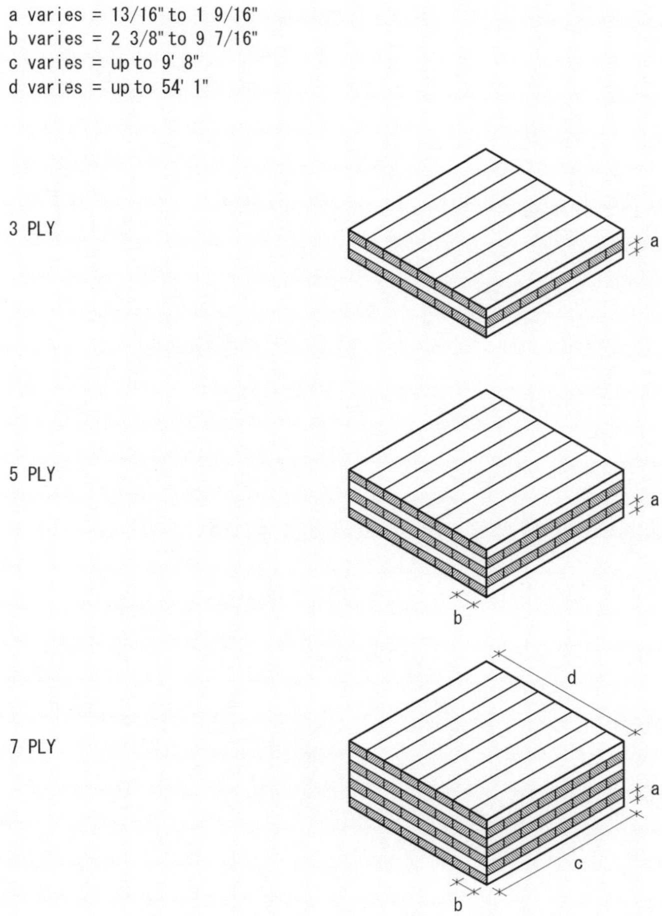

Components and typical associated dimensions of CLT panels

in domestic interiors reimagined as connected volumes, opening up living rooms and bedrooms that might be subdivided otherwise. On the other hand, when blanks are distributed as load-bearing walls in another type, the mid-rise tower, the interior space planning of the open office comes under siege. The open plan shifts radically into a more compartmentalized organization.

The blank offers similar leeway for elevations. One architect might use the blank like a brick, incrementally assembling a facade, while another cuts up the blank in order to serve specific geometry. And then there is what might be the blank's most significant contribution: the potential reunion of structure and finish material. The blank is both, at a much larger scale than brick and stone.

The material's ability to span two directions—to act as wall and floor, with endless cuts for apertures and thresholds—allows blanks to be rotated in any direction and connected seamlessly through a series of linear joints along their longitudinal edges. When creating panel-to-panel connections, engineers are concerned with the in- and out-of-plane forces.[2] Solved with surface splines or half-lapped joints, the connection of two blanks swiftly doubles the blank's surface. To demonstrate sheer heft, imagine a scenario where the blank is repeated multiple times, scaling up the single unit into yet another mega-unit, an expanded surface in elevation (or plan). A large wall or roof plane measuring 50 feet tall and 50 feet wide is quickly achievable with only five blanks.

The architectural duo Ultramoderne, whose principal Yasmin Vobis is a contributor to this book, understood both the efficiency and the theatrics of the blank's expanded surface in the 2015 project Chicago Horizon. Vobis and Aaron Forrest, working with engineer Brett Schneider, significantly advanced the two-way spanning capacity of the blank by using seven three-ply blanks in one direction laminated with seven three-ply blanks rotated 90 degrees. Splined together and then stacked, their 8-foot-by-56-foot blanks—cross-laminated twice, in both their assembly and application—produced a 56-foot-by-56-foot roof plane for a pavilion that spectacularly demonstrates what the blank can do.

Regardless of how manufacturers, architects, and engineers define and dimension the material unit, the blank's seemingly limitless nature announces a pivotal moment in the discipline of architecture. The field is always in search of materials that not only maintain generic properties, but can also be individually interpreted and implemented across a wide range of scales. The blank's ability to accommodate any building type, along with a comprehensive gamut of design and engineering scenarios, has made it architecture's next darling.

But before we continue exploring the implications of the blank, a practical note: Although we have made a series of claims around the lack of determination, inconsistency of sizing, and the scale-shifting quality of the blank as a building unit, we would like to leave the reader with a fixed size in mind in order to anchor our extrapolations. For the remainder of the book, when you read the term *blank*, imagine a panel roughly 9 feet wide and 50 feet long.

Blankness

The blank is a central object in the many interpretations of CLT put forward by the book's contributors. But *blank* is an adjective, too, not only a noun. The book positions the properties of the blank parallel to a conceptual inquiry into *blankness*. For us, this sort of blank does not

CLT Handbook, US edition (Point-Claire, QC: FPInnovations and Binational Softwood Lumber Council, 2013), 7.

mean minimal or empty. Instead, it defines an architecture that engages the aesthetic and conceptual qualities of the blank.

In this sense, more important than the blank's precise dimensions—the size at which a specific blank might enter the world—is its proportion. A quick survey of examples from everyday culture and art practice illustrates how other objects we might describe as blank suggest particular proportions. Whether oriented in portrait or landscape format, US letter or A4, the ubiquitous, iconic white sheet of paper is not square. You may not know the exact number of pixels that make up a PowerPoint slide, yet you know it to be a horizontal frame, a screen-like proportion. Kazimir Malevich's 1918 *Suprematist Composition: White on White* is recognizable as a square format that depicts a tilted square (well, almost a square). Likewise, the CLT blank carries an implied association with the proportion of another known industrial object: the 2-by-12, one of the many pieces of lumber used in traditional wood framing. Linear, long, and board-like, the blank recalls its stick-frame predecessor.

White paper, a white screen, and *White on White* all rely on a lack of color to define an infinite condition. The CLT blank exchanges colorlessness for the graphic of a soft wood grain. This swap suggests an important distinction: such blankness is loaded with the aesthetics of a material, and for CLT this means the inconsistent, infinite variation of knots. At a particular distance from the blank, the wood's grain is not detectable; it appears merely beige in color. Up close, the blank exhibits a characteristic series of soft squiggles, as the grains of wood are identifiable, idiosyncratic, and filled with personality. Because of its many potential applications, the blank is fundamentally tied to these two readings, which the observer witnesses at two different distances. As the blank moves from facade to interior and back, its wood grain flickers in and out of focus—an effect the blankness of a white piece of paper could never produce. Although some might consider the blank cold and industrial, it's not bare or bleak. Its blankness is materially specific, filled with grain and multidirectional.

Blankness also flattens. In her contribution to this book, Courtney Coffman explores techniques of redaction and composition to distinguish between forms of blankness in art and visual practices. But she makes another important claim, one that's less visual and more metaphorical: the blank is a structural system that both flattens materials and integrates architecture and engineering during the construction process. We think she's right. Sam Jacob is in agreement; his essay points to the cartoon-like quality of CLT, an ability to be surface and structure all in one, that flattens the "arcane knowledge" of architecture and brings drawing and building closer together. Flat-packed and installed on-site, the blank is also reminiscent of architectural model-making supplies—foam core, chipboard, and cardstock. Planar blanks deployed to make a three-dimensional volume still somehow appear flat and thin when hoisted into place, a sleight of hand that elides the difference between model and building. Yasmin Vobis's essay, "Ten Points on CLT Models and Public Performance," explores these themes, converting model-making clichés into new ways of reading CLT. Paired with images of Ultramoderne's Chicago Horizon, her points zoom in and out of physical models, wandering into fantasy and then re-grounding the reader in what she calls models' "wrongness"—a provocation that upends any notion that there is a "right" way to build with this material.

Lamination

Blank is a constellation of essays centering contemporary topics of architecture, such as flatness, materiality, surface, and representation, in discussions of and projections around CLT. It recognizes and addresses the immediate need to conceptualize the CLT blank before defaulting to a case-study approach based on limited examples of built work. Simply put, our ambition—which has governed our editorial process and the selection of contributors—is to make claims for the discipline that challenge, enrich, and expand upon the dominant North American discourse on mass timber.

As editors, we have made a conscious effort to assemble a group of writers with varied backgrounds in the field. Some authors are architects who have built with mass timber (like Vobis, Chris Lee, and Nader Tehrani), while others have only just begun to engage the material (like Sean Canty). Some are scholars or designers who haven't worked with CLT at all (like Coffman and Jacob)—but we believe their research and approaches have something to offer to our understanding of the material. It is our intention to establish purposeful intersections and adjacencies among these perspectives.

Although a few of the contributors and their practices are based in Europe or Asia, their academic ties are to North American universities and institutions. We leverage this common ground in order to frame thinking about the CLT blank through two types: the American house and the mid-rise tower (which are most often identified with wood-frame and steel construction, respectively). By overlaying mass timber onto these two historically loaded types, we are suggesting a rapid exchange of material tectonics and volumetric consequences, while at the same time redirecting the field.

Chris Lee references the historical Chicago frame and the contemporaneity of CLT in "Essential Planes," a consideration of the structural grammar of plates and planes in the design of towers. Erin Putalik, a historian of plywood, draws parallels between the ready-made CLT blank and the manufacturing of plywood sheets and surface patterns via a series of experimental houses built in the 1930s and 1940s. Sean Canty continues in this vein of material experimentation by situating the design of three houses with "absent spatial centers" alongside elisions in the practices of Ellsworth Kelly, Lucio Fontana, Céline Condorelli, and SANAA. To enable the curvature that has become a key aspect of his larger project, Canty's houses work with the CLT cassette, a blended construction technique composed of CLT blanks and stressed-skin balloon frames. Nader Tehrani and NADAAA have built extensively with laminar wood as part of a larger engagement with what Tehrani calls a "mono-medium ethic." His piece convincingly lays out how a precise focus on a single material, including a full embrace of its complexities and implications for construction, can advance design thinking. His position captures the essence of the book: directing twelve contributors' attention to the CLT blank teases out inventive trajectories for architecture's immediate future.

To escape architectural hang-ups about technique, we also look to art practices. The book presents a visual essay around works by two Los Angeles–based artists: Lauren Halsey's *The Crenshaw District Hieroglyph Project (Prototype Architecture)*, and a series of works by Jennifer Bolande, including *Plywood Curtains*. In *The Crenshaw District Hieroglyph Project*, Halsey etches figures, representations of materials, and graffiti tags into white drywall assembled as a pavilion in the context of South Central Los Angeles. She fills in blankness with messages for the audience; her cuts both define an aesthetic and communicate meaning. We see direct correlations between her cut-and-scored drawings and the computer numerical control (CNC) machine fundamental to any CLT manufacturer, whose typical fabrication of a blank might involve routing drawings into a panel's surface. Similarly, we can imagine Bolande's curtains as a digitally routed bas-relief; milling the sacrificial outer layer of CLT might also produce curtain-like plays with depth. "Surface Tension," an essay by Victoria Camblin that accompanies Halsey's and Bolande's works, unpacks the meaning and misconceptions of surface in the built environment across the artists' two approaches. Her text forms the middle of this three-ply section on contemporary art. Just before this interlude, Nelson Byun contributes an essay on Matisse's cut-outs, describing the artist's shift from painting to drawing with scissors. Whether 1/4-inch engravings into blank material or compositional "left-overs" (the remainders of cut-outs), these works of art offer another useful entry point for thinking about architecture anew—especially since the blank is ready to be cut into and cut up.

Another significant motivation of this book is to link pedagogy and practice, specifically the collaborations between architects and engineers that tend to exist primarily in practice. *Blank* began as a pedagogical experiment between its editors—Jennifer is an architect, and Hanif is an engineer. We have each pioneered CLT on our respective continents: Jennifer in Haus Gables (2018), a house in Atlanta developed in collaboration with Hanif, and Hanif in Hunsett Mill (2009), a collaboration between his practice, AKT II, and ACME in Norfolk, the United Kingdom. In the spring of 2020, we co-taught an advanced design and research studio at the Harvard University Graduate School of Design titled "Mass Timber and the Scandinavian Effect." Many of the design and structural investigations and positions on the blank that frame this book emerged directly from the design methodology of the studio and discussions with its fourteen graduate students. Through the book, we hope to expose the innovation that arose within the workings of a studio where practice and academia overlapped in an unusual way. To underline the point, the students' design proposals carry throughout the book; we close with a number of short essays by the studio participants, which we understand as calls to action or pithy projections for the field. Collectively, their contributions map timely cultural events and generational aspirations back onto architectural discourse.[3]

3 See, for example, the essay "Everyone Has a 'Good Side,' and So Does CLT," by Edward Han Myo Oo (page 225), who compares Mariah Carey's favored on-camera angle with CLT's most photogenic "side," which shows end grain and blank surface simultaneously. Jennifer's insistence on vibe in her essay similarly points to new generational concerns.

The graphic treatment of the students' speculative work by the book's designer, Neil Donnelly Studio, poses an intentional physical challenge. Donnelly and Siiri Tännler ask the reader to rotate the book to engage the cross-lamination of the contributors' essays and the student projects. Printed on beige paper (the color most closely associated with the blank), the students' drawings and images are grouped by category: tower plans and elevations, for example, exist separately from tower renderings. We invite readers to connect each student project with the associated text at the very end of the book by following the bread crumbs of page numbers that appear next to each image.

Lastly, we believe it is important to advance the visualization of CLT beyond a nostalgic conception of wood. To do so, we have attempted to place special emphasis on the representation of the blank, oscillating between precisely measured, perfectly abstract two-dimensional drawings, structural analysis diagrams, and renderings that highlight the blank as individual unit within materially exaggerated dioramas. It should be noted that all of these images and drawings were created by two research assistants, Anna Goga and Edgar Rodriguez, after the conclusion of the studio, using each student's inventive design work developed earlier as the basis for visual experimentation. Some images use full saturation to draw parallels between the wooden materiality of a one-to-one building construction and the architectural model. These renderings of towers use a neutral color palette that evokes a Yeezy fashion collection or earthy advertisements promoting healthy lifestyles set against the backdrop of a forest. Forcefully pushing representation beyond the linework of modernist worm's-eye views and one-point perspectives, here, the blank is visceral and shows off lessons learned on blankness. Other images offer quick visual how-tos on constructing the blank in architecture, complete with crane didactically hoisting individual blanks into place. Towers and houses are pulled apart, like toys, to describe how blanks go together. These images imply flexibility in how architects and engineers might slice up a variety of massings, whether house or tower.

Another set of images—including the cover of this book—lays out blanks in an imagined cut list, in implicit opposition to the hallowed figure-ground study of the past. In these drawings, black fill (fill-in-the-blank) illustrates the possible presence of figures, openings, notches, and shape, yet removes the panels from their original building form, as the viewer understands only the visual order of the blanks as a list. Here, the blanks are numbered, dimensioned, and ready for manufacturing. The organization of these drawings is loosely based on the structural capacity of the blank as load-bearing vertical wall panels or horizontally spanning floor and roof panels—i.e., the groupings intentionally suggest structural types. Still other images are codified as a series of micro-surface analytics created by a team of structural engineers at AKT II, further rounding out the final set of representations that speak to disciplinary knowledge. Coated in flashy primary colors, these representations test the physics of two houses and two towers. As a collective set, the images illustrate compression, tension, shear, torsion, and twisting—typical of structural calculations by any engineer. In this case, we hope to frame the blank as "surface structure" moving beyond typical balloon-frame or beam-and-column analysis. All the image-based media, whether material tectonic or analytics, together present a non-nostalgic view of timber within the application of house and mid-rise tower.

When we started this book, we wanted to resist the formulas that develop all too easily when a new material arrives on the architectural scene and gets absorbed into teaching, practice, and construction. Our immediate goals included debunking what we saw in current discourse (almost like the "spoilsports who uncurtained the Wizard of Oz," to use the writer Mark Forsyth's phrase). By approaching CLT from multiple other angles, some unexplored or unproven—which felt, in some ways, like cooking blindfolded[4]—we found support from colleagues and collaborators who have contributed to the book, and have arrived at what we hope is a pivotal moment in understanding the potential of CLT, aiming to shine a light on the full breadth of good it can bring into architecture.

4 Another phrase of Forsyth's. Both appear in *The Elements of Eloquence* (New York: Berkley, 2014), 5, 7.

The ideas and projects included in the pages that follow signal a shift in the field—an architectural reset—made possible by the far-reaching, multivalent capacity of the CLT blank.

House 01: Plan
Elevation: p. 52
Blank Panels: pp. 85, 100
Structural Analysis: pp. 210–12
CLT Forecast: p. 237

House 02: Plan
Elevation: p. 46 (top)
Exploded Blanks: p. 178
CLT Forecast: p. 233

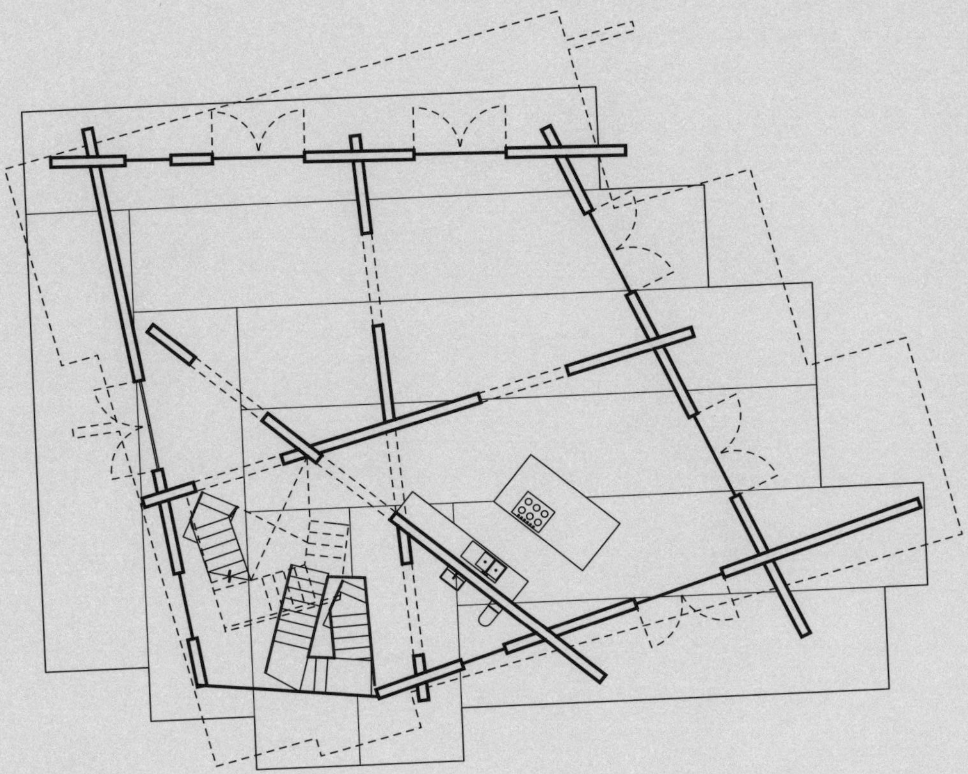

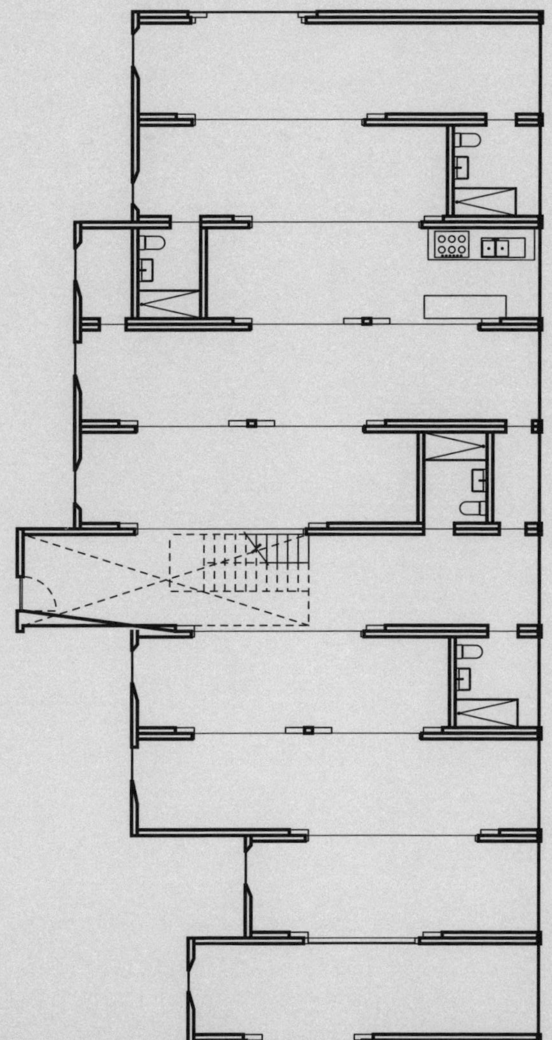

House 03: Plan
Elevation: p.51 (bottom)
Blank Panels: pp.86-87

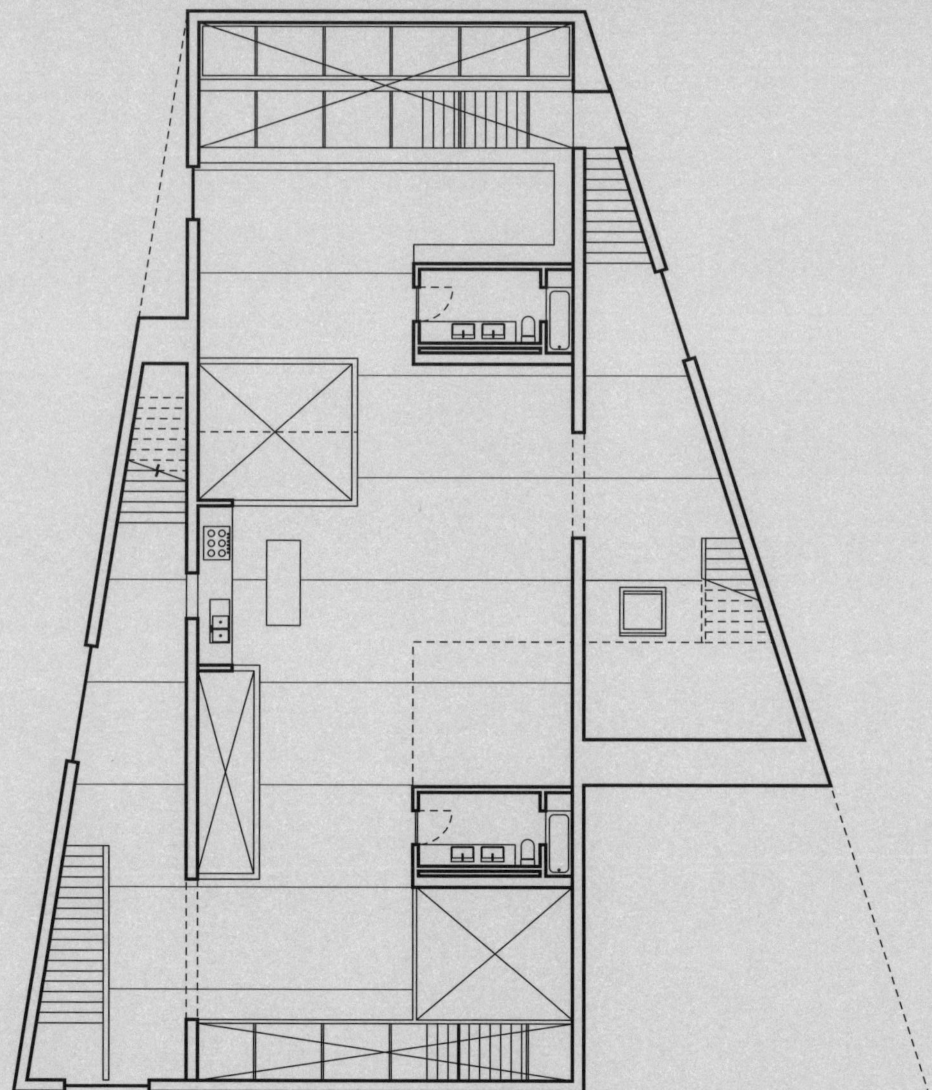

House 04: Plan
Elevation: p. 46 (bottom)
CLT Forecast: p. 230

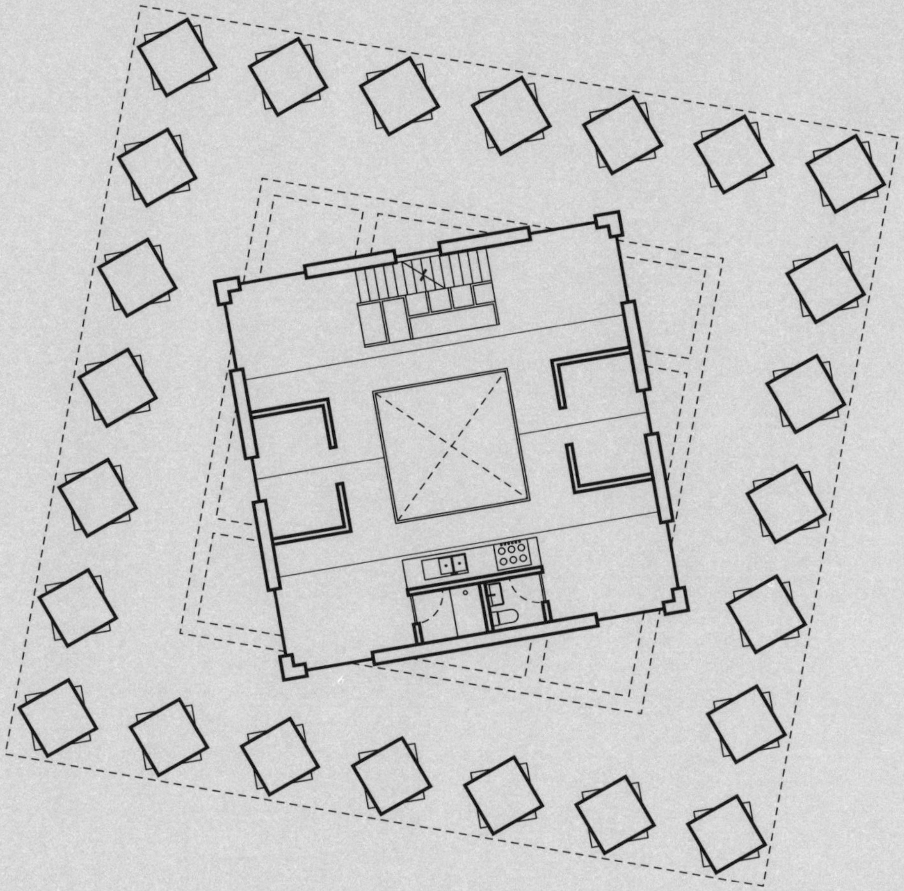

House 05: Plan
Elevation: p. 48 (top)
CLT Forecast: p. 235

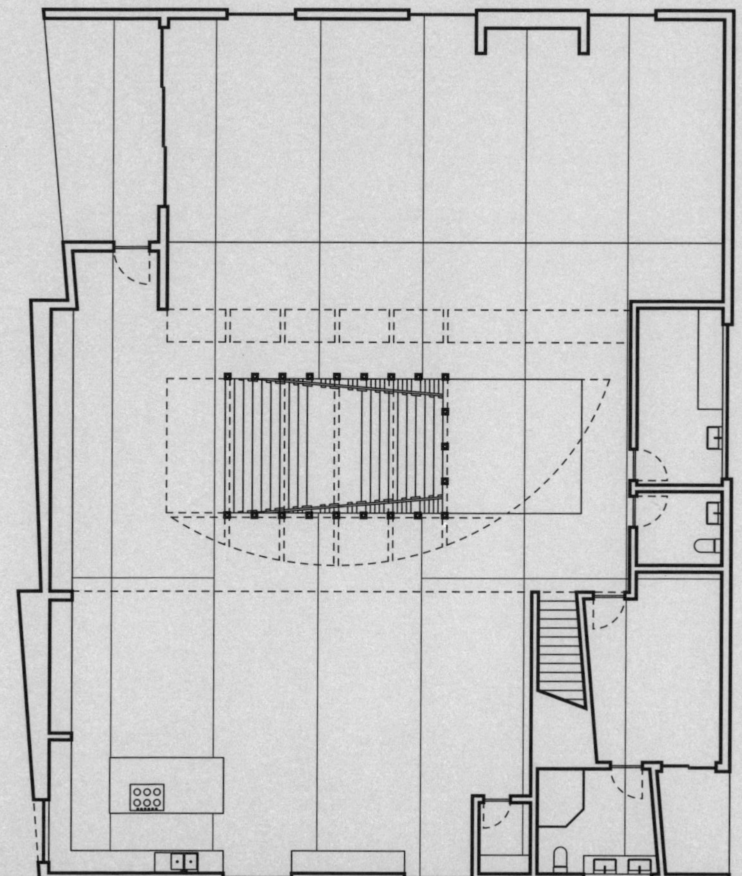

House 06: Plan
Elevation: p.48 (bottom)
CLT Forecast: p.231

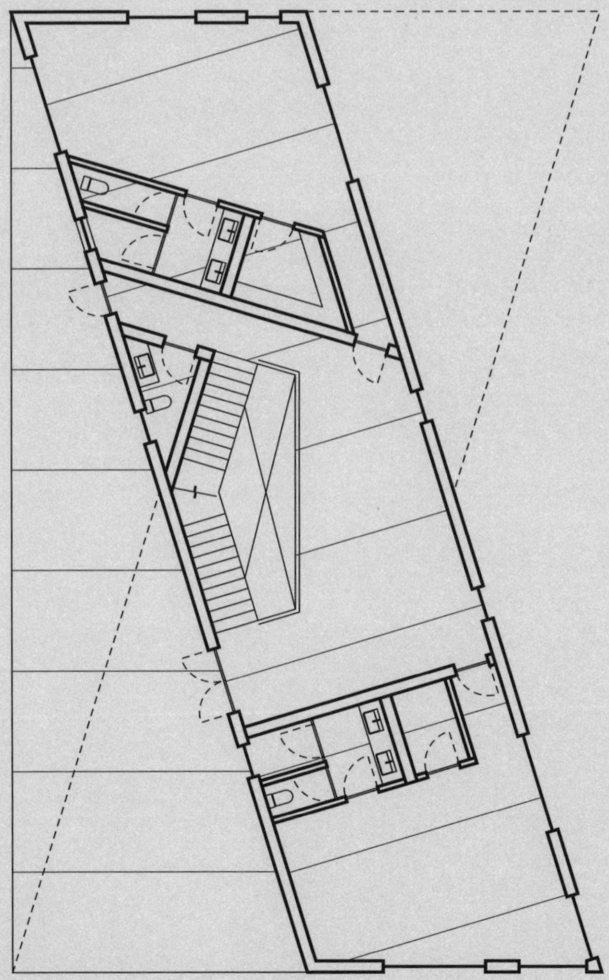

House 07: Plan
Elevation: p.47 (top)
CLT Forecast: p.227

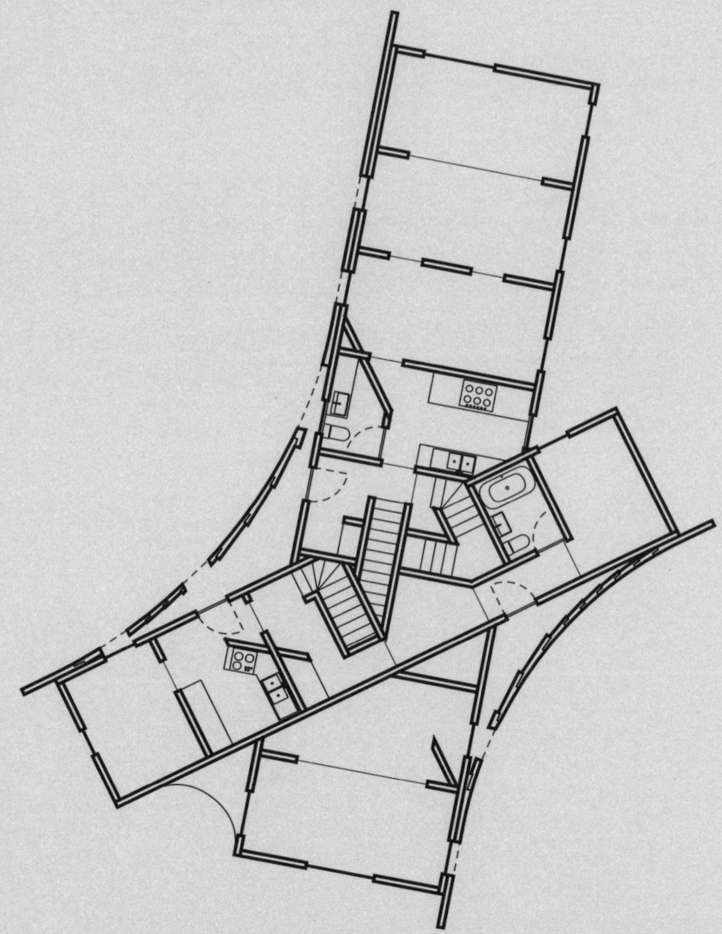

House 08: Plan
Elevation: p.47 (bottom)
Exploded Blanks: p.180
CLT Forecast: p.229

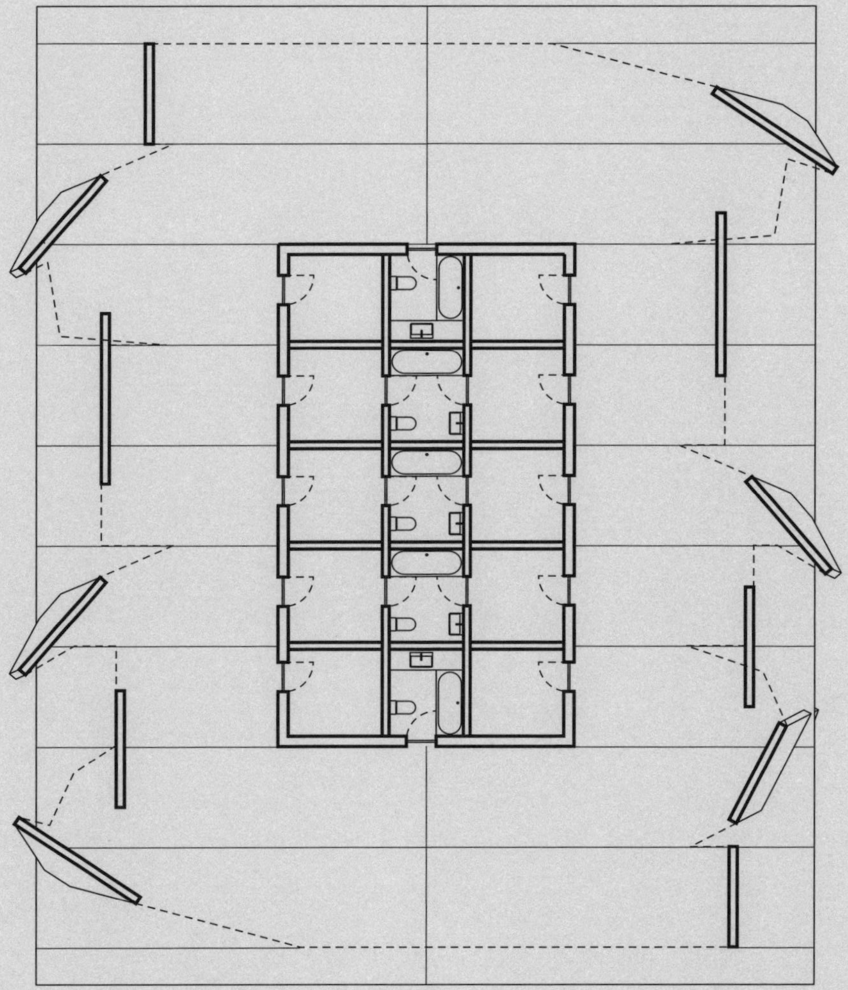

House 09: Plan
Elevation: p. 49
Exploded Blanks: p. 179
Structural Analysis: p. 201
CLT Forecast: p. 225

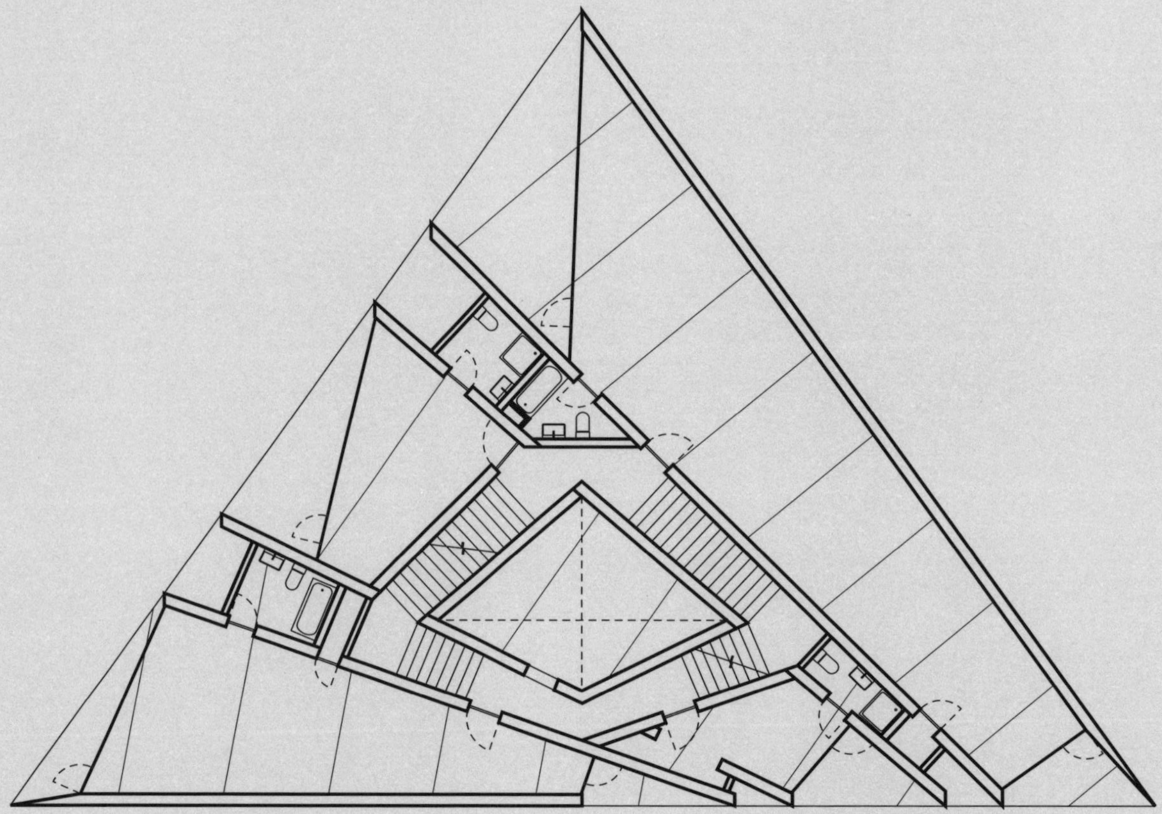

House 10: Plan
Elevation: p. 45
Blank Panels: pp. 90–91
CLT Forecast: p. 226

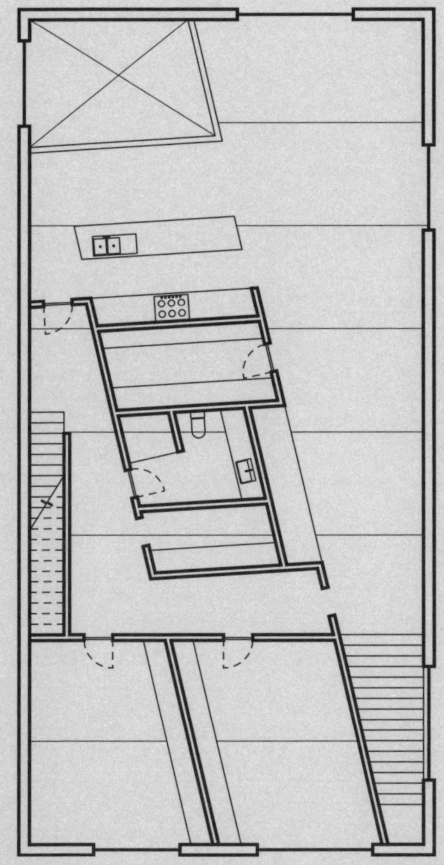

House 11: Plan
Elevation: p. 50 (bottom)
Exploded Blanks: p. 177
CLT Forecast: p. 234

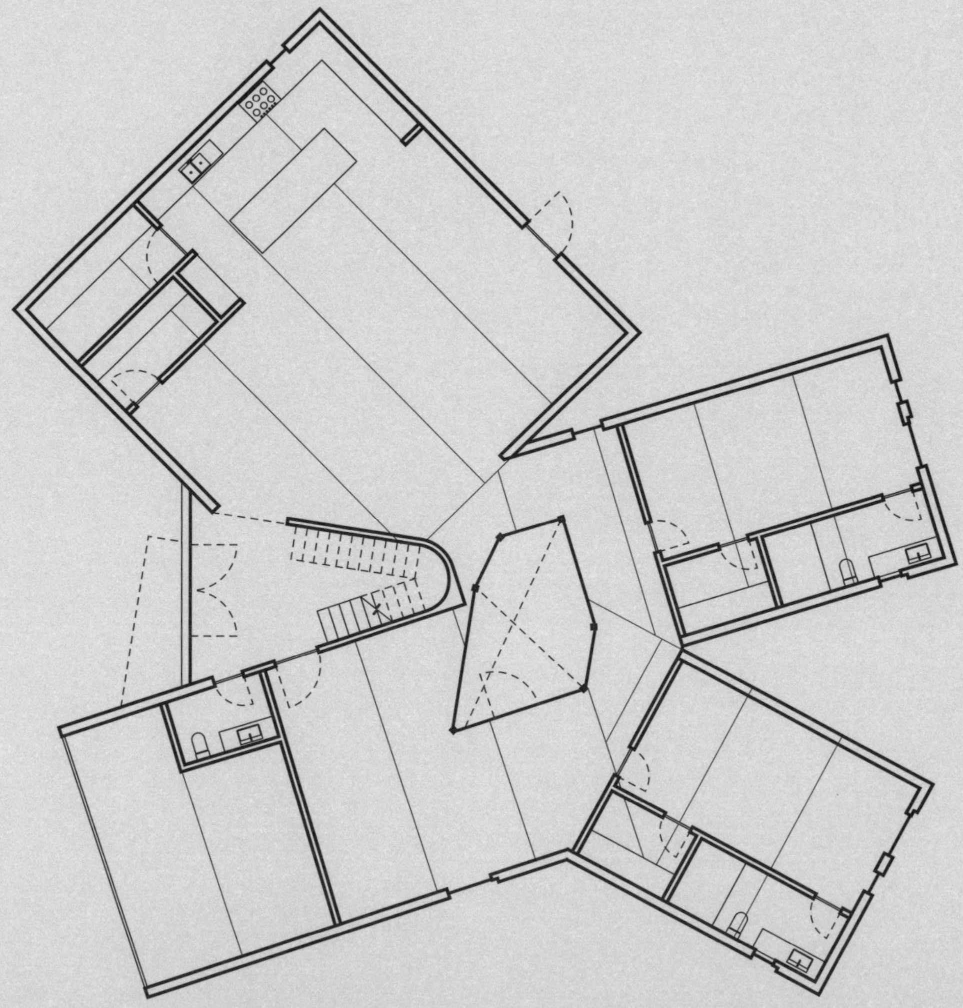

House 12: Plan
Elevation: p. 50 (top)
CLT Forecast: p. 232

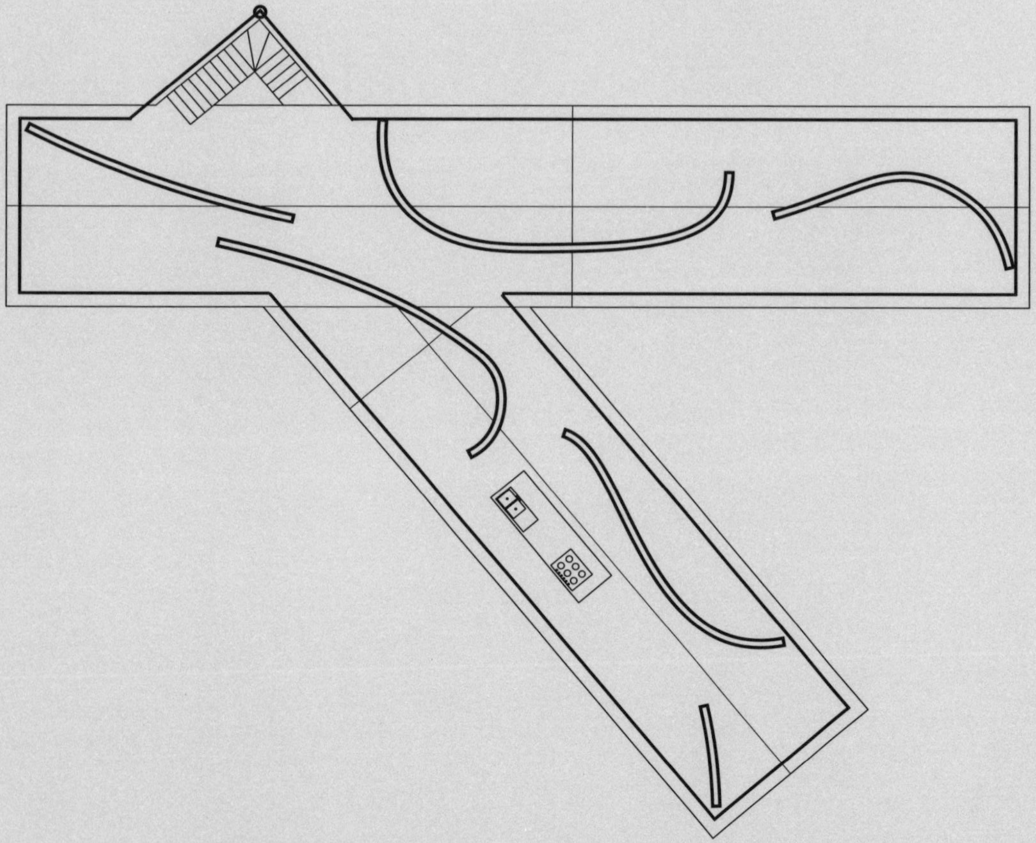

House 13: Plan
Elevation: p. 51 (top)
Blank Panels: pp. 88-89
CLT Forecast: p. 236

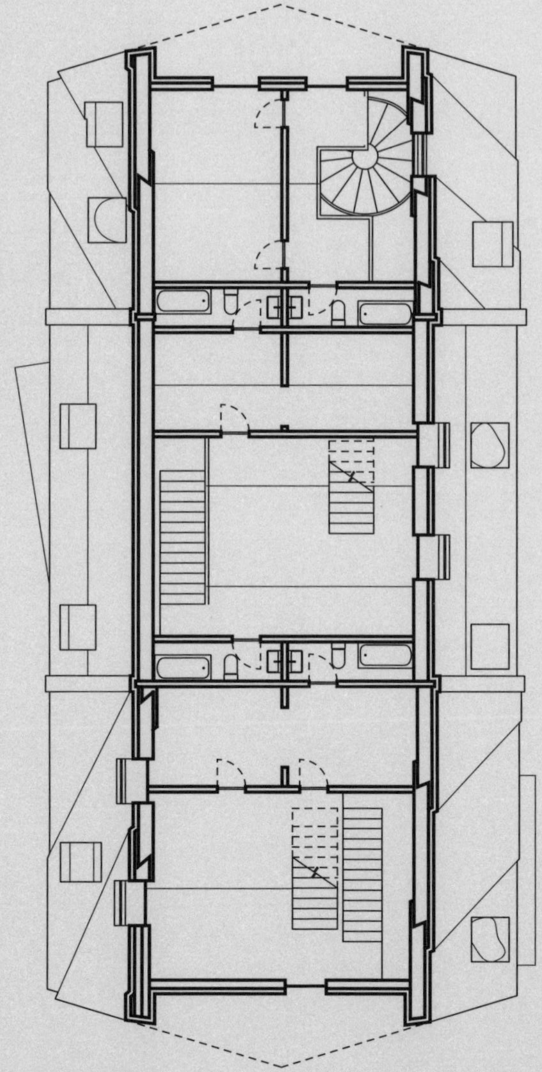

House 10: Elevation
Plan: p. 43 (left)
Blank Panels: pp. 90–91
CLT Forecast: p. 226

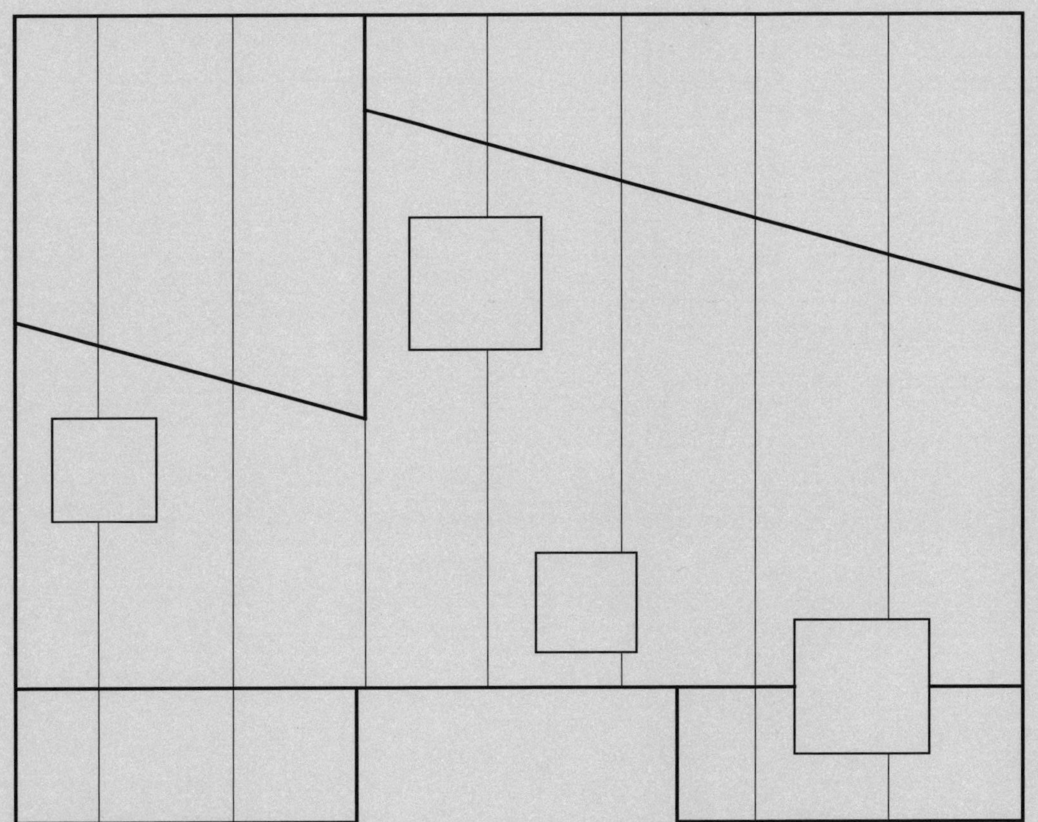

House 02: Elevation
Plan: p.37 (right)
Exploded Blanks: p.178
CLT Forecast: p.233

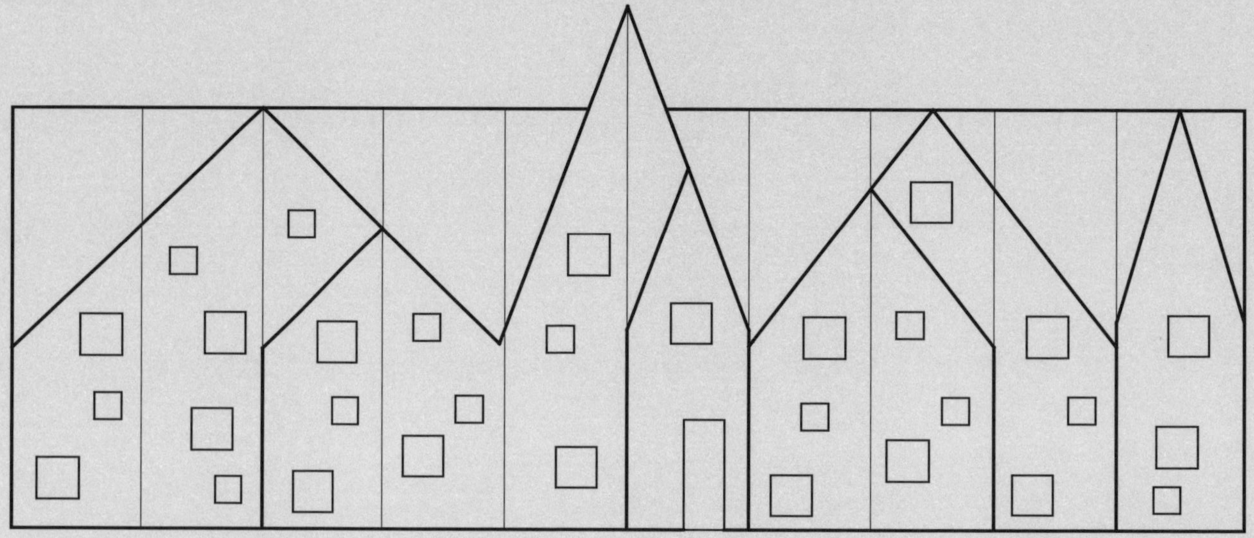

House 04: Elevation
Plan: p.39 (left)
CLT Forecast: p.230

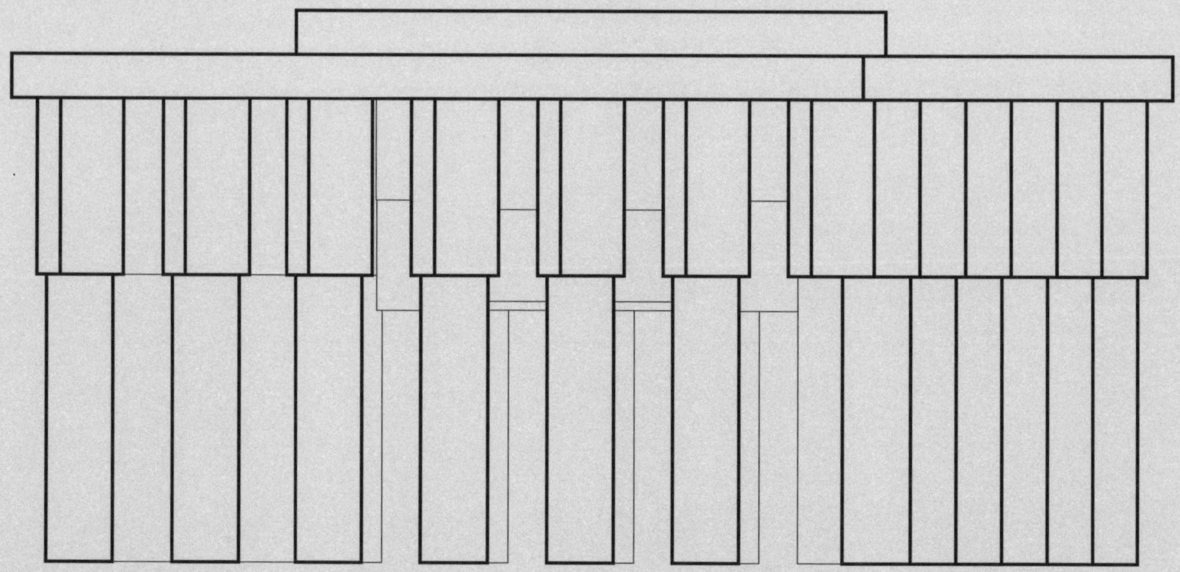

House 07: Elevation
Plan: p. 40 (right)
CLT Forecast: p. 227

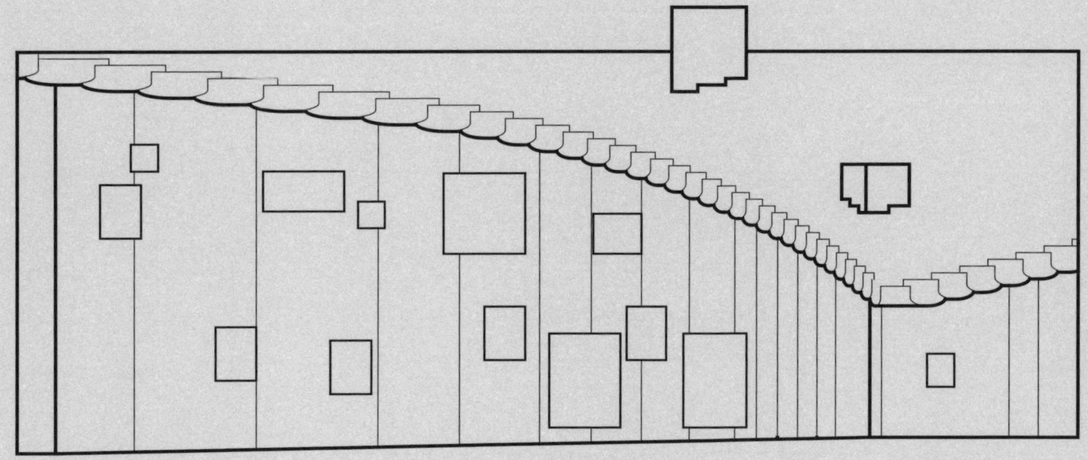

House 08: Elevation
Plan: p. 41
Exploded Blanks: p. 180
CLT Forecast: p. 229

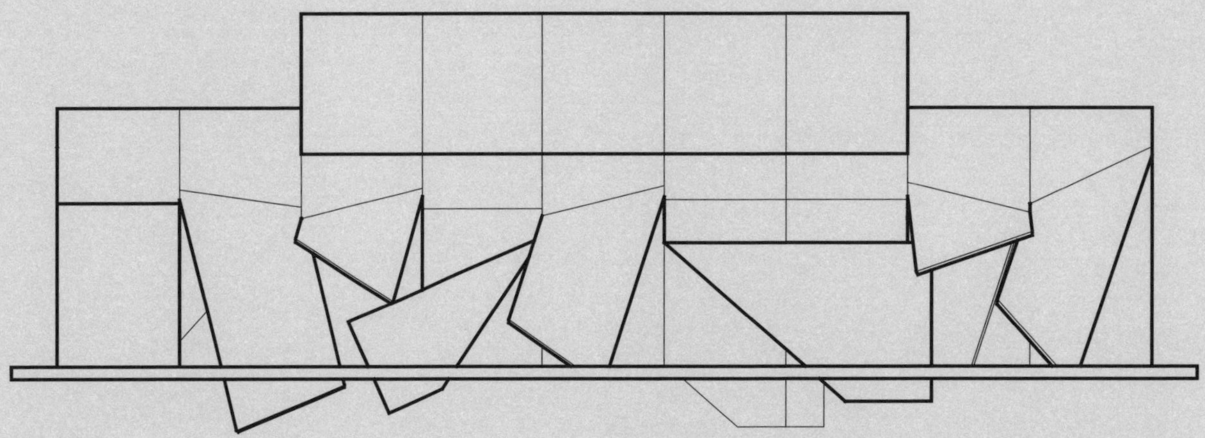

House 05: Elevation
Plan: p. 39 (right)
CLT Forecast: p. 235

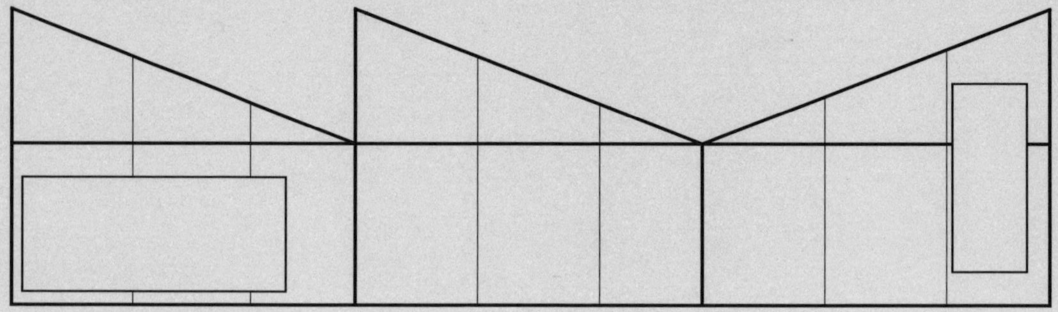

House 06: Elevation
Plan: p. 40 (left)
CLT Forecast: p. 231

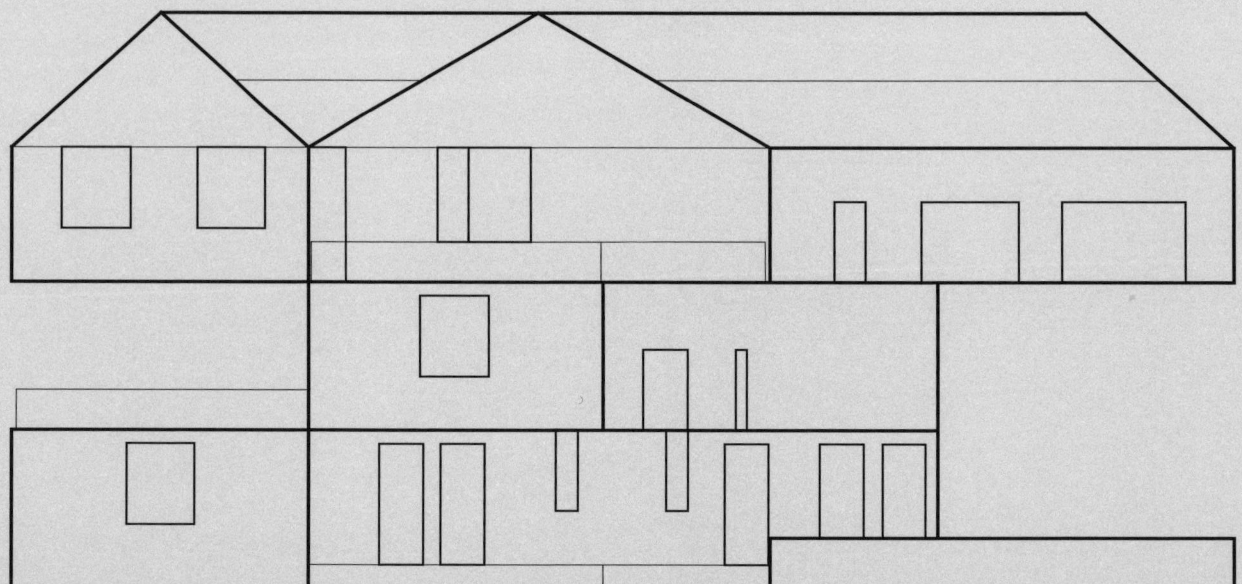

House 09: Elevation
Plan: p.42
Exploded Blanks: p.179
Structural Analysis: p.201
CLT Forecast: p.225

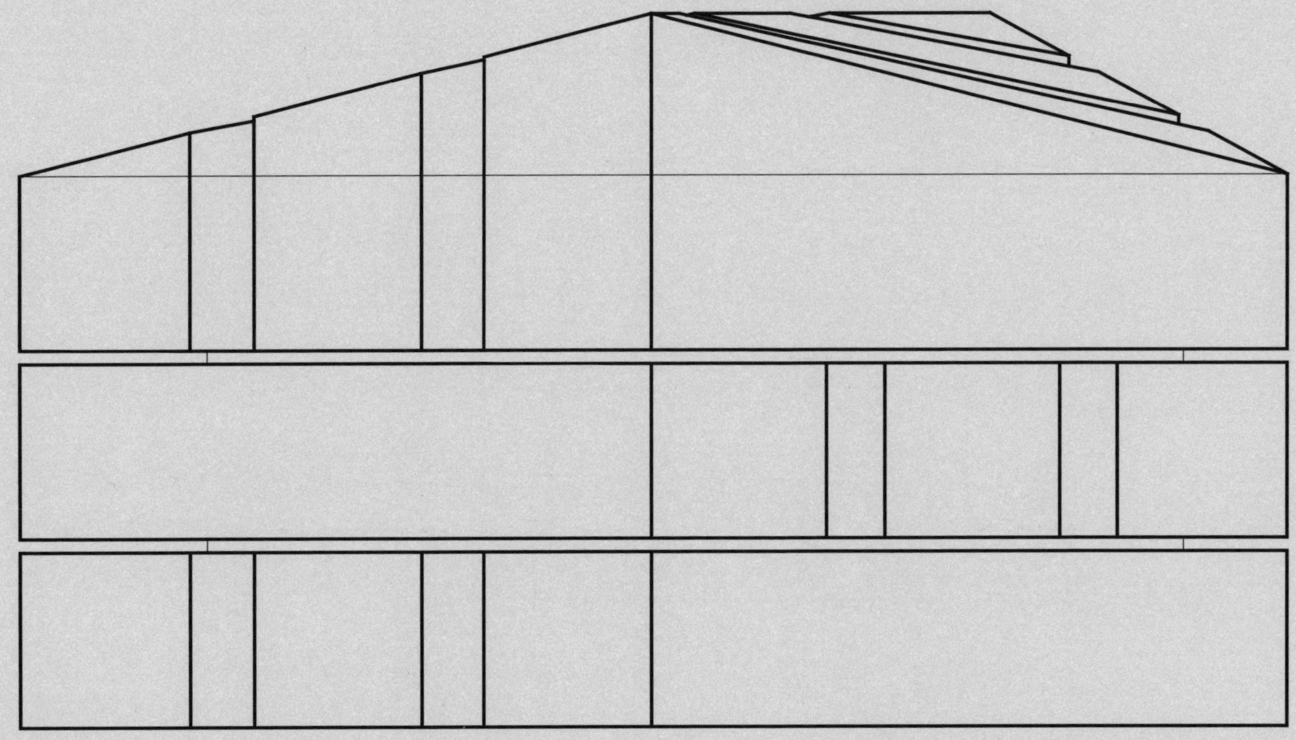

House 12: Elevation
Plan: p. 44 (left)
CLT Forecast: p. 232

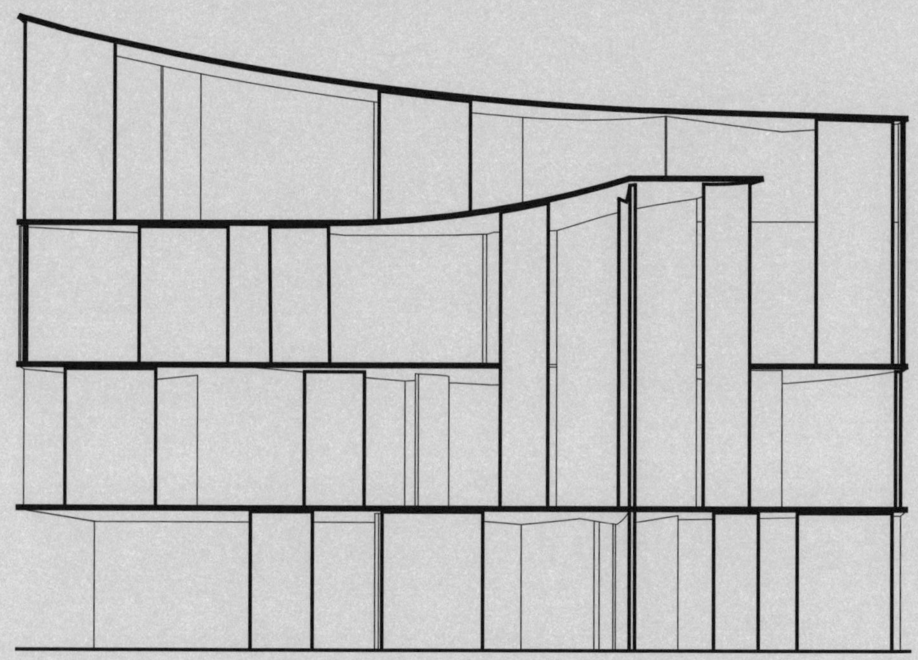

House 11: Elevation
Plan: p. 43 (right)
Exploded Blanks: p. 177
CLT Forecast: p. 234

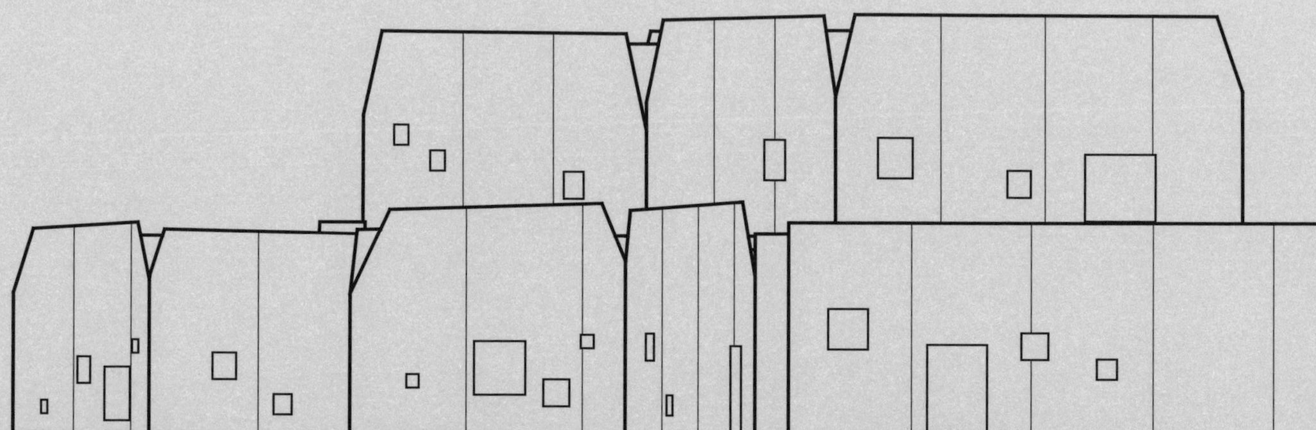

House 13: Elevation
Plan: p. 44 (right)
Blank Panels: pp. 88–89
CLT Forecast: p. 236

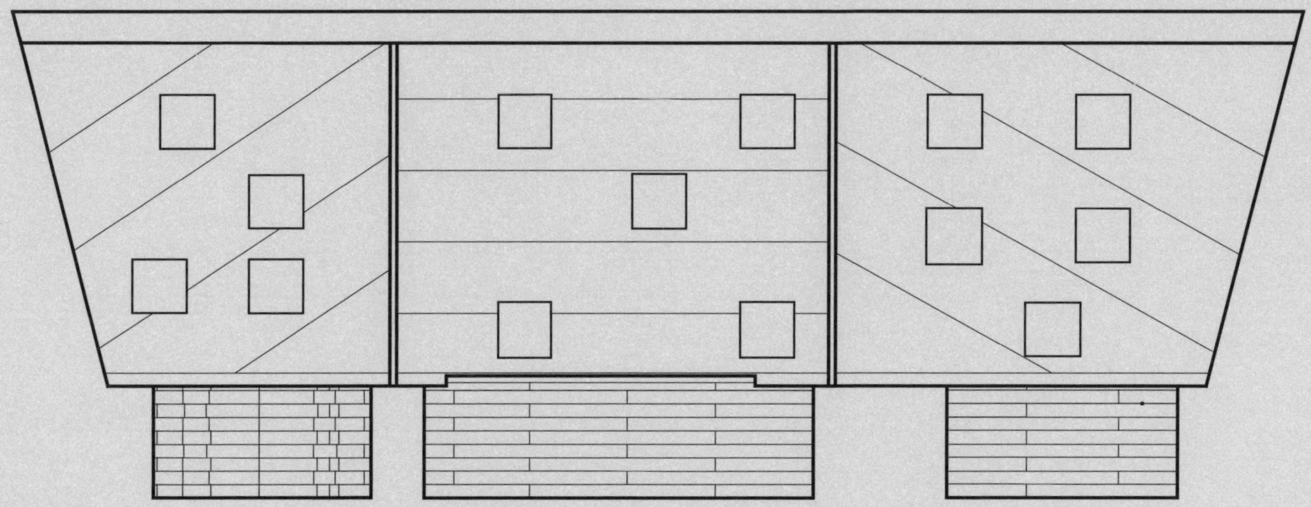

House 03: Elevation
Plan: p. 38
Blank Panels: pp. 86–87

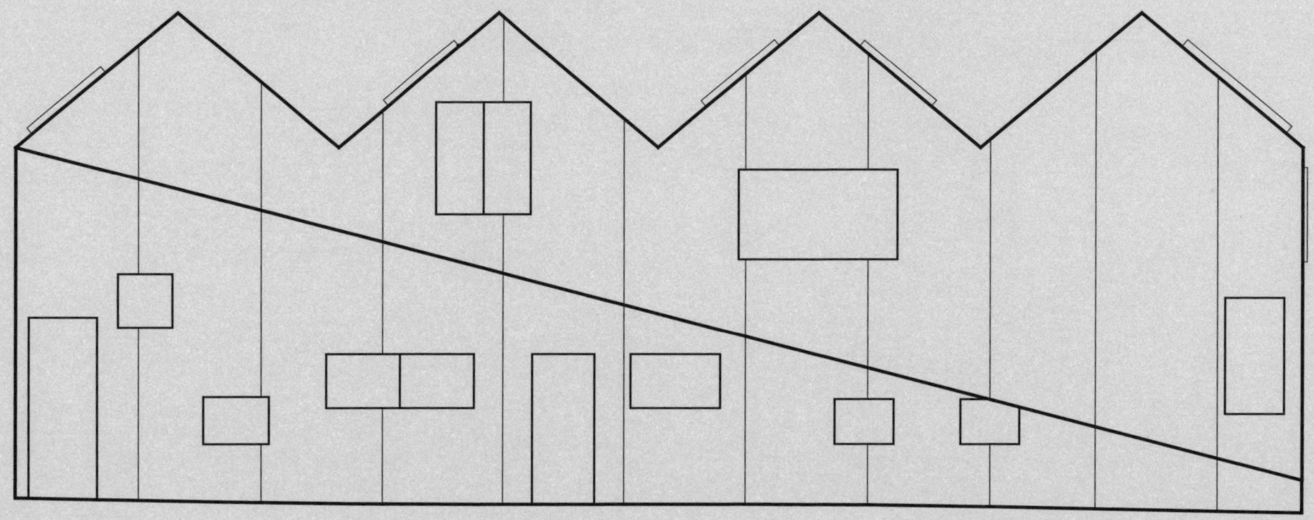

House 01: Elevation
Plan: p.37 (left)
Blank Panels: pp.85,100
Structural Analysis: pp.210–12
CLT Forecast: p.237

Endless Lamellae and Finer Grains: A Brief History of Better Wood

Erin Putalik

As the introduction to this book points out, even when the CLT blank is used speculatively and represented virtually, its surfaces are anything but blank. At its edges, the transverse and longitudinal layers are visible, the alternating grain directions signaling both a natural source and a supersession of the limits intrinsic to such sources. On the faces of the blank, sometimes knotty and often large and open grain patterns create a wild figural effect, interrupted at even intervals by the mechanically perfect splice of the glueline . . . a punctuated rhythm of irregularity checked by precision.

The gluelines, shepherding untold numbers of erratic trees into calculability, are as fundamental to the CLT surface as the grain. Yet it is the grain, and the knots, that retain a surprising uncanniness when used at this scale. Gigantic wood. Dimensionally, the blank is most similar (although still larger by a significant factor) to heavy timber—massive beams and columns gleaned from the nation's primeval forests. But superficially, quite literally on the surface, its knots and widely spaced rings speak of young, faster-growing trees. In this way, in its grain, the blank surface posits an aesthetic paradox: if we understand, somewhere deep in our cultural memory of building, that giant timber has always come from giant trees, how can we make sense of this unnaturally natural surface?

Grain, as a surface pattern of lumber, is the confluence of two factors: growth and manufacture. The growth rings and medullary rays of each tree are revealed in particular ways that depend on how it has been sawn in its transformation into lumber. Grain pattern is thus the fundamental quality that correlates the growing environment of a tree with the physical appearance and structural properties of its wood.

The annual rings of trees trace the shifting needs of the canopy throughout the growing season. The density and coloration of the wood cells within these rings relate to the arc of the season: New wood is formed each year within the cambium, the layer between the bark and the rest of the wood.[1] It is within this new wood that water is brought to the canopy of the tree—its large cell sizes and thin cell walls produce a lighter-weight and lighter-colored wood through which water moves readily. As the growth of the tree slows in late summer, needs for water in the canopy diminish, triggering the growth of narrower cells with thick walls, producing a summer layer that is denser, stronger, and darker.[2]

1 This is a highly simplified account; for a full analysis of how new wood is formed, see Melanie Mauriat et al., "Wood Formation in Trees," in *Tree Biotechnology*, ed. K. G. Ramawat, J. P. Mérillon, and M. R. Ahuja (Boca Raton, FL: CRC Press, 2014), 56-111.

2 Gifford Pinchot, *A Primer of Forestry: Part I—The Forest* (Washington, DC: Government Printing Office, 1899), 20.

Historically, in order to control the appearance and properties of wood, the forests from which the material came had to be either specifically managed or carefully chosen. The management, control, or improvement of the forest was thus closely tied to the improvement of the wood itself. In 1864, George Perkins Marsh argued that "the sooner a natural wood is brought into the state of an artificially regulated one," the better it could satisfy its function of wood production (among others). In doing so, he posited expert control of the forest as roughly synonymous with expert control of what he called the "ligneous texture" of the wood itself. He noted that the production of the best ligneous texture within the white pine, for example, required a dense forest—to protect the trees "from too much agitation by wind, and from the persistence of the lateral branches which fill the wood with knots."[3] A long, straight, knot-free, and tight-grained board of white pine began with the spacing and pruning of trees. The relationship between the grain pattern of lumber, the method of lumber manufacture, and the "life of the forest" was rearticulated by Gifford Pinchot in 1899, in one of America's early texts on forestry. Combining images from Robert Hartig's 1891 *Anatomie und Physiologie der Pflanzen* and contemporaneous photographs of lumber sawn in various ways, Pinchot illustrated the degree to which natural grain patterns, lumber properties, and the forest environment were indelibly linked.[4]

3 George Perkins Marsh, *The Earth as Modified by Human Action: A New Edition of Man and Nature* (1864; New York: Scribner, Armstrong & Co., 1874), 369.

4 Pinchot, 16-20.

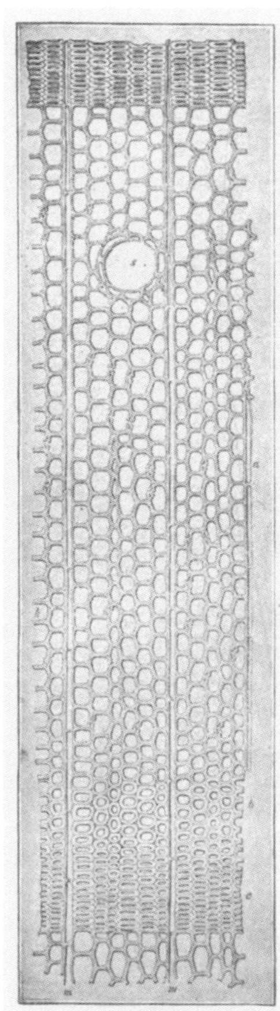

Fig. 20.—Wood of a Spruce, greatly magnified. (From Hartig. Anatomie und Physiologie der Pflanzen, Berlin, 1891.)

Magnification of spruce wood, printed in Gifford Pinchot, *A Primer of Forestry* (Washington, DC: Government Printing Office, 1899)

Finer Grains

Despite an increasing emphasis on the expert management of its environments of growth during the early twentieth century, wood resisted. Its stubborn irregularity in the face of an increasingly mechanized building culture—and in particular an emerging obsession with factory-built homes by the late 1920s—threatened its centrality as America's de facto building material. As two members of the Forest Products Laboratory explained at a 1924 meeting of the American Society of Testing and Materials, "The non-homogenous character of wood and the many factors which affect its strength have long caused it to be regarded as an erratic structural material of indefinite strength."[5] Although couched in the terse and colorless parlance of technicians, this was a truly damning evaluation of wood as a building material. Such analyses increasingly raised the question of whether wood was an inadequately standardizable building material for modern times.

J. A. Newlin and R. P. A. Johnson, "Structural Timbers: Defects and Their Influence on Strength," *American Society for Testing Materials Proceedings*, vol. 24 (1924): 975; cited in Charles M. Haines, "Industrialization of Wood" (PhD diss., University of Delaware, 1990), 319.

The erraticism and indefiniteness of solid wood was overcome in its transformation into an engineered material.[6] In the 1920s and 1930s, the most omnipresent form that this wood improvement took was plywood. Its lightness, large sizes, and structural uniformity and predictability made plywood perfectly suited to a new architectural focus on economies of construction. Plywood was not a new material in the twenties and thirties, but it underwent rapid improvement and became much more widely used during this period. Its development during these years responded to an intense push to standardize building practices and procedures, which increasingly required materials that were uniform and predictable. This predictability was essential for the mass-production and factory-construction techniques that were the focus of so much architectural interest and experimentation.

Researchers at the Forest Products Laboratory also defined laminating structural timbers from small-dimension stock as an arm of their work in the early 1930s. They increasingly looked at the production of large-scale structural wood lamination, focusing on glue-laminated arches and other structural forms. See Forest Products Laboratory, "Project 1052-J55: Laminated Wood Arch Construction," *Annual Research Report* (1935–36): 86.

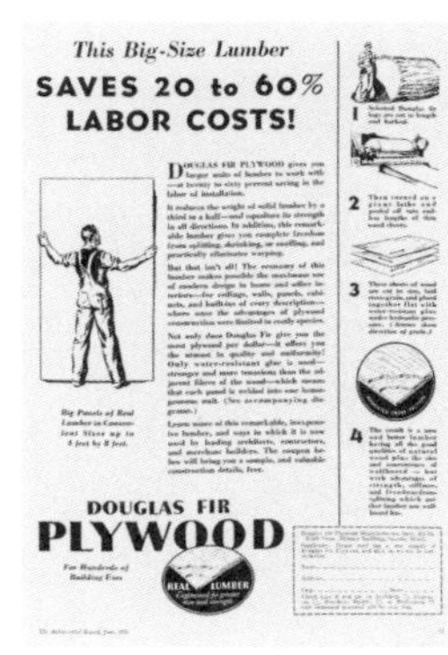

Advertisement for Douglas Fir Plywood Manufacturers, *Architectural Record*, June 1931

Through a process of peeling thin sheets from large logs and then gluing the sheets with alternating grain directions, plywood manufacturers created a form of wood that was also of uniform strength in all directions across its surface. A Douglas Fir Plywood advertisement of 1931 illustrated this process in detail and described its outcome as follows: "The result is a new and better lumber having all of the good qualities of natural wood plus the size and convenience of wallboard—but with advantages of strength, stiffness, and freedom-from-splitting which neither lumber nor wallboard has." The tagline for the material, embedded in a small oval featuring a cutaway illustration of the layers of plywood, echoed this message: "Real Lumber: Engineered for greater size and strength."[7] In this way, entities such as the Douglas Fir Plywood Association acknowledged the natural limitations of the source material while leveraging an unfettered faith in technological innovation to transcend these limitations—all while carefully retaining claims to realness.

Douglas Fir Plywood Manufacturers, advertisement for Douglas fir plywood, *Architectural Record*, June 1931, 59.

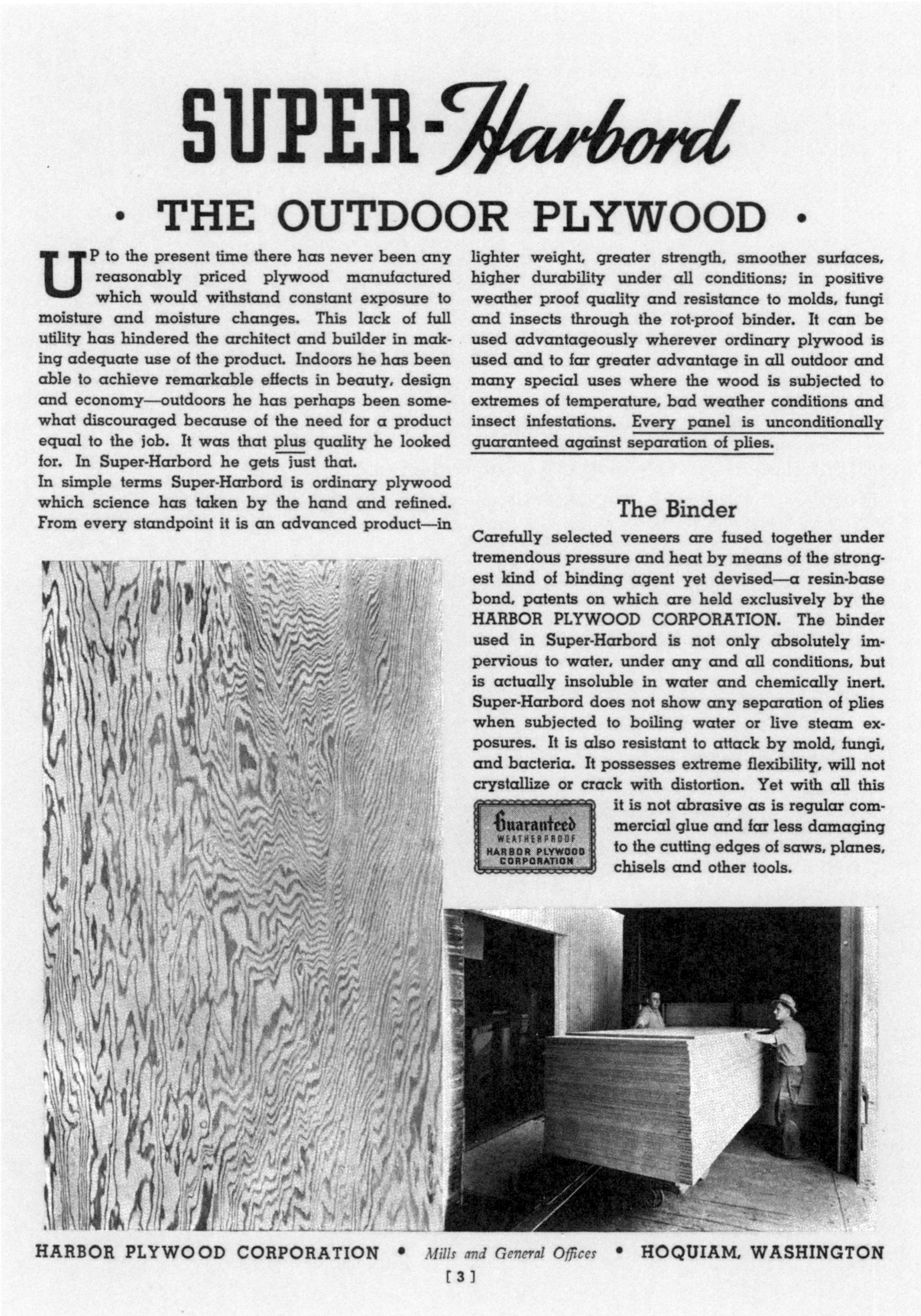

SUPER-*Harbord*

• THE OUTDOOR PLYWOOD •

Up to the present time there has never been any reasonably priced plywood manufactured which would withstand constant exposure to moisture and moisture changes. This lack of full utility has hindered the architect and builder in making adequate use of the product. Indoors he has been able to achieve remarkable effects in beauty, design and economy—outdoors he has perhaps been somewhat discouraged because of the need for a product equal to the job. It was that plus quality he looked for. In Super-Harbord he gets just that.

In simple terms Super-Harbord is ordinary plywood which science has taken by the hand and refined. From every standpoint it is an advanced product—in lighter weight, greater strength, smoother surfaces, higher durability under all conditions; in positive weather proof quality and resistance to molds, fungi and insects through the rot-proof binder. It can be used advantageously wherever ordinary plywood is used and to far greater advantage in all outdoor and many special uses where the wood is subjected to extremes of temperature, bad weather conditions and insect infestations. Every panel is unconditionally guaranteed against separation of plies.

The Binder

Carefully selected veneers are fused together under tremendous pressure and heat by means of the strongest kind of binding agent yet devised—a resin-base bond, patents on which are held exclusively by the HARBOR PLYWOOD CORPORATION. The binder used in Super-Harbord is not only absolutely impervious to water, under any and all conditions, but is actually insoluble in water and chemically inert. Super-Harbord does not show any separation of plies when subjected to boiling water or live steam exposures. It is also resistant to attack by mold, fungi, and bacteria. It possesses extreme flexibility, will not crystallize or crack with distortion. Yet with all this it is not abrasive as is regular commercial glue and far less damaging to the cutting edges of saws, planes, chisels and other tools.

Guaranteed
WEATHERPROOF
HARBOR PLYWOOD CORPORATION

HARBOR PLYWOOD CORPORATION • *Mills and General Offices* • HOQUIAM, WASHINGTON

[3]

Page from Harbor Plywood Corporation insert, *Sweet's Catalog*, 1938

By 1938, the Harbor Plywood Corporation, one of the first American plywood manufacturers to develop a fully waterproof glueline, was carefully differentiating its Super-Harbord exterior plywood from "ordinary plywood" with claims that its product was "In simple terms . . . ordinary plywood which science has taken by the hand and refined."[8] Advertisements prominently featured panels of loudly grained plywood, with surfaces richly rendered and shaded to bring out the grain. These images of the natural surface sat aggressively alongside

8 Harbor Plywood Corporation, insert in *Sweet's Catalog*, Section 8-4 (1938), 3.

TECHNICAL NEWS AND RESEARCH

Large panel of Phemaloid Compound Lumber produced by Haskelite Manufacturing Corporation.

NEW PRODUCTS: WOOD, TEXTILES, PAPER

Haskelite compound lumber featured in *Architectural Record*, April 1933

detailed claims of the manners in which Super-Harbord had overcome all of the shortcomings intrinsic to natural wood, including its vulnerability to termites and molds, but especially its uneven strength, small sizes, and relative heaviness.

Even as the size and strength of these new engineered woods were touted, the texture of their grain remained a prominent feature in their representations, both in advertisements and in renderings of interiors and exteriors. The grain of Douglas Fir Plywood and Harbor's Super-Harbord was both an inherent quality of better-than-natural wood and evidence of material improvement. The surface patterns of these woods, like those of most structural fir plywood, deviated widely from the grain of solid lumber. Solid lumber can be sawn in various ways—most commonly, plain/flat sawn, quarter sawn, or rift sawn—that involve different relationships between the cut and the growth rings of the tree. Each of these methods produces a solid lumber with different degrees of dimensional stability and different surface grain; generally, the closer the cut aligns with the radial plane of the trunk (perpendicular to the tangent of the tree ring), the smoother and tighter the grain and the more dimensionally stable the wood.[9]

9 The quantity of material wasted in each of these processes also varies widely.

In contrast, in the production of structural fir plywood, veneers are not sawn but peeled, using a large blade held tangent to the log's face. As the log rotates, a thin veneer of a uniform thickness is removed, unfurling like a large sheet of paper from a roll. This process, in which

MODERATE-COST HOUSE CONSTRUCTION AND EQUIPMENT

Prefabricated wood panels being assembled in model house built by Forest Products Laboratory.

NEW WOOD CONSTRUCTION

The assembly of a Forest Products Laboratory house, printed in George Trayer and Hamilton Beatty, "New Wood Construction," *Architectural Record*, August 1935

the blade moves slowly inward toward the center of the tree, creates a very different grain, with markings revealed as the blade crosses through an annual tree ring. Unlike the linear and lightly curving grains of sawn lumber and veneers, which often retain evidence of their original position within the tree trunk, the grain of a peeled veneer is frequently florid, swoopy, and almost baroque. Left natural and unfinished, this grain pattern telegraphs both a natural origin and a highly specific process of wood improvement. The referent of the original tree has been distanced, even as the specificity and prominence of the grain has been foregrounded.

The grain geometries of the CLT surface communicate a different sort of improvement, but one that is similarly legible. Small-dimension stock is laminated on the exterior faces, with the orientation of these boards communicating the major strength direction. The knots and grain deviations stand out—they are loud and active textures, like the grain of peeled veneers, and also unmistakably aligned with a very particular form of wood improvement. These surface features, generally associated with lower-strength wood, are subsumed into the pervasive grid of the gluelines, and these signatures of wood weakness become instead signs of strength. The grid of glue renders this surface infinitely extensible, hypothetically, limited only by technologies of fabrication, transport, and construction.

Endless Lamellae[10]

The large size of the CLT blank—and the way in which this module and its scale signal the possibility of new approaches to construction—has a clear precedent in early experiments with plywood and related wood-based sheet goods. Just as the irregularity and unpredictability of solid wood were transcended by the remanufacture of peeled veneers into dimensionally stable sheets, so too were the size limitations innate to solid wood overcome by laminating peeled veneers into larger modules. These large, light sheets were perfectly suited to prefabricated panel systems in which fully constructed sections of plywood-clad walls could be factory-fabricated and site-assembled.

Between 1934 and 1937, the Forest Products Laboratory built a series of such houses that would, in many ways, transform how wood and plywood were used in factory-built homes for decades to come. Using a stressed-skin principle adopted from airplane construction, researchers at the laboratory experimented with various ways to attach plywood panels to the inner and outer faces of a wood frame such that it might work as a single structural unit.[11] These lightweight panels were then assembled into relatively conventional-looking houses, with basic designs and boxy appearances[12]—but their widespread publication in architectural journals of the time ensured a decades-long fascination with lightweight, stressed-skin panel systems.

The size of the 4-by-8-foot sheet of plywood figured prominently in many of the all-plywood experimental houses that were constructed during the 1930s and into the 1940s, either in the context of the fully assembled wall panel (as with the Forest Products Laboratory houses) or as a governing module of the plan and elevation of more conventionally constructed houses. One example of the ways in which the module of the plywood sheet itself became rich territory for experimentation is Eleanor Raymond's plywood house for Amelia Peabody, built in 1941. Raymond's drawing set for the Peabody Plywood House is illustrative of the manner in which a prolific architect who was exceedingly talented at detailing, but who also forged a career building more normative and non-modern homes, encountered these new sheet goods. Raymond embraced the inherent modularity of the plywood sheet, using it in its full size as frequently as possible. The floor plan was gridded in a 4-foot module, with the facade and its associated fenestration tightly constrained within this dimension. Fundamentally, the Peabody Plywood House, like other houses on the Peabody estate, was conceived as a low-cost

10 "Endless lamellae" is a phrase that CLT manufacturers use frequently to explain the way in which wood pieces composing each CLT layer are integrated with each other, often with finger joints, such that they are structurally continuous. See, for example, "Manufacture," BSP Holz, accessed January 1, 2021, https://www.en.brettsperrholz.org/cross-laminated-timber-clt-x-lam/manufacture/mn_45176.

George W. Trayer, "Plywood as a Structural Covering for Frame Walls and Wall Units" (Forest Products Laboratory internal research report, March 1934), 14, accessed at the Forest Products Laboratory Archives, Madison, WI.

12 See T. J. Moseley, "The Forest Products Laboratory Develops a Prefabricated All-Wood House System" (Report B35692, May 22, 1935), 1–3, accessed at the Forest Products Laboratory Archives, Madison, WI.

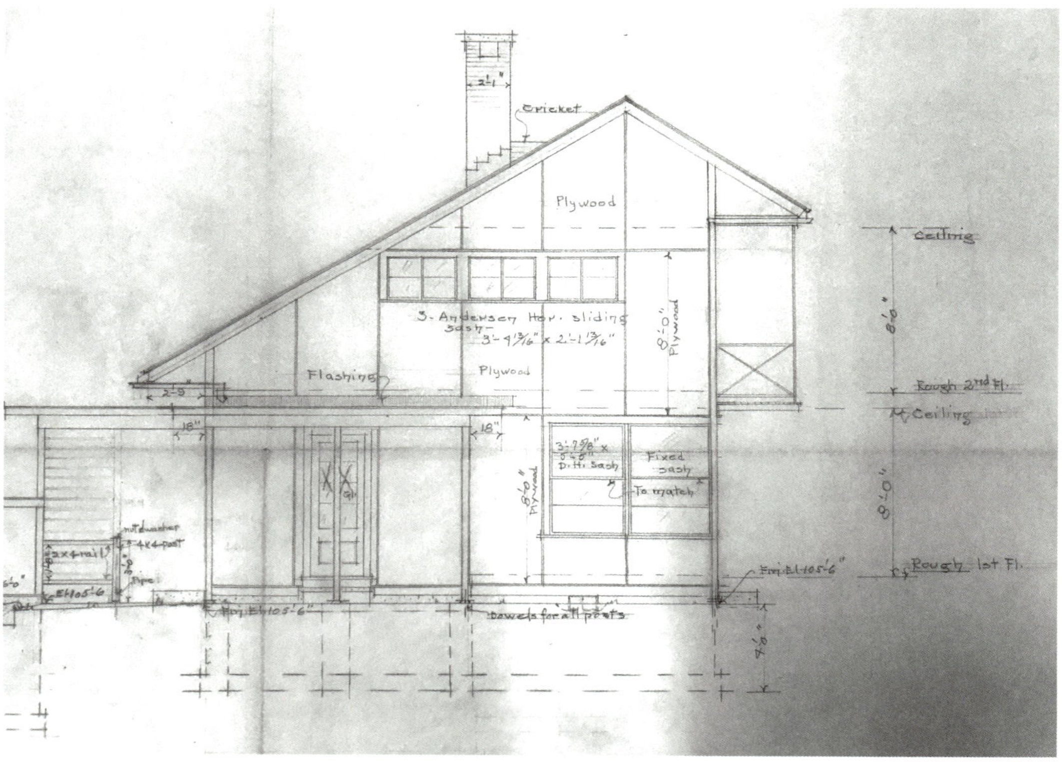

Top: Eleanor Raymond, Peabody Plywood House, Dover, Massachusetts, 1940-41

Bottom: Peabody Plywood House, elevation, 1940-41

Eleanor Raymond, Parker Plywood House, Winchester, Massachusetts, elevation, 1941, 1945–46

housing prototype, an agenda manifested in Raymond's visible ethos of material efficiency, particularly evident in her desire to use full plywood sheets in the house's cladding.

Following her work for Amelia Peabody on the experimental plywood house, Raymond was enlisted by the Parker family—themselves lumber dealers—for the design of their home. On the exterior of the house, she used plywood in a manner that emulated standard clapboard siding. In fact, elevations label this material treatment as "plywood clapb'ds," indicating that this traditional siding technique, typically done with pine boards, had been recreated with plywood. If the implicit message of the facade of Raymond's Peabody Plywood House was that the most logical and efficient use of the material, given its inherent dimensions and properties, was a highly simplified surface with a low cost per square foot and relatively unfussy installation, then the message of the plywood clapboards used in the Parker house was that plywood could do everything that regular wood could do—and in fact would be indiscernible from wood, except perhaps in its resistance to weathering and warping.

The tendency to express the full dimension of the plywood sheet as the basic module of the experimental house dwindled after the Second World War, for reasons that likely included its extensive use in low-cost and mass-produced wartime houses, but architectural interest in the material itself continued unabated. Panel-based building systems of the kind pioneered by the Forest Products Laboratory were widely used in the construction of thousands of nearly identical housing units, associating the legible 4-by-8-foot module with cheapness and expediency. As the war drew to a close, architectural competitions proliferated, inviting

William W. Wurster, Carquinez Heights defense housing under construction, Vallejo, California, 1941–42

entrants to envision the materials and spaces of the postwar dream house. *Arts & Architecture*'s 1943 competition "Designs for Postwar Living" was one such endeavor. Two-thirds of plans submitted to this competition involved the use of plywood, with seven of eight finalists clearly

California Panel & Veneer Co. advertisement in *Arts & Architecture*, August 1943.

specifying plywood in their designs.[13] The winning entry was submitted by Eero Saarinen and Oliver Lincoln Lundquist and entitled PAC (Pre-Assembled Component). The PAC unit, made of a "resin bond stressed skin plywood hull," contained a residential core of sorts; the units were shown configured in groups of two or three, called the BiPAC and TriPAC by Saarinen and Lundquist. Spanning between each PAC unit was a massive flat roof, and a cutaway perspective revealed that the construction of the roof was also a stressed-skin panel. The airy and spacious indoor-outdoor living area, so emblematic of West Coast incarnations of the postwar dream home, was fundamentally enabled by the stiff, lightweight, and structurally efficient combination of plywood and frame.

In the years following the war, even as architectural enthusiasm for all things factory-built began to ebb, the large figural grains of the plywood sheet continued to make their way into proposals for the modern postwar home—less because of the material's technical distinction, and more for its ability to impart a warm and livable character to a home's interior. In their sketches for Case Study House #3, produced in 1945, William Wurster and Theodore

Wurster and Bernardi, interior perspectives of Case Study House #3, printed in *Arts & Architecture*, July 1945

Bernardi prominently drew the grain figure of the peeled fir veneer as the interior wall surface. Referring to their decision to use fir plywood as a finish material, they spoke of its atmospheric, not technical, qualities, noting that it imparted a "rich mellow surface that we don't think can be beat."[14]

14 *Arts & Architecture*, July 1945, 37-38.

Back to Blanks

One could argue that in the last century, the valence of wood grain has changed just as drastically as the material properties of the myriad forms of improved wood that emerged during the same period. While the tight grain of old-growth pine had once assured builders of the timber's strength and density, the new graining of the plywood surface came to signify the strength and lightness that was intrinsic to any modern wall section. Likewise, the CLT blank is frequently rendered with an unfinished or natural surface, allowing a specificity up close—and an increasingly recognizable, pervasive beige from afar. If plywood led the way in associating remade grains with material improvement, the blank extends this position. Its legibility as wood—proffered by irregular grain and occasional knots—is fit within a larger grain-matrix of the gluelines, which are relentlessly regular. These knots and grains still speak of wood, but better wood—the next logical step in a long history of selectively editing material properties.

Also like plywood, which played a central role in tempting architects to creatively engage with sheets (and their inherent flatness, troublesome edge conditions, and generic modularity), the CLT blank arrives ready-made. The plywood sheet and CLT blank pose the same question—is this an object or a material?—similarly compounded by the persistence of the grain. In the first decades of the twentieth century, the transformation of wood into sheets enabled the material to remain relevant to a building culture that increasingly required objects, not materials. The emergence and proliferation of sheet goods, many of wood, fundamentally transformed the way houses were constructed in the United States. This new sheet is barely a sheet anymore, now that it is sometimes nearly a foot thick, and the transformations it will prompt remain to be seen. Architects have a new "better wood," but we have been making wood better for generations.

Essential Planes

Christopher C. M. Lee

Technological advancements in the construction industry, especially in structure and materials, often trigger speculation on their transformative potential for architecture. These conjectures can be broad, covering the processes and the product of the discipline itself, or the how(s) and what(s), and the wider reasoning and meaning that validate the adoption of the latest technology, or the why(s). The advent of steel and reinforced concrete frames in the nineteenth century enabled not only the multistory high-rise building as a new type, built with speed, but also the ideological bearings for architectural modernism—the conflation of the image of the machine and mechanical processes as architectural embodiment of a progressive, industrialized modern society. This is most evident in Le Corbusier's Maison Dom-Ino, an iconographic distillation of the promise of reinforced concrete construction into a set of principles and standards that would galvanize an entire generation of architects.

That was more than a century ago. The latest in similar breakthroughs is an ancient construction material, timber, now processed and reengineered as thin structural panels. Among other advantages, CLT promises quick on-site assembly and more economical construction for large-scale projects. Its arrival—as the planet faces a climate emergency—cannot be timelier. Because of carbon sequestration, timber is the most sustainable material there is for construction today, and the more we build in timber from renewable forests, the more carbon will be taken out of the atmosphere, limiting the rise in Earth's temperature. As CLT's adoption by architects and clients accelerates, the speculation that would naturally follow involves whether this structural system will shift the way we understand and create architecture, just as the "five points of a new architecture" propounded in the Maison Dom-Ino displaced the tropes of classicism in the 1920s. These are early days for such speculation, considering that the five points came twenty-four years after the first reinforced concrete building was built—a reasonable gestation period for a cogent and didactic promulgation. It is not the ambition of this essay to proclaim that another new architecture is just within

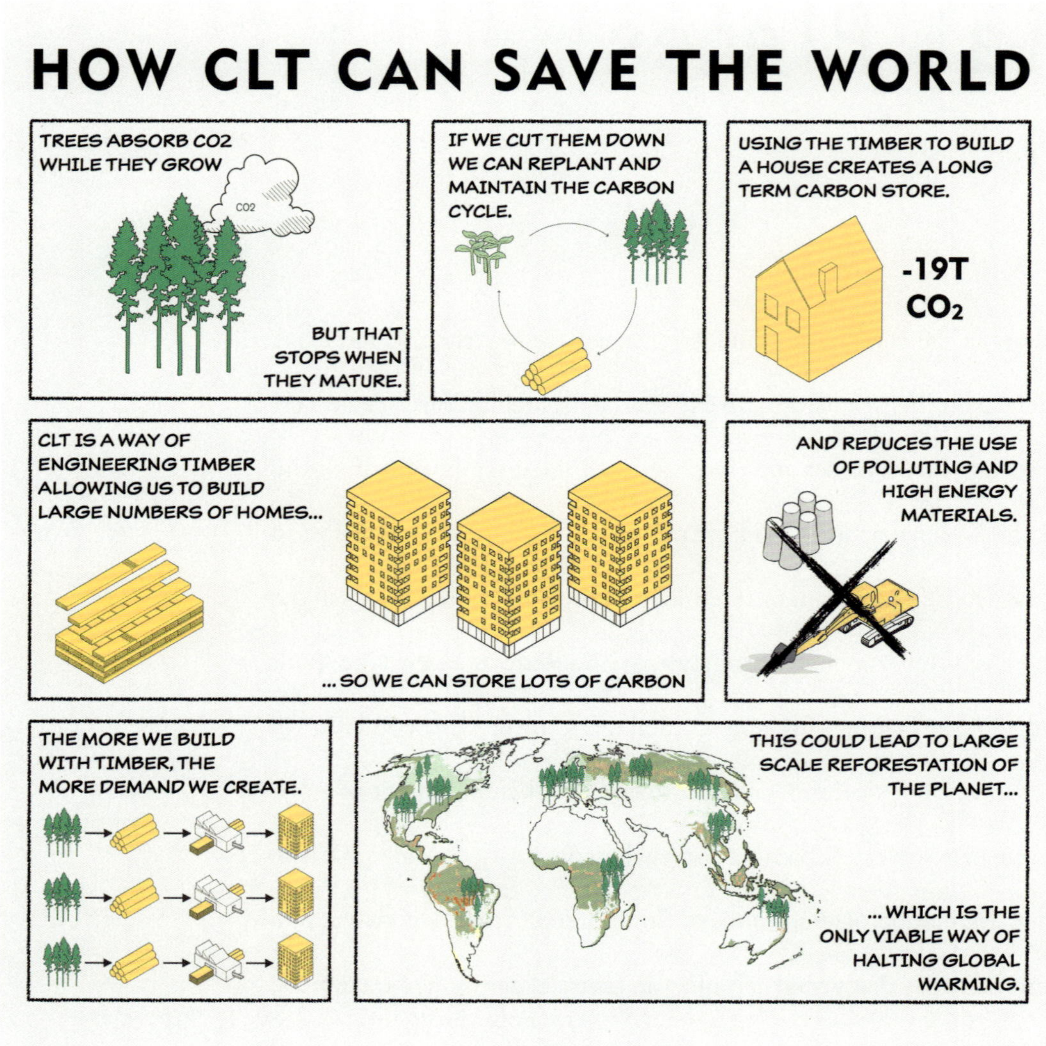

Waugh Thistleton Architects, "How CLT Can Save the World," 2019

grasp. What we can do, however, is feel our way around the contours and textures of CLT's potential.

Multistory timber structures are not new; as early as 725, Kohfukuji, a five-story Buddhist temple in Nara, Japan, was constructed entirely out of timber and reached a height of more than 150 feet. In North America, two- and three-story houses have been constructed in timber for centuries. What is novel is not the material but the structural system that accompanies this new method of processing and treating wood. The temple was constructed from an intricate post-and-beam system, the homes with balloon frames. In both cases, the irreducible element of structure and construction is a line. CLT, on the other hand, is *planar* structure. Each plane is made from several timber ply glued together under high pressure, with each layer rotated 90 degrees in alternation following their grain. These planes form a rigid frame when assembled as connected walls and floors.[1] This is the most significant difference, the major breakthrough of the technology. And this quality furnishes a path we might follow to speculate on the

1 "This material minimizes the inhomogeneity and anisotropy (directional dependency) inherent in wood's fibrous structure and allows high-performance, precisely calculable planar building materials to be made with dimensions that are limited only by manufacturing conditions." Hermann Kaufmann, Stefan Krotsch, and Stefan Winter, *Manual of Multi-storey Timber Construction* (Munich: Detail, 2018), 38.

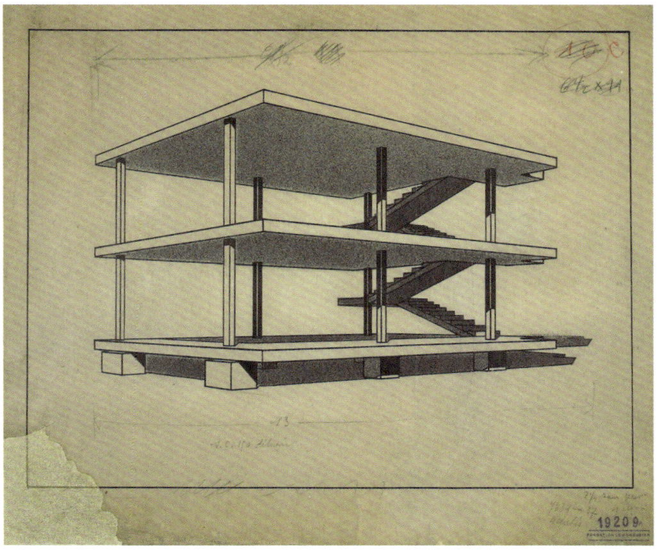

Left: Le Corbusier, Maison Dom-Ino, 1914

Right: Five-story wood pagoda, Kohfukuji Temple, Nara, Japan, 1426 (originally constructed in 730)

possibilities of CLT, and particularly its application within towers, the site of so much structural innovation in the past one hundred years.

CLT panels have an outstanding strength-to-weight ratio—20 percent higher than structural steel, and four to five times higher than unreinforced concrete in compression. Their lightness makes for easier transportation to site and higher workability on-site compared with steel and concrete. CLT's thermal insulation is fifteen times better than concrete and four hundred times better than steel. Based on the material's structural tectonics, CLT frames create compartmentalized rooms, allowing for more efficient heating compared with larger volumes of space afforded by skeleton frames. The most compelling reason and important factor for the adoption of CLT, and indeed the reason for its recent development, is that mass-engineered timber is a renewable and resource-efficient material. The embodied carbon of steel, concrete, and the hybrid of the two is estimated at 225 kilograms of CO_2 per square meter for the superstructure of a typical open plan commercial building from "cradle to site," considering extraction, processing, and delivery. Using CLT for the same superstructure, on the other hand, yields only 63 kilograms of CO_2 per square meter. Considering the sequestered carbon of timber is 900 kilograms of CO_2 per cubic meter, CLT panels have promising potential to achieve carbon neutrality.

For low-rise buildings, CLT uses more material than a conventional post-and-beam timber structure.

Given that CLT was first developed for mid- and high-density housing,[2] its adoption has been most pronounced in the mass-housing sector, especially in the United Kingdom and northern Europe. At first glance, most of these projects display no overt signs that they were built using CLT, as the timber structure has been cladded over by brick, precast concrete, ceramic, or metal panels. Only when the CLT is left exposed in the interior is its presence seen and felt. This is not surprising, because CLT must be protected from the elements. Even when treated, timber used as external cladding will turn from its natural brown and beige to silver and needs resealing every few years to prevent further deterioration. This makes it unviable as an external material for a multistory building. There are also other reasons to hide CLT. In the context of planning in the UK—where consent is based on qualitative judgements, such as appearance and maintaining visual harmony in the immediate context—brick facades are staple. Here, paradoxically, it is in its silence and concealment that CLT has been most conspicuous in overcoming the two immediate challenges of building today, securing consent to build by contextual conformity and emitting as little CO_2 as possible in the process.

This brings us back to how architecture, as cultural discourse and disciplinary knowledge, advances when it is prodded by new building technology. We can consider the issue through two interrelated questions, of coherence and invention: should architecture and structure form a coherent whole, and does the introduction of a new structural frame displace the prevalent tropes of architecture? Colin Rowe, in his 1956 essay "Chicago Frame," argued that the skeleton steel or concrete frame was integral to the search of a new architecture at the turn of the twentieth century and had almost become certainly the most recurrent motif in architectural modernism:

> The frame has established relationships, defined a discipline, and generated form. The frame has been the catalyst of an architecture; but one might notice that the frame has also *become* architecture, that contemporary architecture is almost inconceivably in its absence.... The frame has come to possess a value for contemporary architecture equivalent to that of the column for classical antiquity and the Renaissance. Like the column, the frame establishes throughout the building a common ration to which all the parts are related.[3]

3 Colin Rowe, "Chicago Frame," in *The Mathematics of the Ideal Villa and Other Essays* (Cambridge, MA: MIT Press, 1976), 90.

Rowe's essay traces the early development of the skeleton frame in Chicago in the second half of the nineteenth century through the works of Chicago School architects, namely Louis Sullivan and Daniel Burnham, and conducts a comparative analysis between the buildings produced by these pioneers of the high-rise and those by the pioneers of the modern

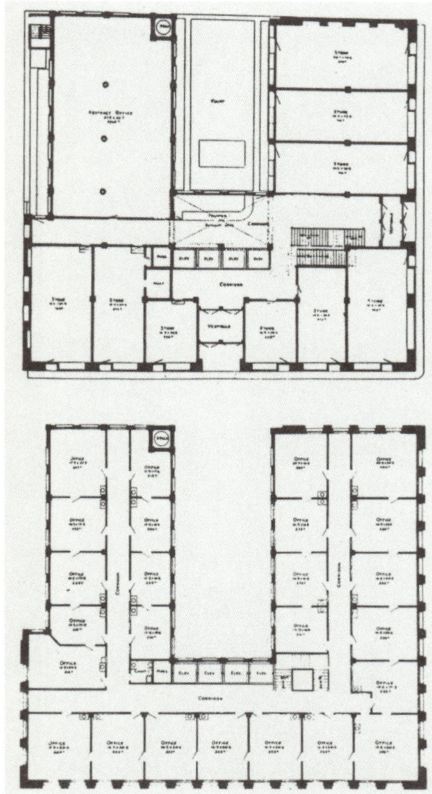

Clockwise from top left: Frank Lloyd Wright, St. Mark's-in-the-Bouwerie Towers, New York City, aerial perspective, ca. 1927–31

Adler & Sullivan, Wainwright Building, St. Louis, plans of first floor (above) and second through ninth floors (below), 1891

Decorated columns on the facade of the Wainwright Building

movement, Frank Lloyd Wright and Ludwig Mies van der Rohe. His analysis is split into two parts. The first concerns the expressive nature of the skeleton frame—whether it is treated as an expressive column or in pursuit of expressive space. The second asks if the structure is made to carry a functional or an ideological content.

In the first analysis, he pits Sullivan against Wright, contrasting the buildings of the former, including the Wainwright Building, in St. Louis (1891), and the latter's St. Mark's

Left: Burnham and Root, Reliance Building, Chicago, 1890–95

Right: Ludwig Mies van der Rohe, Glass Skyscraper, photograph of model, 1922

Tower, for New York City (1929). Sullivan's plans are undistinguished, a series of partitioned office spaces with the skeleton frame hidden behind an elaborately decorated facade. In this regard, Rowe argues, Sullivan accepted the technological breakthrough of the skeleton frame as a given and an enabler of a flexible interior for speculative commercial building, and no more. Attention was instead lavished on the design of expressive columns, just as a Renaissance architect would with a load-bearing system of masonry walls. The plan of St. Mark's Tower, on the other hand, is a result of Wright's rejection of the grid frame: he treats the tower's structure as a gigantic mushroom column supporting large trays of living spaces. This expressive space is instigated by the exploration of the structural limits and plasticity of concrete and steel and is fused with the structure as a coherent whole. This contrast unlocks the second thread of the argument: for Rowe, the work of the Chicago School was a response to immediate commercial needs and failed to adequately address a notion of society, and therefore were not appreciated as facts of culture.

Comparing Burnham to Mies, Rowe points out that the Reliance Building (1894), in Chicago's Loop, answers a particular problem: the existing needs of a commercial capital burgeoning with new high-rises. Mies's glass skyscraper for Berlin (1921), on the other hand, is an abstract solution to a general problem, envisioned to serve a future need and lifestyle, a vision made obvious in the way it rises against the backdrop of a wooded hill and a typical low-rise European city. In its physical and social context, there is no immediate necessity for (or ability to realize) Mies's skyscraper. It is therefore less a project for an office building than an "advertisement for a cause"[4]—a charged symbolic statement, and an implicit social criticism. For Rowe, the glass skyscraper engages both the moral and the aesthetic of our utopian sentiments; the high-rise is a symbol of a technologically oriented future society. In this reading, the advent of the skeleton frame is harbinger to a future society and its architecture, and Mies used the new structure prophetically, to frame an ideological content.

4 Rowe, 106.

In a similar vein, but drawing attention to the more ambiguous relationship between history and architectural modernism, Alan Colquhoun, in his 1972 essay "Displacement of Concepts in Le Corbusier," argues that the work of Le Corbusier differs from that of most other modern architects in the way it refers to architectural traditions, but at the same time stresses the need to reject them in favor of a new architecture informed by new technology and modern societal demands. As such, Corbusier's five points could have been formulated and fully understood only "with reference to the old, in absentia." Each of the five points departs from an existing and received practice, but then proceeds to reverse it:

> The use of *pilotis*, for example, is a reversal of the classical podium; it accepts the classical separation of the piano nobile from the ground but interprets this separation in terms of void rather than mass. The *fenêtre en longueur* is a contradiction of the classical window aedicule. The roof terrace contradicts the pitched roof and replaces the attic story with an open-air room. The free facade replaces the regular arrangement of window openings with a freely composed surface. The free plan contradicts the principle by which distribution was constrained by the need for vertically continuous structural walls and replaces it with a free arrangement of nonstructural partitions determined by functional convenience.[5]

5 Alan Colquhoun, "Displacement of Concepts in Le Corbusier," in *Essays in Architectural Criticism: Modern Architecture and Historical Change* (Cambridge, MA: MIT Press, 1981), 51.

These five conceptual displacements are afforded by none other than the concrete frame of the Maison Dom-Ino. The examples of Villa Savoye and Pavillon Suisse serve to illustrate

Amin Taha Architects, Barretts Grove, London, 2014–16

Clockwise from top: Barretts Grove and neighboring Victorian buildings; exposed CLT structure; brick screen

these points and have been well-discussed in the history of the movement, but Colquhoun's insights continue to resonate today, for they point to the productive intercourse between technological breakthroughs and received traditions.

Returning back to our central question and drawing from the above heuristics, we can postulate that the new structural frame is planar, and should therefore lend itself to a grammar of plates and planes. The combination of vertical and horizontal planes naturally produces rooms, or a series of rooms—a departure from the space of the free plan arising from the skeleton frame. Working through the problem of arranging rooms of multiple scales and proportions without the constraints of linear load paths may prove a rich territory for discovery.

In this early phase of CLT's adoption, the conceptual and technical separation between facade and structure is the norm and mirrors the early days of the skeleton frame's intrusion into architecture—as exemplified by Sullivan's expressive columns, developed without any meaningful acknowledgment of the potential of new spatial organization arising from an open frame. If coherence is unattainable and undesirable, this dichotomy can be approached with and wit and delight. Amin Taha's Barretts Grove in London ticks all the boxes of the requirement to "keep with its surroundings"—the five-story housing block's form and exterior materials are drawn from its immediate neighbors. But closer inspection reveals that the brick is expressed not as a faux load-bearing facade, a staple in London housing projects today, but as a screen, with open gaps between each brick where the mortar should be. This immediately suggests that the screen is placed on a supporting plane, which turns out to be a CLT frame, legible only when one enters the building. Openings glide across the planes, following no discernable linear load paths. The combination produces a building that is unusually light in appearance and proportion for its kind.

Three noteworthy attempts to bring about the fusion between facade and structure are still under construction. LAN's Wood'Up housing project, in the 13th arrondissement of Paris, and C.F. Møller's HSB 2023—Västerbroplan, in Stockholm, are both attempts to externalize the internal cellular arrangements of CLT rooms. LAN's housing block has an open, crate-like facade, with the exposed edges of the CLT panels clad in a transparent material. C.F. Møller's thirty-five-story apartment complex deploys the cellular aggregation of rooms to create a truncated tower form. The entire timber structure, adhering strictly to the

Top: LAN Architects, Wood'Up tower, Paris, 2017–21

Bottom: C.F. Møller, architect, and AKT II, structural engineer, HSB 2023—Västerbroplan, Stockholm, 2013

dimensions of rooms, is visible from the exterior, as glazing is hung from the structure like a curtain wall. Serie Architects' project in Porte de Montreuil, Paris, part of the winning bid for the C40 Reinventing Paris 2019, spans across the city's eastern ring road. The project uses CLT panels to create cellular rooms for a micro hotel and coworking building. The exposed timber takes on the rhythm of its internal structure but is expressed instead as a porticoed facade, alluding to the classicism of Haussmann's Paris. This can be read as an attempt at cultivating a grammar of timber tectonics from the the site's fertile historical context, informed by the logics of a newfound structure.

Serie Architects, Plot 3C, Collective for Climate, Porte de Montreuil, Paris, 2019. The project features a trabeated grammar of the external timber frame regulated by an internal structural modularity and the spacing of CLT rooms.

Of all the qualities and properties of CLT, one that should resonate with our increasing focus on and panic about our planet and its finite resources is that this new structural frame is resource-efficient—the structure *is* the space, *is* a room; it insulates; it is renewable and captures the very gas that threatens the extinction of our species. This redeeming efficiency is accompanied by a flat and smooth appearance, save for the inherent timber grain of ply, a blankness that points to a certain essentialism in the way we go about creating architecture and inhabiting our planet. It should point to a way of conceiving architecture that focuses on the judicious use of materials and resources, beautifully and delightfully considered, of course, guided by the speculation of the needs of society in the not-too-distant future.

On Blankness

Courtney Coffman

It's hard to get excited about material specifications, but there is a certain allure in CLT construction. Perhaps it took post-post aesthetic movements, like Normcore, to make such materials appealing for architectural exploration; CLT suggests possibility within its standardized economy.[1] Blankness has aesthetic value in these present days of "boring" and "not interesting" projects, which push long past the aughts' "Hokusai Wave" and "Reasons to Get Back into Shape."[2] Moving beyond the identifiable architectural icon and its didactic diagram, this moment isn't as easily digestible, despite the perceived simplicity of its method.

1 For more on self-designations of disciplinary movements, see Andrew Holder, "Forever After Or, The Work of Architecture in the Age of its Chronological Superfluity," *PRAXIS* 15, "Bad Architectures" (2019): 111-23.

2 See, for example, Paul Preissner's *Kind of Boring* and Andrew Atwood's *Not Interesting*, in contrast to Alejandro Zaera-Polo's "The Hokusai Wave" and "The Politics of the Envelope" and R. E. Somol's "12 Reasons to Get Back into Shape."

One of the pervasive challenges of CLT is how to manage its scaleless quality—an issue Jennifer Bonner and Hanif Kara interrogated in their CLT research studio at Harvard's Graduate School of Design.[3] Like most prefabricated materials, CLT implies an economy of iterative sameness, a generic architecture with a rather blank austerity. According to Bonner, the studio worked hard both to undo the blankness of CLT—to deny the reading of the blank—and to use the reading of blankness as a desirable design methodology. It is precisely in these dual readings of blankness, in its relentless self-similarity, where a conceptual ripeness occurs. A certain elegance rests in the *un*-iconographic form, where multiple readings and misreadings purposefully create an open-endedness, dissolving the instantly identifiable, or its iconic representation. Of course, the rub here is that blankness, like Normcore, cannot escape representation, despite its indifference to it.

3 Led by an architect (Bonner) and an engineer (Kara), the studio is a metaphorically apt vehicle for research on CLT—given that as a structural system, CLT flattens both materials and the distinction between architecture and engineering in its construction process.

Nonetheless, blankness conveys a milieu of visual imagery and historiographical arguments distinctly connected to the architectural object. This particular notion of blank expands beyond void space or erasure; it is an ontological abstraction that simultaneously questions reality. In this blankness, there's always a given: the blank is a response to a context or object covered or obscured, a technique to draw attention to what's really important.[4] Instead of relying on the same canonical architectural and art historical references to trace this trajectory, let's redistribute some *other* references to create a new trajectory: a visual culture of the blank.

4 *blank*, transitive verb: "cover up, obscure, or cause to appear blank or empty."

The blankness of Kazimir Malevich's *Black Square* begins this visual inquiry. Within the deep black of the canvas, there is a Suprematist composition lurking just below the cracked surface; an X-ray of the painting reveals abstract geometric shapes colliding in space. Our familiar reading of the simplistic black square grows more suspicious with art historian Aleksandra Shatskikh's assertion that "Malevich's understanding of *Black Square* also manifested itself in his resolute transformation of historical reality itself."[5] She divulges that Malevich backdated *Black Square* from its creation in 1915 to 1913, post-rationalizing not only the painting, but also a crucial though short-lived movement called Fevralism, a prequel to Dada:

Aleksandra Shatskikh, *Black Square: Malevich and the Origin of Suprematism* (New Haven, CT: Yale University Press, 2012), x.

> By August 1915 there were already quite a few absolutely nonobjective works, and Suprematism's creator had already pushed back its birth to December 1913. This meant that Fevralism, which is fixed in letters and the "1915 Painting Exhibition," appeared chronologically after the discovery of Suprematism, something which, according to Malevich, should not have been.
>
> The artist sacrificed Fevralism to Suprematism by depriving it of its place in time and space.... Malevich's first personal "ism" cleared the way for his chief "ism."[6]

Shatskikh, 32, 33.

In essence, *Black Square* embodies a quintessential blankness in both its articulation, covering the underlying composition, and its conceptual power to obscure chronology. But even more interesting is to consider *Black Square* in relation to another Malevich piece, also created in 1915, titled *Alogisme 29. Derevnya (Alogism 29. Village).* This modest work also contains a black square—a heavy-handed pencil outline—with the Russian word for "village" written inside. Below the slightly off-center village square is a lightly scrawled description: translated to English, "instead of drawing the huts of nature's nooks, better to write 'Village' and it will appear to each with finer details and the sweep of an entire village."[7] The wordplay of the art object forges yet another sense of blankness, an ontological provocation of multiple readings through our individualistic experiences of language and meaning.[8] This open-ended gesture invites the viewer to call into question reality—what constitutes not only a work of art, but also the feigned structures of our world.[9]

Quoted in Shatskikh, 14.

"Fevralism erased the boundaries of what was customarily designated by the word 'art.'" Shatskikh, 33.

As Shatskikh demonstrates, *Village* is a precursor to works such as Joseph Kosuth's chair(s).

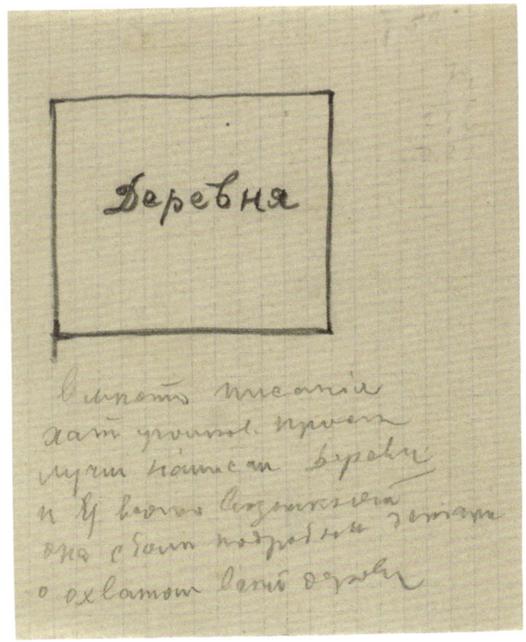

Clockwise from top left: Kazimir Malevich, *Black Square*, 1915

Kazimir Malevich, *Alogisme 29. Derevnya (Alogism 29. Village)*, 1915

Virgil Abloh: "PAY PER VIEW", Kaikai Kiki Gallery, Tokyo, 2018

The designer Virgil Abloh deploys this technique of self-explanatory descriptions in a more contemporary context, calling attention to the overt objectness of readymades. Not only does Abloh's work quote those who also notoriously quote precedent though clever swerves, but he further elevates—and authors—*his* iterations with the proper punctuation of quotation marks.[10] In his 2018 exhibition *"PAY PER VIEW"*,[11] Abloh sources the graphic power of Malevich's *Black Square* through the "hot" media of billboards rendered completely blank with black paint.[12] In a Decaux-does-Rothko gesture, each gallery wall carries the cultural weight of these chromatically deep rectangular canvases while a black-pile rug that reads "Oil on Canvas" rests on the floor, expertly performing the function of museum label. Here, the white Helvetica letters on the plush wool provide information on the media of the billboards, but they also designate the slippage of the institution and its signifiers with a candid blankness.

Five years prior, Abloh worked on one of the most influential blank images of recent: the album art for Kanye West's *Yeezus*. The simplicity of the album's design rests in its "less-but-better" approach—a squeaky-fresh reflective compact disc shines behind the clear plastic crystal case, which is sealed with an orange sticker.[13] The image of a blank compact disc missing its album sleeve was commonplace in the early days of online music-sharing services, where the medium of the blank disc transcended genre in favor of random masses of downloadable content. The everydayness of this object-cum-artifact bookended the era of digital downloads for streaming subscriptions; the ear trained for curated mixes succumbed to the analogous (autonomous?) algorithm. The blank disc as album art hammed up the death rattle of yesterday's "burned" music—further lamented by the nostalgic packaging tape that was once physically broken by our fingers to open the album for play, a ritual now reduced to a click.

Yet it's the tape that binds in another visual example, proving that the structure of the blank is rather prudent. Like Abloh, the jazz musician Jason Moran is a multifaceted creative who moves between disciplines and relies on open-ended structure to allow for improvisation. The cover of the catalog that accompanied Moran's 2018 exhibition at the Walker Art Center, in Minneapolis, depicts a floating matte-black square in which empty music staffs appear as a series of debossed lines—sheet music awaiting notation—adhered to chipboard with faux tape in a ripe tomato red.[14] The *trompe l'oeil* cover evokes both the limitlessness of the blank space found on sheet music and Moran's musical methodology:

When asked by a student about his "practice routine"—in parallel to the basketball player Allen Iverson's notion of practice—during a lecture at the Harvard Graduate School of Design, Abloh replied, "I've trained my eye to be creative. That's what I'm doing now with the quotes. Do some random activity that forces your eye to see things it normally wouldn't." Virgil Abloh, *"INSERT COMPLICATED TITLE HERE"*, *The Incidents* (Berlin: Sternberg, 2018), 71.

11 Takashi Murakami's Kaikai Kiki Gallery, in Tokyo, proved a fitting choice of venue, considering Murakami himself is no stranger to the subversive power of consumerism within the white box.

12 Consider the collapse of commercialization—the medium is the message—with the obfuscation of Hugh Ferriss's architectural forms rendered in dark charcoal.

13 Note that the Baldessari-like sticker appears redder on the digital album than on the actual compact disc, where it's more construction orange. This discrepancy speaks to the iterative process of developing the album's artwork; see Michael Darling, ed., *Virgil Abloh: "Figures of Speech"* (Munich: DelMonico Books / Prestel, 2019). For a commentary on the similarity between the "finished" *Yeezus* artwork and Peter Saville's shelved design for a 2001 New Order album, see, for example, Sydney Gore, "Who Does the 'Yeezus' Artwork Really Belong To?," *Highsnobiety*, September 27, 2018, https://www.highsnobiety.com/p/kanye-west-yeezus-artwork-controversy. The parallels are not just visual: "The revelation that [West] listened to

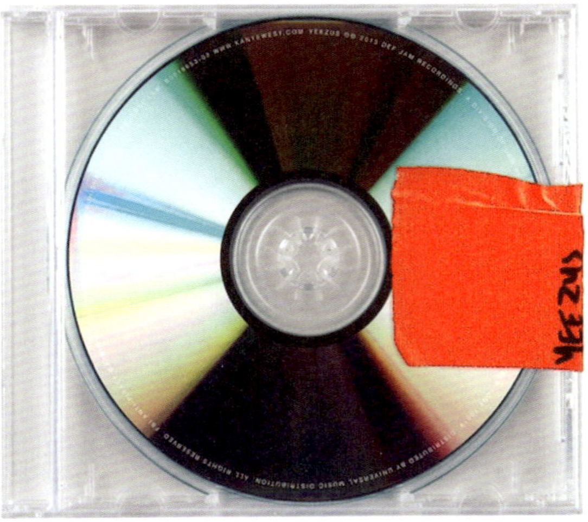

Left: Virgil Abloh, album concept art for Kanye West's *Yeezus*, 2013

Right: Cover of *Jason Moran* (Minneapolis: Walker Art Center, 2018). Exhibition catalog designed by 12:01 — Office of Hassin Rahim.

> When I'm in the midst of a solo, I like to play phrases of music "over the bar line." This means that I resolve the phrase far past where/when the ordinal resolution occurs. I stack the phrases, kind of like run-on sentences. That tug on the music also pulls the musicians and the listener, so we all tilt together.[15]

This is the moment when Moran's technical craft breaks free of transposed structure in favor of space for improvisation. His expansion of time and (paper)space may be abstract—perhaps it takes a trained ear to hear when he goes "over the bar line"—but his spontaneous actions break down the parameters of musical notation to create new expressions, filling the empty edges with musical marginalia.

Leaping from analog musical notation to digital artifacts, there is a particular resonance between Moran's blank space beyond the end bar—the site of musical infinity—and Hito Steyerl's vision of viewing the world through its infinite pixels. Hidden among the California desert is a large-scale digital resolution target, and like a typical resolution test card, it consists of various white lines against a black background—in this case, a square asphalt slab. "This is a resolution target. It measures the resolution of the world as a picture," a voiceover reveals in Steyerl's 2013 video work *How Not to Be Seen: A Fucking Didactic Educational .MOV File*.[16] As Steyerl moves between analog and virtual space during the video's presentation of five lessons, she demonstrates how our exploration of data easily slips into our exploitation as data, how the distinction between bodies and pixels can help us disappear by allowing us to recalibrate ourselves, assimilating a digital vision. To master Steyerl's disappearing act, our built environment must either become hyperspecific—for example, by blending into a gated

a lot of Joy Division is extremely instructive as to how *Yeezus* sounds," the critic Claire Lobenfeld observed in a *SPIN* roundtable marking *Yeezus*'s release, noting "the dark cloud of Ian Curtis looming over the album." "Sheezus Talks: A Critical Roundtable," June 21, 2013.

14 The cover references *WINDS*, a 2015 work by the artist.

15 Jason Moran, "Artist's Statement: Closer," *Jason Moran*, ed. Adrienne Edwards (New York: D.A.P./Distributed Art Publishers, 2018), 10.

The resolution test screen looks a lot like the CLT kit of parts. Composed of gray targets in the California desert by US forces, the resolution target site was used to test now outdated methods of aerial photography, and has been decommissioned since 2006.

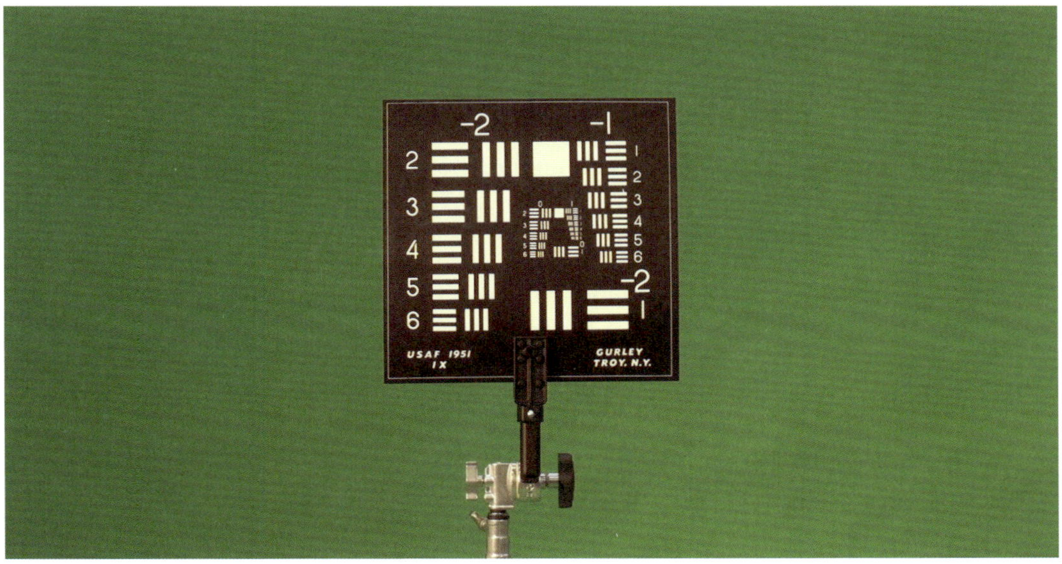

Stills from Hito Steyerl, *How Not to Be Seen: A Fucking Didactic Educational .MOV File*, 2013

suburban community—or extremely emptied out into the blankness of a green screen, wherein artificial experiences manifest. It's interesting then, strictly as a superficial observation, to consider the aesthetic similarities between the resolution card/target and the mill files for CLT construction—the blank lines calibrating our built environment. As with green screen, our resolution problems dissolve with the blank: we can be anywhere and yet nowhere. The blankness hides us in plain sight and emphasizes our context.

In her fifth instruction, "How to Become Invisible by Merging into a World Made of Pictures," Steyerl uses the green screen to project the audience into a series of highly produced architectural renderings of generic, siteless luxury developments. The sequence immerses viewers in the amenities of the building project and boasts blandly titled programmatic spaces, such as a lush public square labeled "Exquisite Green," while semitransparent ghosts (scale figures) walk about the community. As the audience, we also blend into this virtual space; the familiar journey of pixels within pixels is akin to the digital stream of infinite content architects both produce and consume, manifesting our disciplinary sameness. The blank, as a "slower" space, stands in opposition to the context of highly resolved images and megapixels; through its blankness, it both resists (as an object) and projects (as a screen) the constant design porn churning on our devices.[17]

17 See Christopher Hawthorne's "Boring Architecture? Yes, Please" (*Los Angeles Times*, November 16, 2017), in which he references Sam Kahn's essay "The Triumph of the Quiet Style."

Riffing on the iconicity of stararchitect structures, the artist Jose Dávila's series *There But Not* extracts the architectural object at the core of his photographs, leaving an empty white space.[18] Dávila photographs various buildings in situ and then removes them with surgical precision, soliciting viewers to consider the iconicity of architectural form and pointing attention to contextual details that may have been previously overlooked. The compositions excise certain landmarks—such as the Köln Cathedral or the Empire State Building—and demonstrate the impact of their removal on the city by suddenly foregrounding the heterogenous density that surrounds the flat, figural void. Dávila's technique recalls John Baldessari's "dots," where the editing of an "as-found" object, the photograph, reorients both the viewer and the work itself. Here, Baldessari obscured the object, and Dávila extracts it, yet both techniques culminate in a figural blankness. The early iterations of Baldessari's "dots" use newspaper clippings of random events and announcements to draw attention to the nuances of context—body language, objects on a table or in someone's hands—by covering faces with round price stickers. He later forgoes as-found faces and stickers altogether and scales up his subjects, obscuring building facades with hand-painted circles.

18 See also page 132 of *S, M, L, XL*, where OMA's Villa dall'Ava is shown as a blank, white silhouette (New York: Monacelli Press, 1995).

While their respective techniques vary—subtractive (Dávila) versus additive (Baldessari)—the end result transposes a blank into a given context, much like Bonner's debut CLT project, Haus Gables. One of the first CLT residential projects in North America, Haus Gables demonstrates how the blankness of CLT lends itself to formal provocations like Dávila's and Baldessari's. In an aerial drone shot, the slim, white home is nestled in the sprawl of residential Atlanta, its distinctive form photographed as if it were an axonometric rendering. Deceptive in both scale and material, the house reads as a paper model photomontaged into a stock image of a neighborhood. Subtle hints—such as the roof, with its many "hats"—suggest that this isn't a Photoshop job, but rather a successful performance of the

Clockwise from top left: Jose Dávila, *Buildings You Must See Before You Die*, 2009

John Baldessari, *National City (W, 1, 2, 3, 4, 5, 6, B)* (detail), 1996/2009

Jennifer Bonner / MALL, Haus Gables, Atlanta, 2018

Left: Jennifer Bonner and Germane Barnes in Opa-locka, Florida. Part of the project Made in Opa-locka, by Bonner+Stayner (Jennifer Bonner and Christian Stayner).

Right: John Baldessari, *Cutting Ribbon, Man In Wheelchair, Paintings (version #2)* (detail), 1988

blank, here as support for equally blank surface. Further proof rests in a portrait of Bonner and her collaborator Germane Barnes, who don Baldessari-like circles while standing in the streets of Opa-locka, Florida. Their "dots" are more complex than "as-found" stickers: they are massing models of the project Made in Opa-locka possibly the seedling of Haus Gables's roof.

Projects like Haus Gables, and the speculative proposals in this book, demonstrate how the challenge of resolving CLT's blankness can be mined for latent possibilities. Each methodological example reveals a new strategy on how this can be done—whether by celebrating this quality or subverting it—through language and shifting ontologies, reconsidering cultural artifacts, or simple handmade gestures. The built environment becomes ripe with new *subjective* readings. Instead of denying blankness as a consequence of production, it's time for a little improvisation, to go past the bar, to situate the potential of CLT as not only a mere building material, but a medium of possibility.

House 01: Blank Panels
Plan: p. 37 (left)
Elevation: p. 52
Blank Panels: pp. 85, 100
Structural Analysis: pp. 210–12
CLT Forecast: p. 237

House 03: Blank Panels
Plan: p.38
Elevation: p.51 (bottom)

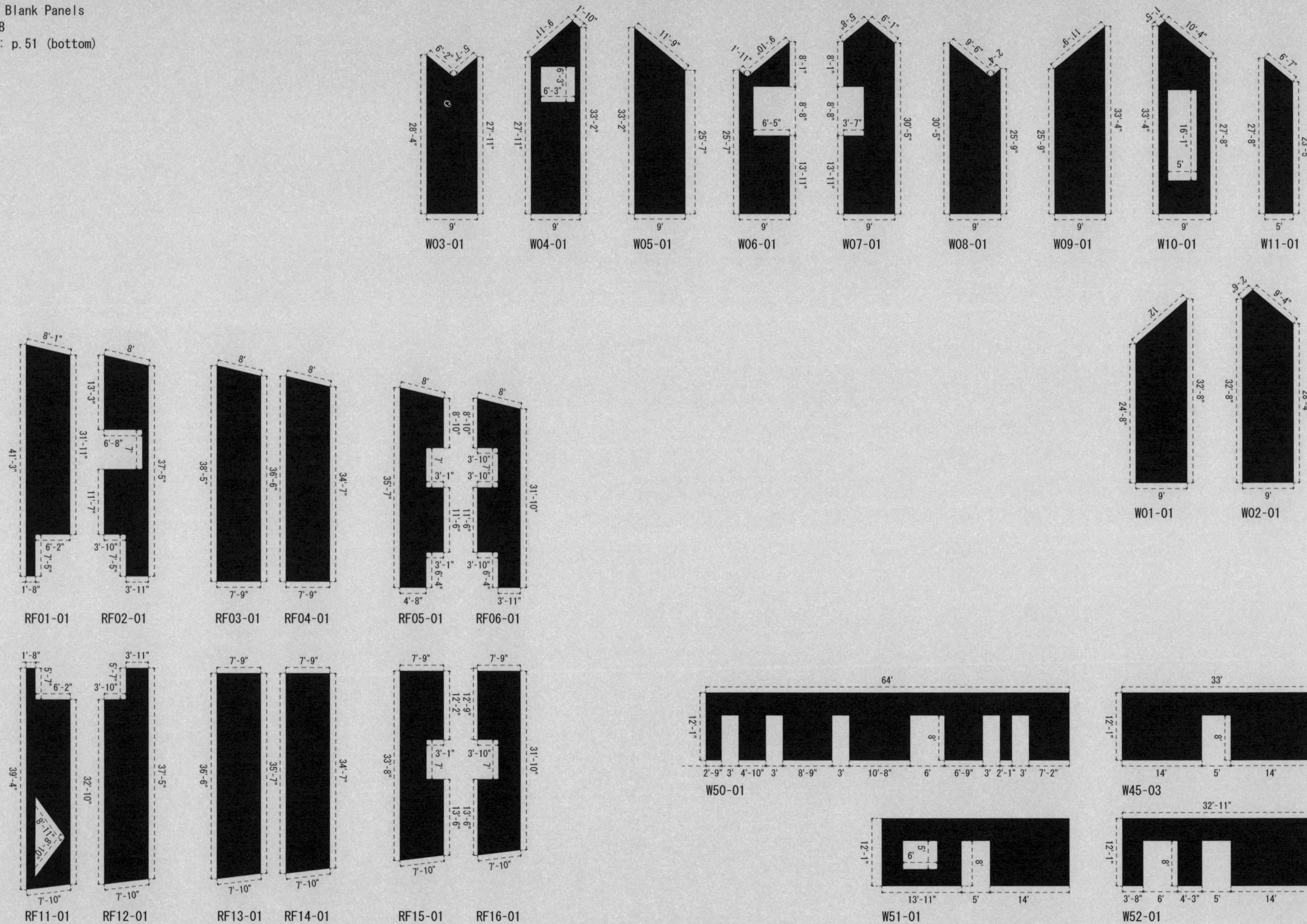

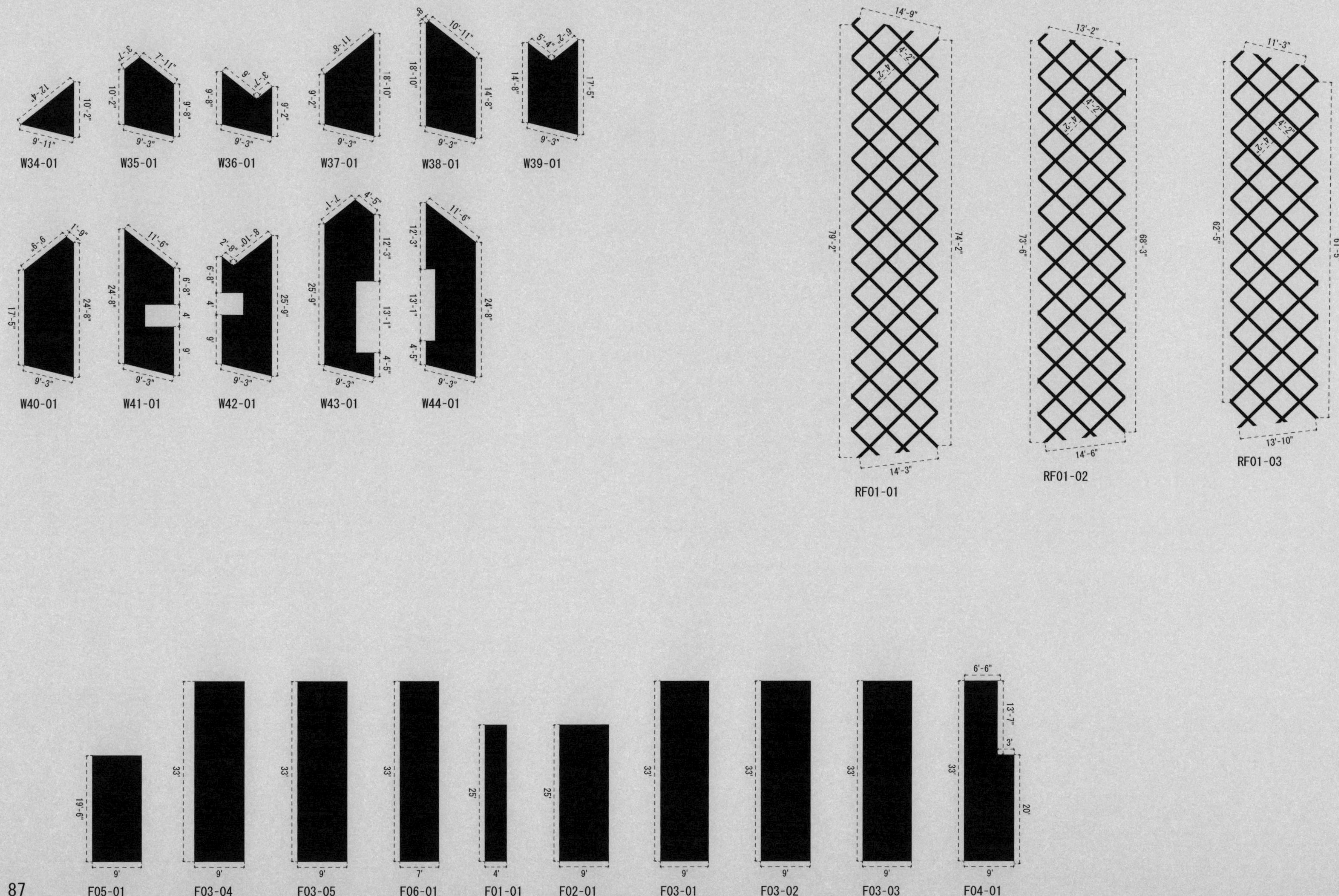
W34-01
W35-01
W36-01
W37-01
W38-01
W39-01
W40-01
W41-01
W42-01
W43-01
W44-01
RF01-01
RF01-02
RF01-03
F05-01
F03-04
F03-05
F06-01
F01-01
F02-01
F03-01
F03-02
F03-03
F04-01

House 13: Blank Panels
Plan: p.44 (right)
Elevation: p.51 (top)
CLT Forecast: p.236

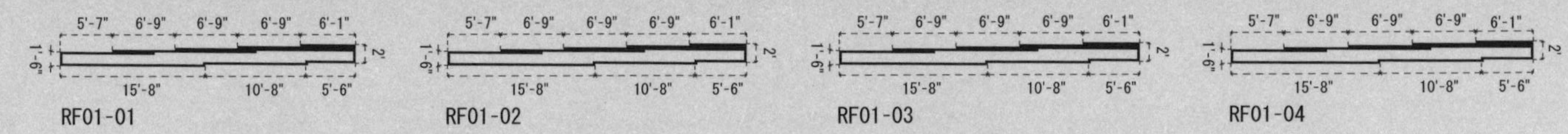

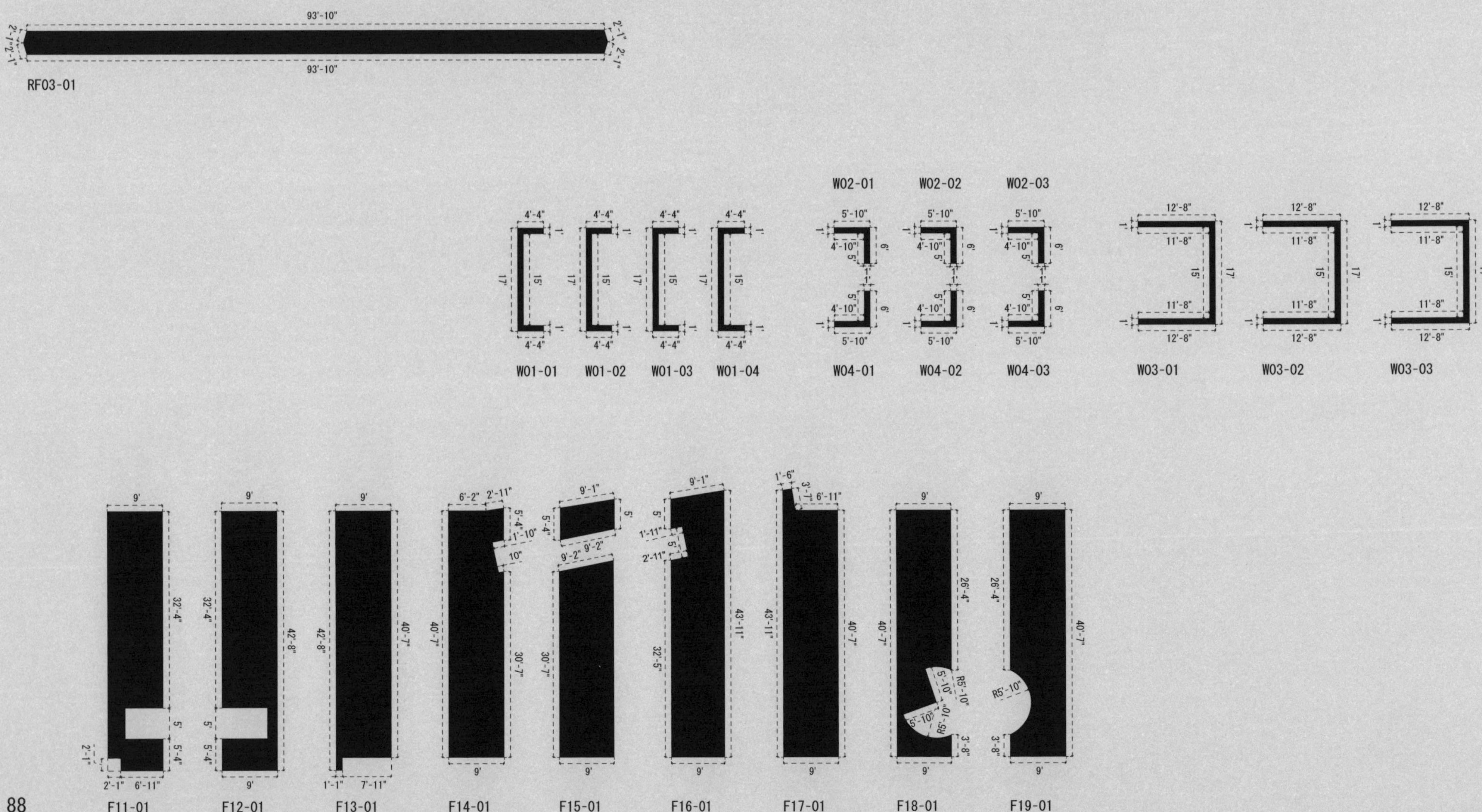

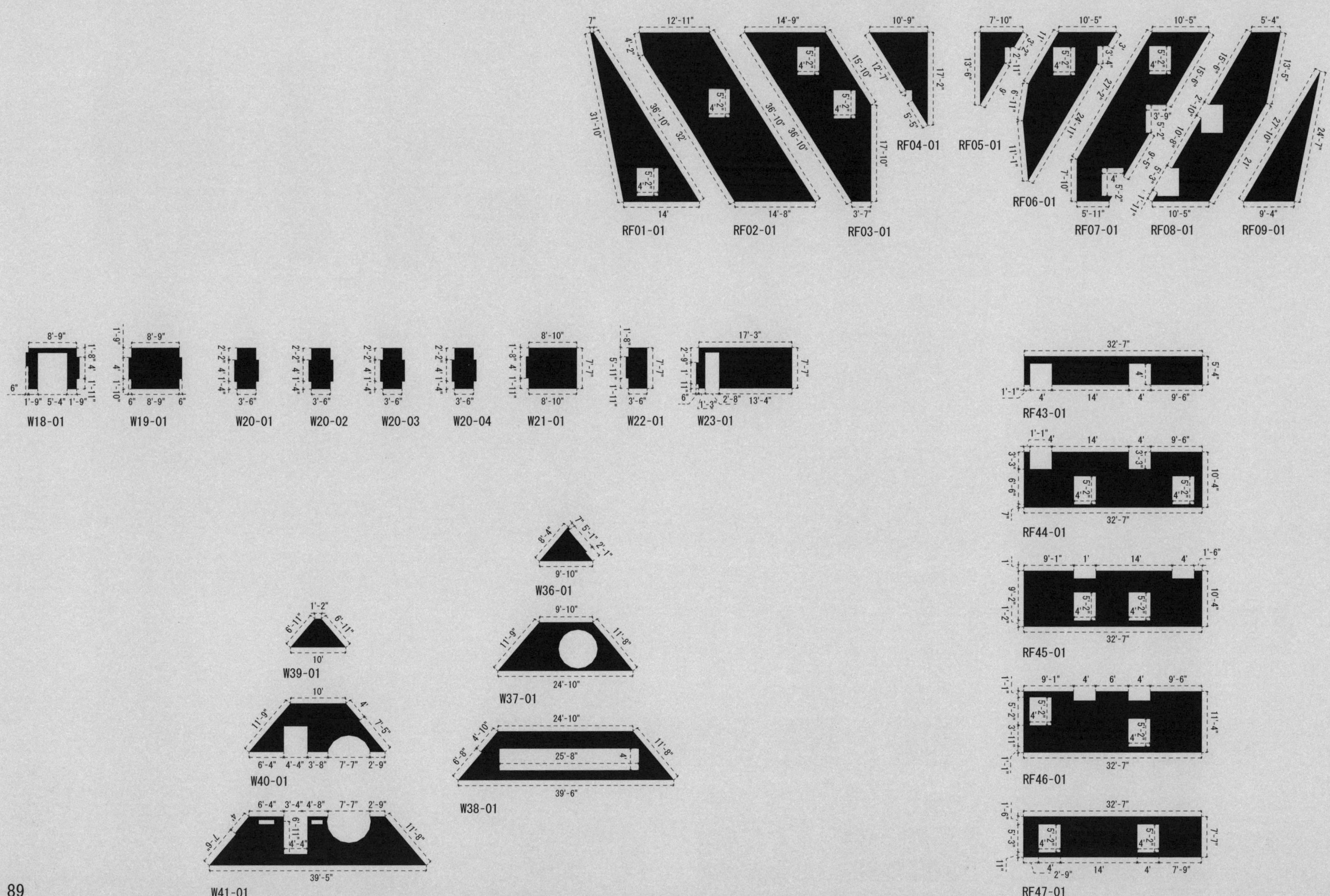
RF01-01
RF02-01
RF03-01
RF04-01
RF05-01
RF06-01
RF07-01
RF08-01
RF09-01
W18-01
W19-01
W20-01
W20-02
W20-03
W20-04
W21-01
W22-01
W23-01
RF43-01
RF44-01
RF45-01
RF46-01
RF47-01
W36-01
W37-01
W38-01
W39-01
W40-01
W41-01

House 10: Blank Panels
Plan: p.43 (left)
Elevation: p.45
CLT Forecast: p.226

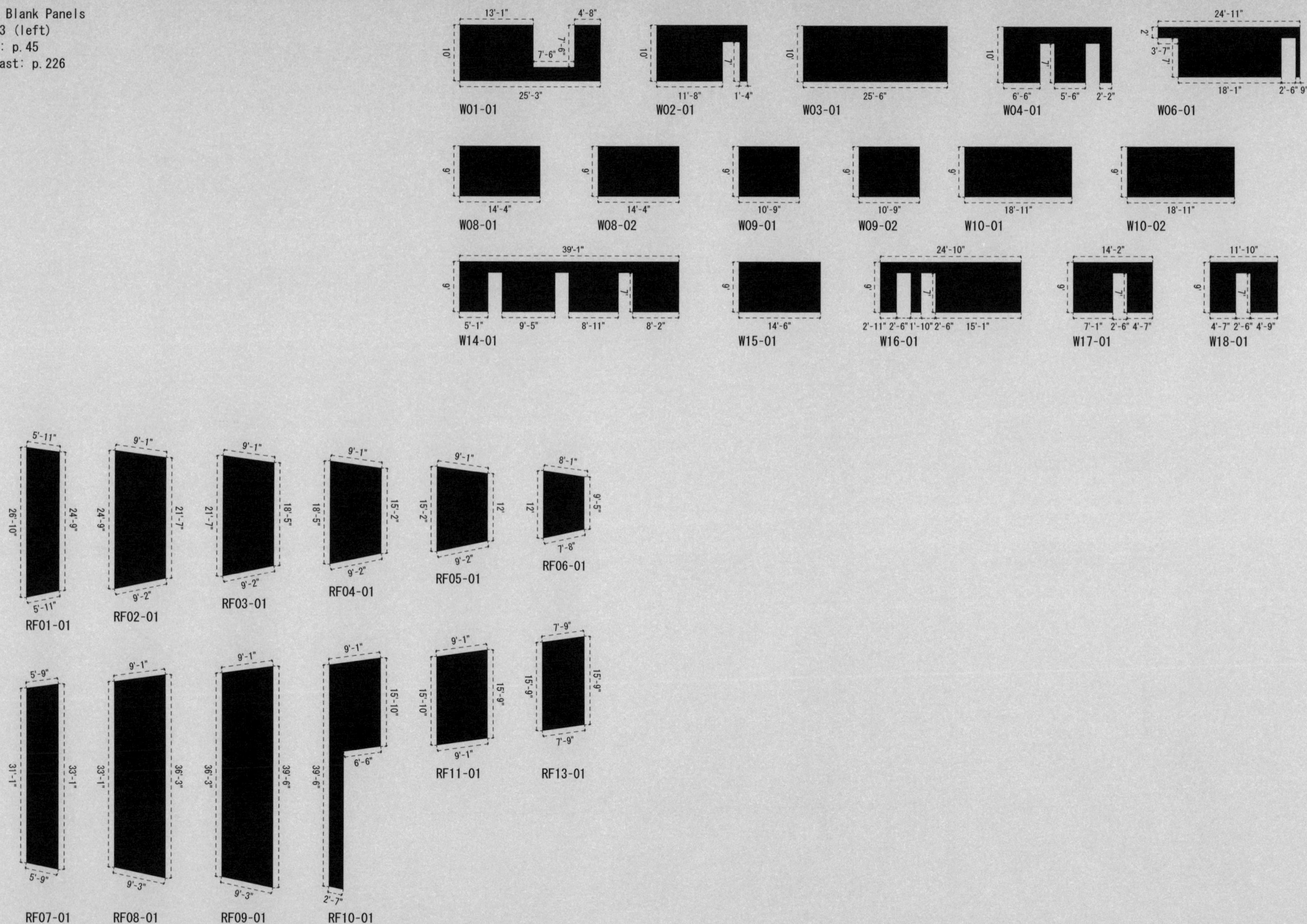

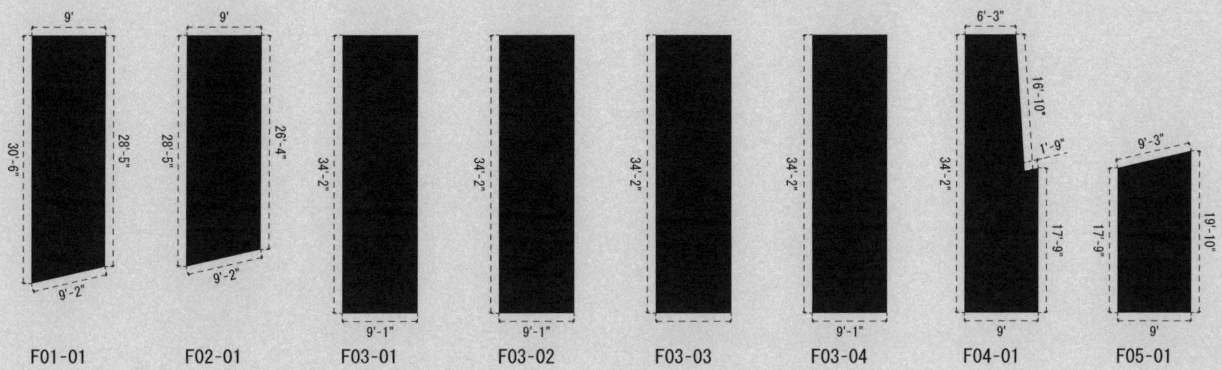
F01-01
9'
30'-6"
28'-5"
9'-2"
F02-01
9'
28'-5"
26'-4"
9'-2"
F03-01
34'-2"
9'-1"
F03-02
34'-2"
9'-1"
F03-03
34'-2"
F03-04
34'-2"
9'-1"
F04-01
6'-3"
16'-10"
1'-9"
34'-2"
17'-9"
9'
F05-01
9'-3"
17'-9"
19'-10"
9'

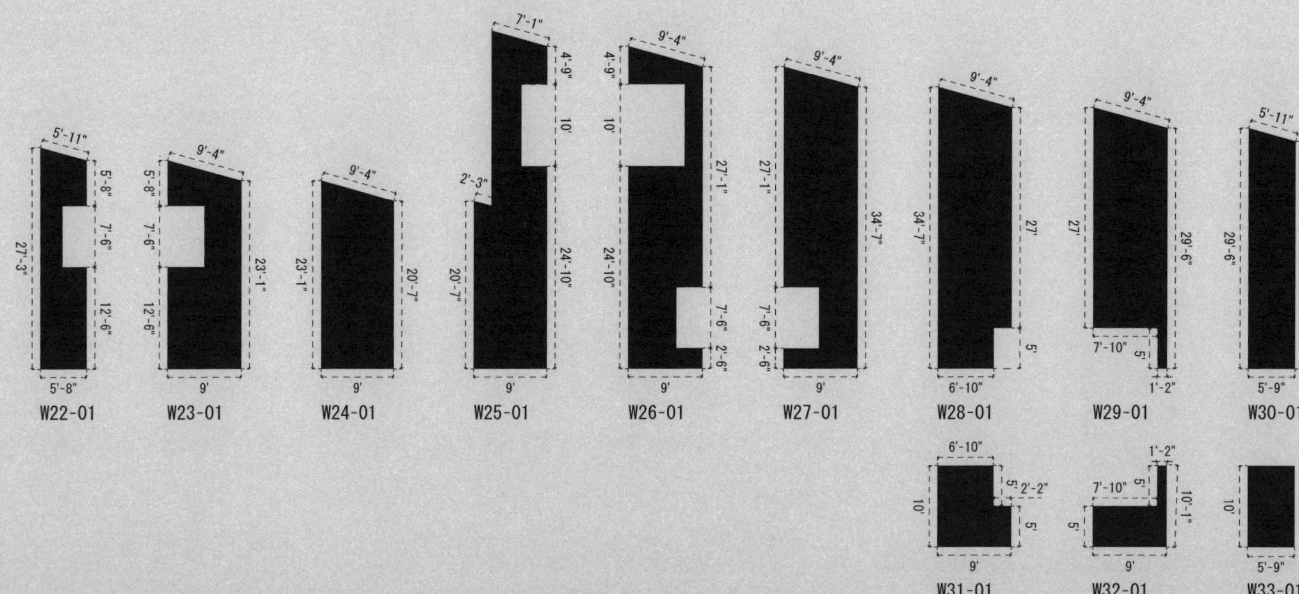
W22-01
5'-11"
5'-8"
7'-6"
12'-6"
27'-3"
5'-8"
W23-01
9'-4"
5'-8"
7'-6"
12'-6"
23'-1"
9'
W24-01
9'-4"
23'-1"
20'-7"
9'
W25-01
7'-1"
4'-9"
10'
2'-3"
20'-7"
24'-10"
9'
W26-01
9'-4"
4'-9"
10'
27'-1"
24'-10"
7'-6"
2'-6"
9'
W27-01
9'-4"
27'-1"
34'-7"
7'-6"
2'-6"
9'
W28-01
9'-4"
34'-7"
27'
5'
6'-10"
W29-01
9'-4"
27'
29'-6"
7'-10"
5'
1'-2"
W30-01
5'-11"
29'-6"
27'-11"
5'-9"
W31-01
6'-10"
5'
2'-2"
10'
5'
9'
W32-01
1'-2"
7'-10"
5'
10'-1"
5'
9'
W33-01
10'
5'-9"

Tower 11: Blank Panels
Plan: p. 7 (left)
Elevation: p. 14 (left)
Wood Grain Model: p. 140
Structural Analysis: pp. 206-9
CLT Forecast: p. 229

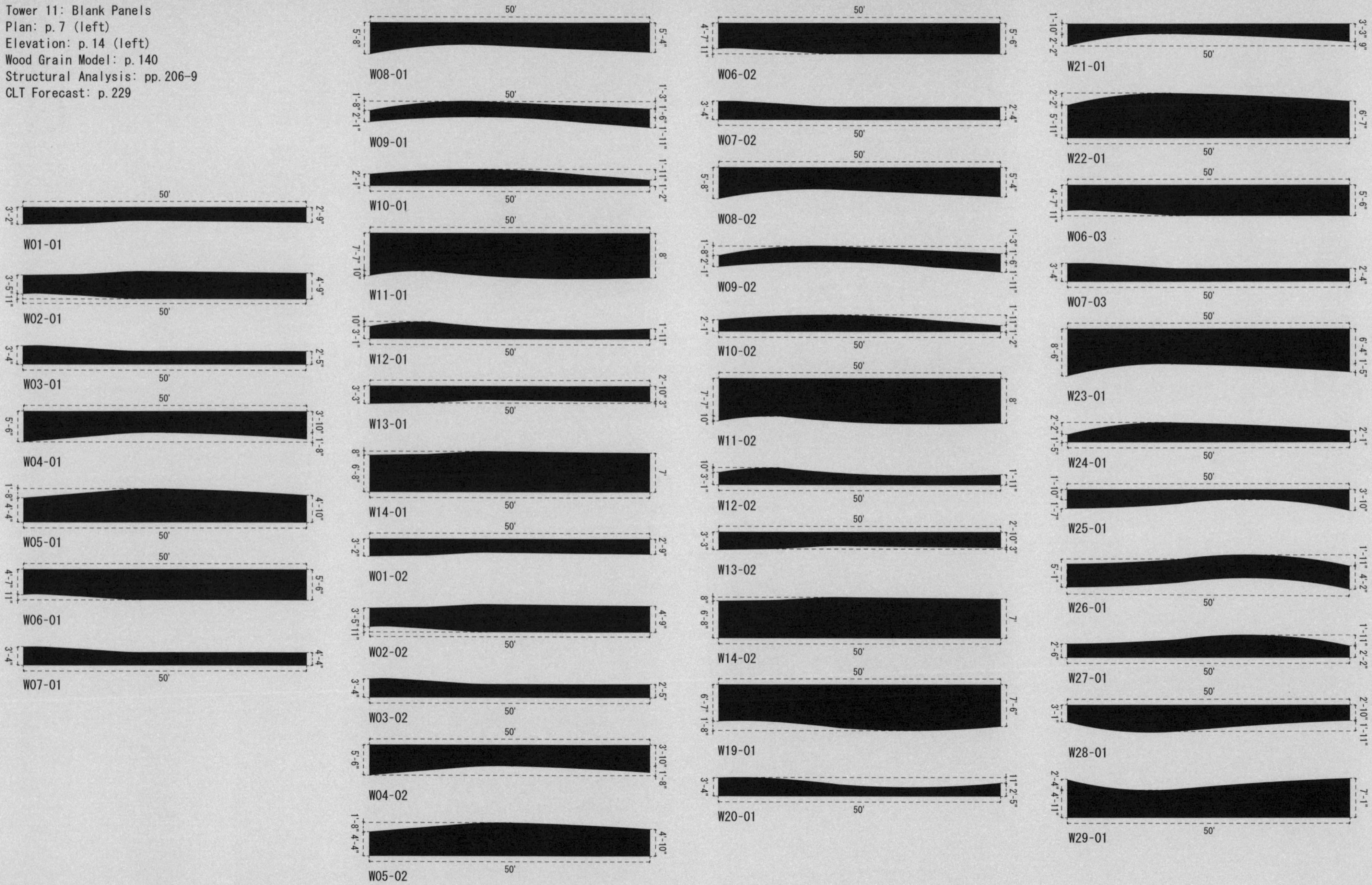

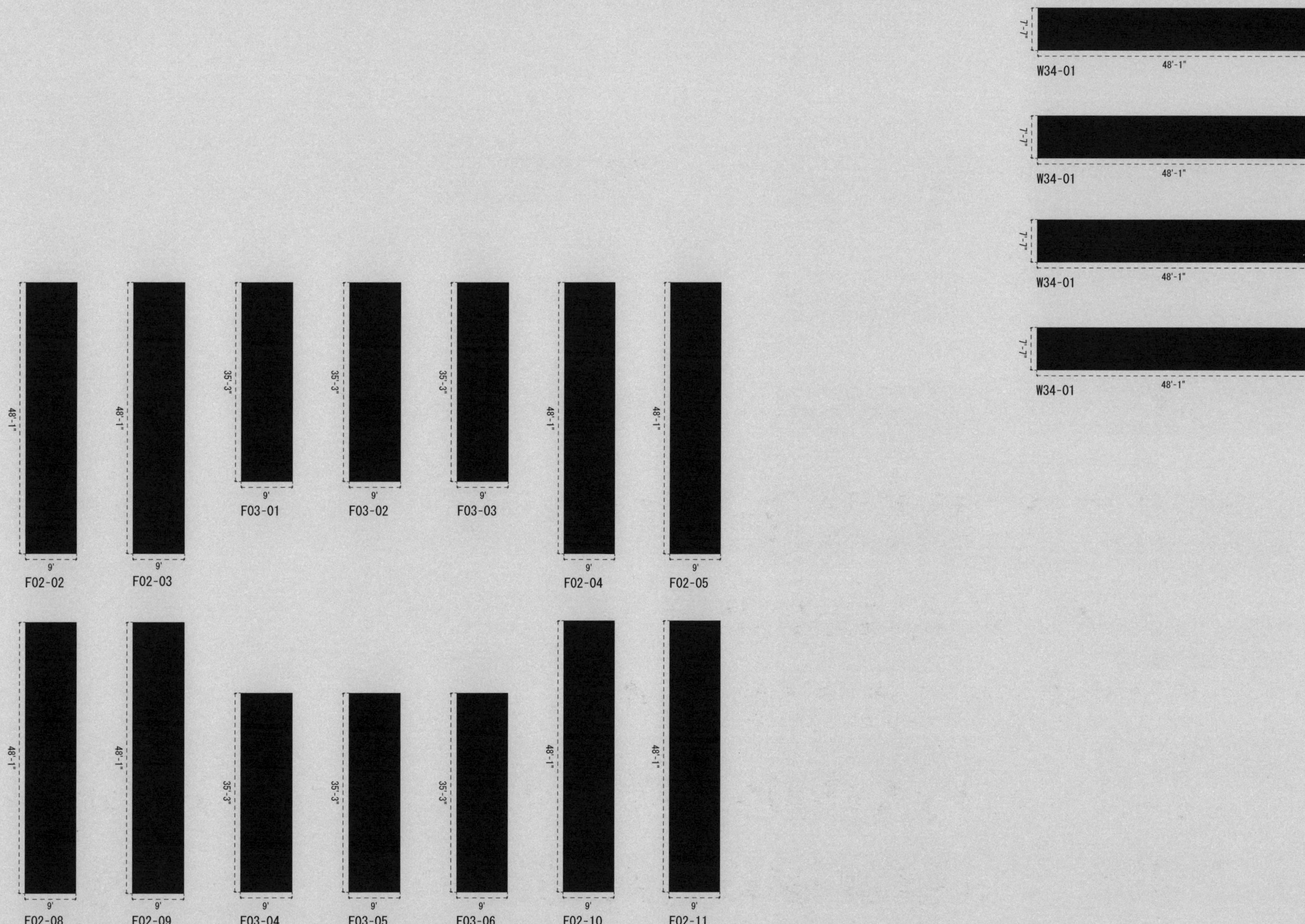
W34-01
48'-1"
7'-7"
W34-01
48'-1"
7'-7"
W34-01
48'-1"
7'-7"
W34-01
48'-1"
7'-7"
F02-02
F02-03
F03-01
F03-02
F03-03
F02-04
F02-05
F02-08
F02-09
F03-04
F03-05
F03-06
F02-10
F02-11
48'-1"
35'-3"
9'

Tower 01: Blank Panels
Plan: p.1 (left)
Elevation: p.9 (right)
Wood Grain Model: p.131
CLT Forecast: p.235

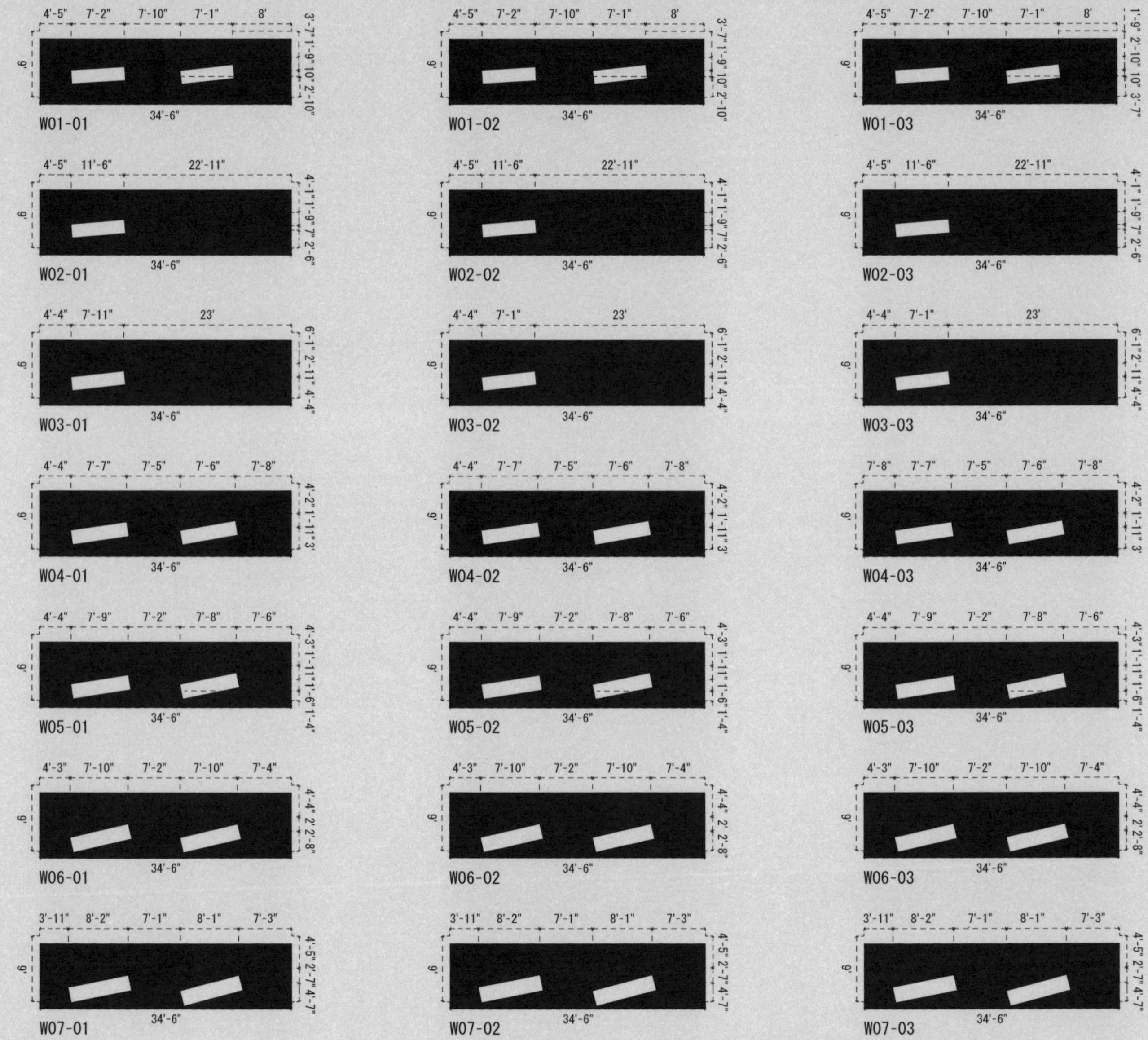

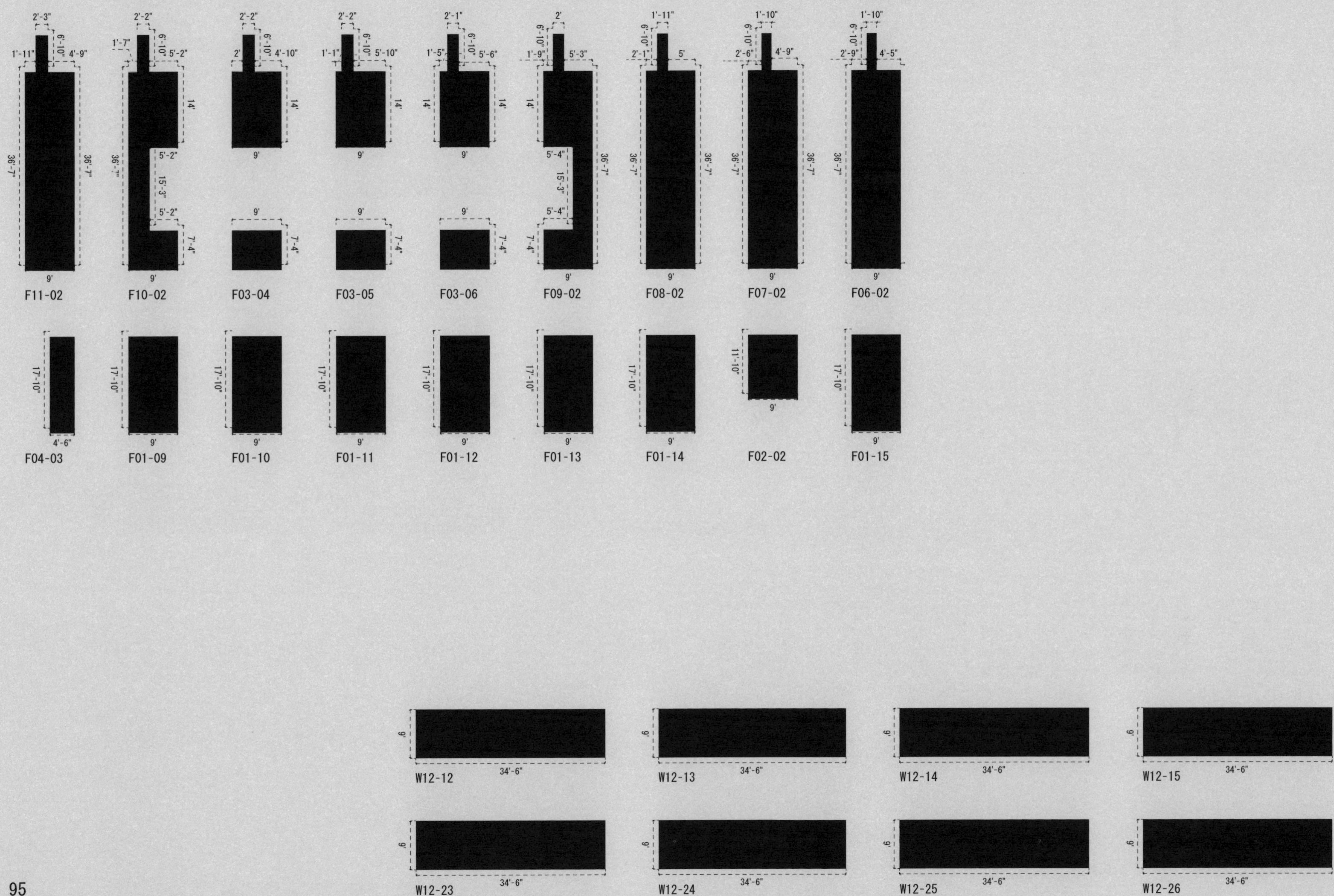
F11-02
2'-3"
1'-11"
6'-10"
4'-9"
36'-7"
9'
F10-02
2'-2"
1'-7"
6'-10"
5'-2"
14'
15'-3"
7'-4"
36'-7"
9'
F03-04
2'-2"
2'
6'-10"
4'-10"
14'
9'
7'-4"
F03-05
2'-2"
1'-1"
6'-10"
5'-10"
14'
9'
7'-4"
F03-06
2'-1"
1'-5"
6'-10"
5'-6"
14'
9'
7'-4"
F09-02
2'
1'-9"
6'-10"
5'-3"
14'
5'-4"
15'-3"
7'-4"
36'-7"
9'
F08-02
1'-11"
2'-1"
6'-10"
5'
36'-7"
9'
F07-02
1'-10"
2'-6"
6'-10"
4'-9"
36'-7"
9'
F06-02
1'-10"
2'-9"
6'-10"
4'-5"
36'-7"
9'
F04-03
17'-10"
4'-6"
F01-09
17'-10"
9'
F01-10
17'-10"
9'
F01-11
17'-10"
9'
F01-12
17'-10"
9'
F01-13
17'-10"
9'
F01-14
17'-10"
9'
F02-02
11'-10"
9'
F01-15
17'-10"
9'
W12-12
W12-13
W12-14
W12-15
W12-23
W12-24
W12-25
W12-26
9'
34'-6"

Tower 10: Blank Panels
Plan: p.6 (right)
Elevation: p.14 (right)
Wood Grain Model: p.134
CLT Forecast: p.234

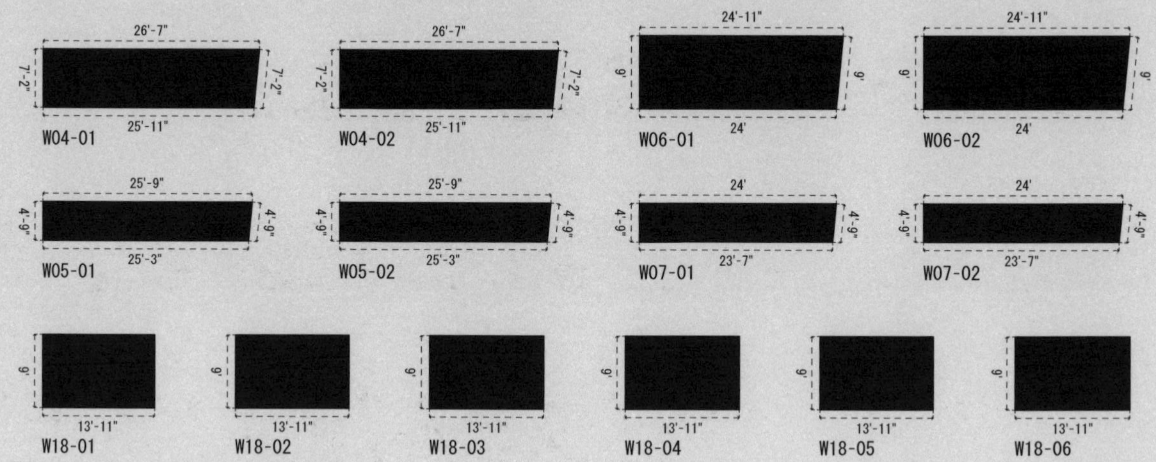

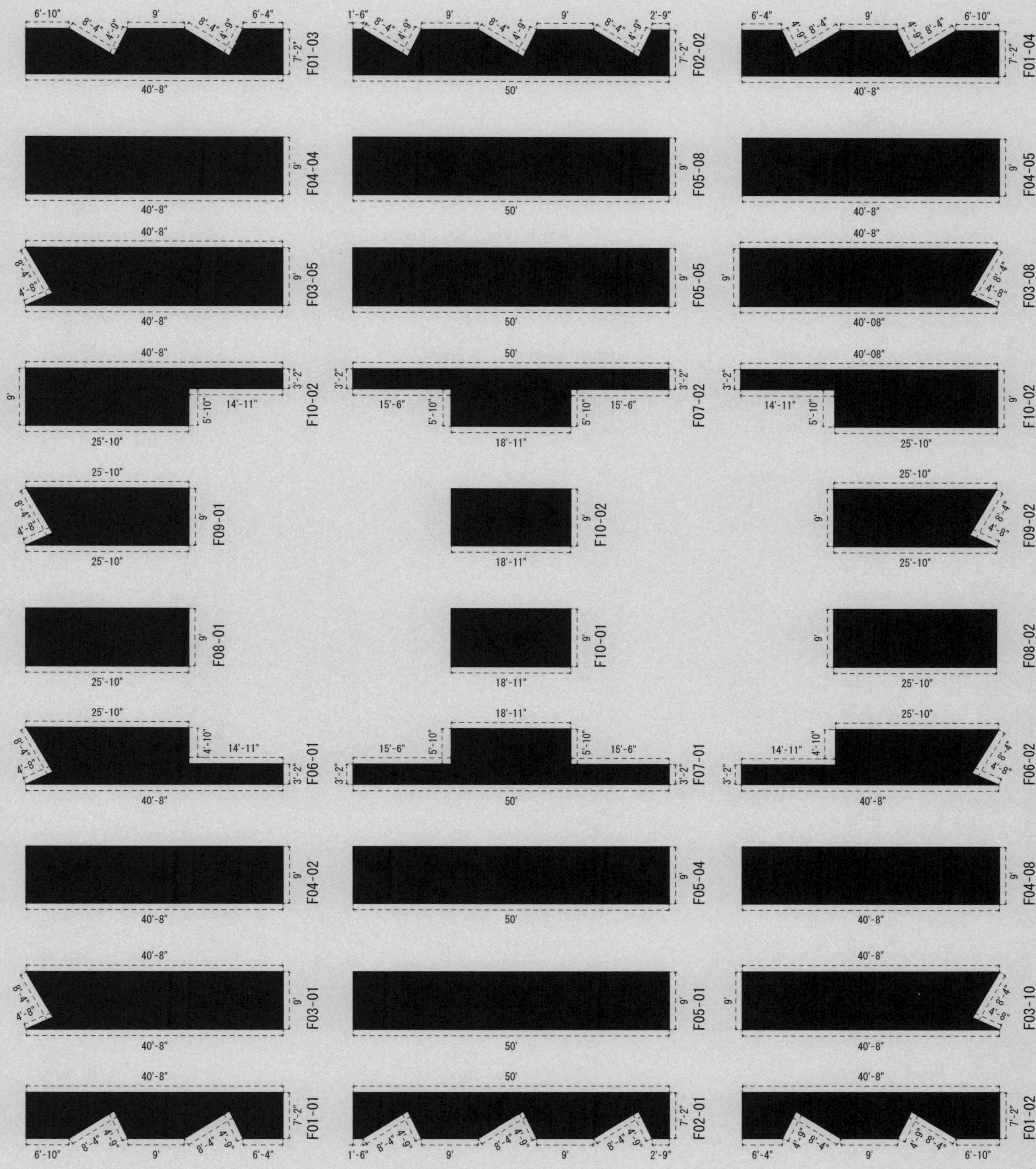
F01-03
F02-02
F01-04
F04-04
F05-08
F04-05
F03-05
F05-05
F03-08
F10-02
F07-02
F10-02
F09-01
F10-02
F09-02
F08-01
F10-01
F08-02
F06-01
F07-01
F06-02
F04-02
F05-04
F04-08
F03-01
F05-01
F03-10
F01-01
F02-01
F01-02

Tower 09: Blank Panels
Plan: p.6 (left)
Elevation: p.16 (left)
Wood Grain Model: p.137
Structural Analysis: pp.202-5
CLT Forecast: p.233

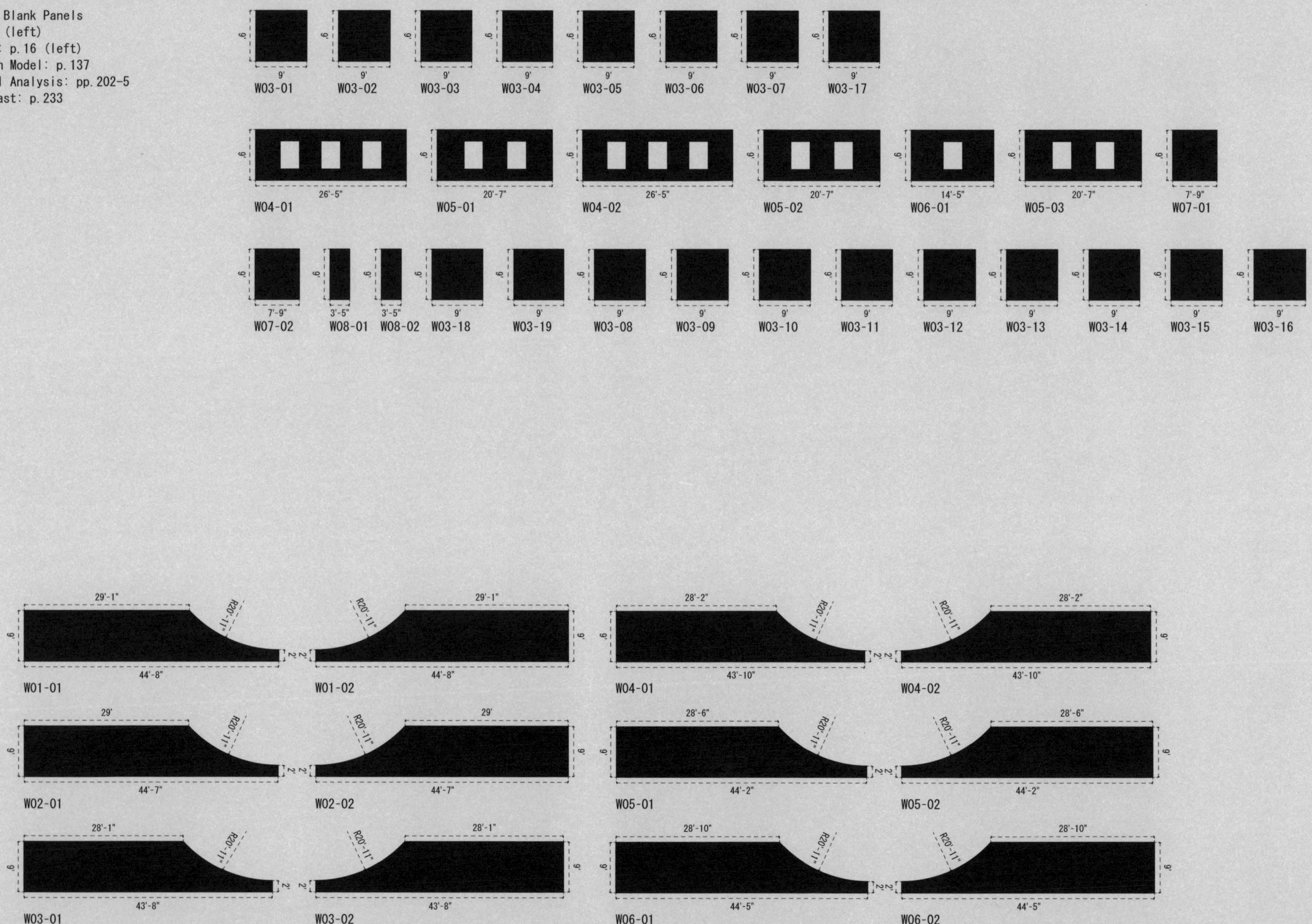

F01 28'-4" 5'-11" 27'-2" 8'-4"
F02 27'-2" 9'-2" 25'-7" 9'
F03 25'-7" 9'-2" 24' 9'
F04 24' 9'-2" 22'-5" 9'
F05 22'-5" 9'-2" 20'-10" 9'
F06 20'-10" 9'-2" 19'-3" 9'
F07 19'-3" 9'-2" 17'-8" 8'-11"
F08 17'-8" 9'-2" 16'-1" 9'
F11 12' 9'-2" 13'-7" 8'
F12 13'-7" 9'-2" 15'-2" 9'
F13 15'-2" 9'-2" 16'-9" 9'
F14 16'-9" 9'-2" 18'-4" 9'
F15 18'-4" 9'-2" 19'-11" 9'
F16 19'-11" 9'-2" 21'-6" 9'
F17 21'-6" 9'-2" 23'-1" 9'
F18 23'-1" 9'-2" 24'-8" 9'
F21 19'-9" 7'-3" 19'-8" 8'-11"
F22 19'-8" 9' 19'-8" 9'
F23 19'-8" 9' 19'-8" 9'
F24 19'-8" 9' 19'-8" 9'
F25 19'-8" 9' 19'-8" 9'
F26 19'-8" 9' 19'-8" 9'
F27 19'-8" 9' 19'-8" 9'
F28 19'-8" 9' 19'-8" 9'
F31 27'-4" 6'-9" 26'-1" 9'
F32 26'-1" 9'-2" 24'-6" 9'
F33 24'-6" 9'-2" 22'-11" 9'
F34 22'-11" 9'-2" 21'-4" 9'
F35 19'-2" 7'-2" 17'-11" 7'
F36 19'-9" 9'-1" 18'-2" 9'
F37 16'-7"
F38 16'-7" 9'-2" 15'
F41 19'-7" 9' 19'-6" 7'-4"
F42 19'-6" 9' 19'-6" 9'
F43 19'-6" 9' 19'-6" 9'
F44 19'-6" 9' 19'-6" 9'
F45 19'-6" 9' 19'-6" 9'
F46 19'-6" 9' 19'-6" 9'
F47 19'-6" 9' 19'-6" 9'
F48 19'-6" 9' 19'-6" 9'
F51 13' 3'-5" 13'-9" 4'-8"
F52 13'-9" 9'-6" 15'-4" 9'-2"
F53 15'-4" 9' 16'-11" 9'-2"
F54 16'-11" 9' 18'-6" 9'-2"
F55 18'-6" 9' 20'-1" 9'-1"
F56 20'-1" 9' 21'-8" 9'-2"
F57 21'-8" 9' 23'-3" 9'-2"
F58 23'-3" 9' 24'-10" 9'-2"

House 01: Blank Panels
Plan: p.37 (left)
Elevation: p.52
Blank Panels: pp.85, 100
Structural Analysis: pp.210-12
CLT Forecast: p.237

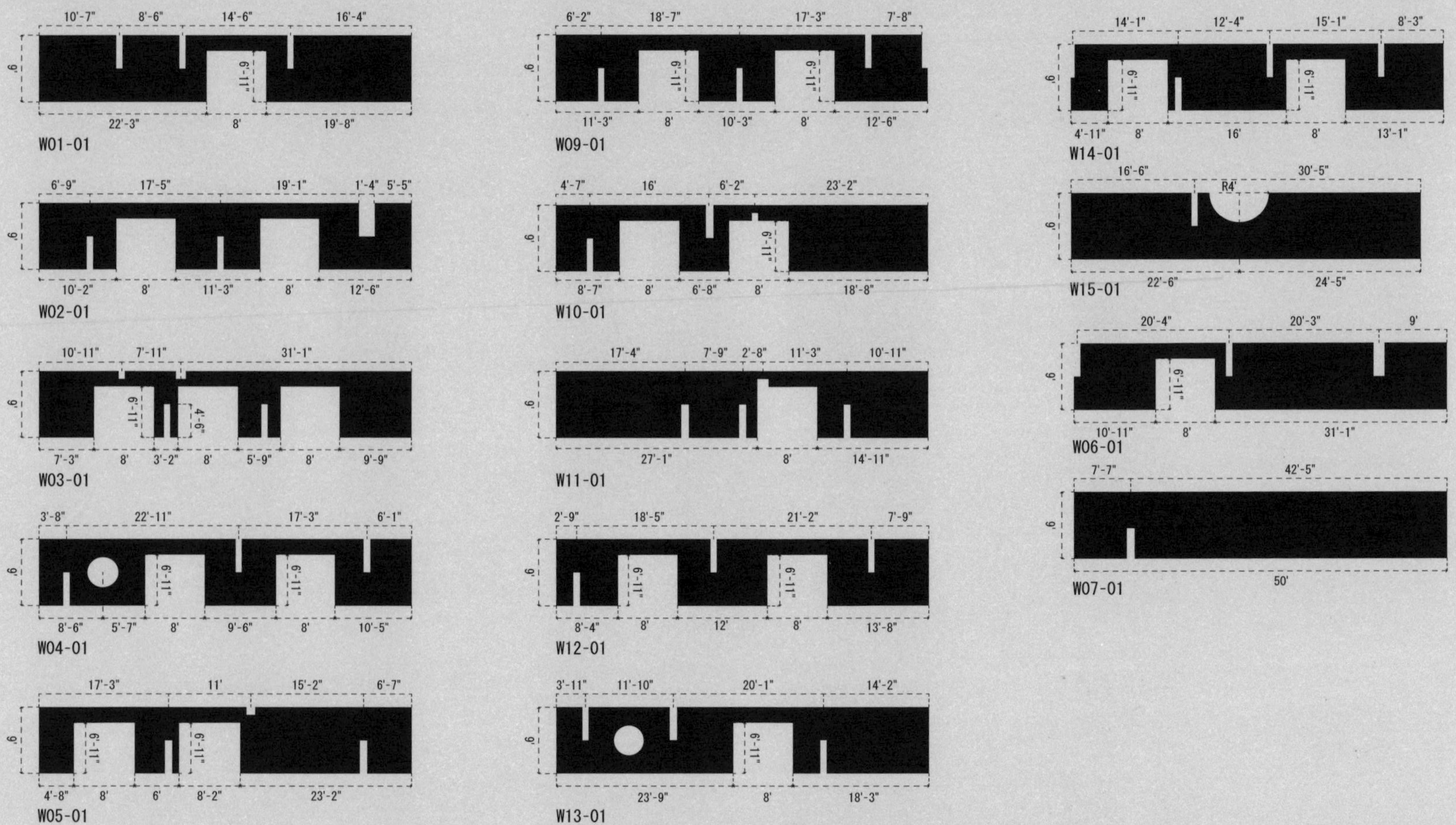

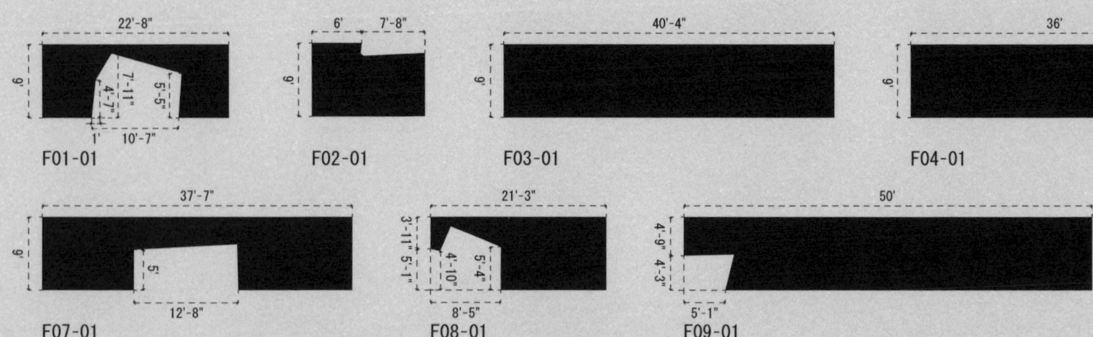

Blank Shots: Monolithic Desires and Laminar Inevitabilities

Nader Tehrani

The Mono-Medium Ethic

Gottfried Semper, Caribbean Hut, published in *Der Stil*, volume II (1863)

Emerging discussions on mass timber have elicited a wide range of responses that engage topics of building technology, sustainability, and legal codes; naturally, all of these subjects have a substantial impact on design thinking, but if we were to pose the challenge of designing in mass timber more holistically, we might yet establish more reciprocity between the technical and conceptual aspects of this cultural project. In turn, this reciprocity may prompt a theoretical position that internalizes the technical as part of its intellectual apparatus. Among the many tendencies that characterize design thinking, one stands out from a material perspective: in identifying a single medium through which to work, the architect is able to force invention from within a genre, and in doing so, to radicalize its ability to transform, evolve, and innovate.

The prospect of working in a single medium defies normative architectural thought, in part because of the immediate, practical differences between architectural elements—the ground we walk on, the wall that supports a building, the roof that protects from the elements. The performative requirements of these elements have produced a history of material research and development that has assigned optimal materials to each. For this reason, the repellent qualities of ceramic tiles have been marshaled toward roofing and wet rooms, while the sturdiness of stone and concrete toward foundations, grounds, and hearths. If indigenous constructions of limited means have not self-organized according to these principles, then architectural theories such as Gottfried Semper's "four elements" have institutionalized the categorical differences among architectural components, approaches toward material specification, and a decorum toward their functional assignment.[1] As such, working within a single medium runs against the current in the context of theory as well.

1 Gottfried Semper's *The Four Elements of Architecture* (1851) cites the connection between the hearth and metallurgy/ceramics, the roof and carpentry, the enclosure and textiles, and the mound and earthwork.

There are significant exceptions to this rule, and often they are associated with exceptional constructions, where architecture stems more directly from a local resource, be it the stone of Matera, Italy, or the forests of Kiso, Japan. If the former site produced wonderous archaic excavations, where architectural spaces are extracted from rock, the latter produced an elaborate culture of wood details, evacuated almost entirely of other mediums, creating a syntax of elements that dispenses with extraneous mediating joinery; instead, the intelligence of the work stems almost entirely from inventions in wood, with linguistic delight to match. To achieve this, centuries of research went into the extraction of resources, the development of transport methods, the testing of different woods and tooling protocols, and the categorization of joinery details under the stresses of compressive, tensile, and lateral forces. Much work has also gone into finishing processes, differentiating between interior and exterior, protecting against the elements and forces of nature.

Still, the insistent appeal to a single material medium is fraught with added complexities, most often addressed through architectural amendments and predictable mediations. In Matera, where stone cannot offer human comfort, furnishings, fabrics, and finishes come to the rescue; meanwhile, black terra-cotta tile (Kawara) protects the Japanese temple's roof from the elements. It is all the more poignant, then, how Ensamble Studio's Truffle adopts hay bales not only as formwork, but also as the index of its entire interior finish, or how Thompson and Rose's Straightsview Barn uses wood shingles for its entire enclosure, without mediating elements, like gutters; such projects display an intellectual insistence that goes beyond the positivism of solving problems.

For these reasons, the predisposition toward the singularity of a material medium is an artifice, and should in no way be confused with nature, nor function. One could claim it is a strategic device, in effect to build adversity from within one's approach, if only to demonstrate the ingenuity of architecture in response. And in the appeal to parasitic details in support of the host material, the ethic of this philosophy remains intact, precisely because the excursions outside of the medium make no claims to dominance.

Clockwise from top left:
Matera Casa Grotta,
Matera, Italy, 2006

Detail of Goryo-jinja
Shrine, Kamakura,
Japan, late Heian period
(794-1185)

Ensamble Studio, Truffle,
Costa da Morte, Spain,
2010

Thompson and Rose,
Straitsview Barn, San
Juan Island, Washington,
1997-2002

Sigurd Lewerentz,
St. Peter's Church,
Klippan, Sweden, 1963–66

The Logic of Strategic Labor

At St. Peter's Church in Klippan, Sweden, Sigurd Lewerentz adopts brick in its many guises, and with it the emergence of a language, a discipline, and an ethic. We recognize that the church's steel structure serves merely as a framework for the brick enclosure; the floors, walls, vaults, and certain key attributes are cast in brick, while allowing the introduction of glass, wood, and steel for critical interventions (windows, furnishings, handrails). However, Lewerentz's use of brick reminds us of the seminal role of mortar. In his refusal to cut the brick (an ethic he imposes on the medium), he is also subsequently required to develop a malleable bonding strategy: the bonding dimension is sometimes called on to increase beyond common reason, and the brick is enveloped by a sea of mortar, inverting their traditional figure-ground relationship, an invention that is entirely unique to him.

The floor of the church is cast in the same bricks as its walls and vaults, and as such biases us toward a monolithic reading of the building as a whole. The space, even if the result of aggregated parts, appears to be excavated out of a stack of bricks, even more so as one inspects the telltale details of the ground: the altar and an interior "hill" are both construed of the same medium, the former a result of brick rotated in a stacked formation, and the latter the result of the conventional running bond deformed to create a topography that allows for a subtle prospect, a vantage point toward the altar. The associated excavation in front of the

Oscillating between practice and research, many early projects were focused on installations and houses, all of which allowed for an investment in a single medium: terra-cotta in Casa La Roca, thin ply in Immaterial/Ultramaterial, ceramics in Boolean Valley, acrylic in the Voromuro installation, corrugated metal in the Zahedi House, and wood at the Beaver Country Day School.

Clockwise from top: Nader Tehrani, Immaterial/Ultramaterial, Harvard Graduate School of Design, Cambridge, Massachusetts, 2001

Adam Silverman and Nader Tehrani, Boolean Valley, MOCA Pacific Design Center, West Hollywood, California, 2009

Office dA, Voromuro, Vita Brevis Georges Island, Boston, 2007

Office dA, Zahedi House, Weston, Massachusetts, 1997

NADAAA, Beaver Country Day School R+D Center, Chestnut Hill, Massachusetts, 2019

Office dA, Interfaith Hall of Prayer, Northeastern University, Boston, 1998. The project required an architectural treatment that would conceal the fact that it had no access to natural light. With the introduction of all-glass cladding, we advanced the mono-material ethic to ensure that the glazing would engage all functional variations at the edge of the room: zones of thresholds, pilasters, and niches where the lighting systems were hidden. The glazing was fashioned in a shingle system to allow for variations, cascading up and down while establishing functional differences in an otherwise self-similar system. In turn, we incorporated stacked laminar plywood to eliminate the traditional division between structural and framing systems for glazing. By absorbing what would otherwise be the purview of varied trades, the system was able to achieve substantial customization without the normative associated costs.

"hill" reveals the bonding system, its depth, and the appearance of the material constitution of the building at large—all brick.

In face of architectural challenges—the navigation of the ground, the compressive forces at work in the walls, and the geometric parameters of the vaults—Lewerentz elects to radicalize the reach of one medium, effectively demonstrating where architectural discipline possibly lies: somewhere in the confines of constraints, and less so in the limitless categories of difference. Here, he calls on those differences to be located within operations onto one medium, erasing the evidence of elemental categories to the eye. Instead, he reveals the nuanced shift in a material's behavior through the sites of its interaction with the human body: the ground onto which we step, the furnishings we touch, and the tactile interface that rituals require.

Most importantly, Lewerentz identifies the way in which labor is harnessed in its most strategic capacity to create a cerebral opulence, where the craft is allowed to remain raw and crude. By essentially eliminating the need for other trades, matters of cost, coordination,

Office dA. Mantra restaurant, Boston, 2001. The Mantra "den" served as a foundational exercise, harnessing our varied abilities in design and construction to overcome what we found to be unnecessary adversities. By absorbing responsibilities of the means and methods of fabrication internally, we were able to eliminate $200,000 in costs and build the structure in less than thirty days. The working drawings indicating the stratification of wood layers were mounted on the ceiling to serve as a jig for the plum bobs that would eventually identify each point of connection. Conceived within the tradition of log cabin construction, the structural system is premised on its compressive strength, while the nonstandard use of geometry introduces torqued ruled surfaces that serve as a surface-active structure, creating a smooth surface out of an incrementally corbelled system.

and craft are redirected toward one mission—brick assemblies—and with it, the rewards not only of the generosity of its affect, but of the advancement of a discipline.

Within this conceptual construct, this essay expands on my investment in mono-medium thinking, through wood. With its conventional use in American construction, our engagement with this medium was inevitable; however, there are various episodes within that trajectory that contribute to a larger narrative about inventions within the medium, and this is an opportunity to bring them to light, and into conversation with each other. If the zeitgeist is calling on everyone to consider mass timber as a sustainable approach, I will instead speak more broadly about wood construction, including mass timber, attempting to identify its conceptual advantages, insofar as they are rooted in the means and methods of their respective uses. Moreover, I will attempt to show that these strategies are not mutually exclusive and sometimes require hybrid approaches not only to optimize material uses, but to also radicalize their architectural potentials. This both amplifies the pragmatic underpinnings of wood tectonics and conveys the idea that tectonics requires more than the orthodox use of matter—and in fact requires an approach that balances out the technical and representational commitments it faces in confronting material facts with requisite expression.

Reengaging Means and Methods

An important first step in engaging materials is to better understand the means and methods associated with their fabrication, and that is a fraught terrain. The construction industry

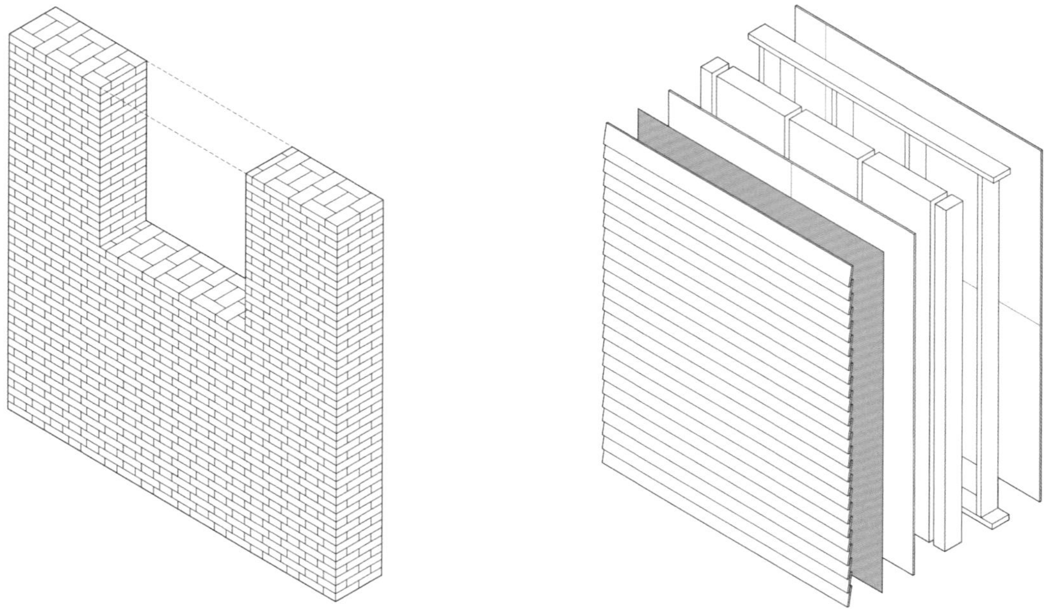

The monolithic load-bearing wall serves structural purposes, while its thickness offers thermal mass as an environmental benefit. In contrast, the contemporary laminar wall adopts individuated layers to create a composite of performative features: waterproofing, structure, insulation, interior finishes, and so on. If the former benefits from a principle of simplicity, the latter endures the redundancy of many layers, each of which has its own respective duties, adding complexity. The aim of this essay, in part, is to reengage the potentials of simplicity, while acknowledging that what appears to be simple involves complications, and what is complex produces simplicity. Mediating between archaic and contemporary systems, this research aims to draw out alternative models of construction originating outside of industry standards.

and its trades have certain expertise, but also exhibit bias, complacency, and indifference to the disciplinary narratives that underlie a work of architecture. This is only reinforced by the American Institute of Architects' legal framework, which divorces the notion of "design intent" from the "means and methods," the former held by the architect and the latter by the contractor. This obvious division is at the root of the dismemberment of the architect's agency over construction and its corollary implications: labor, craft, budgets, and details—in short, the ability to specify the relationship between part and whole.

The challenges of balancing cost, speed of construction, and level of complexity are well-known (as in the cliché that you can control two, but not all three). However, emerging fabrication protocols have helped to upend these trade-offs, especially when the architect takes responsibility for some critical aspects of oversight. So too, as we encounter emerging technologies, it is all the more incumbent on the architect not only to understand the associated means and methods, but to be able to transform architectural culture in response to them. Our particular response has been threefold. The reliance on mono-materiality, while rooted in architectural motivations, has also resulted in the elimination of ancillary trades, resulting in a leaner attitude toward both budgets and schedules. By extension, our concurrent collaborative engagement (and war) with trades has helped to foster either a genuine confluence of design-building thinking, or alternatively a decisive split upon which our team has stepped into the role of fabrication. Otherwise, our incursions into construction have helped advance fabricators' confidence through our mock-ups, which serve as a test bed of ideas and proof of concept. These simple strategies, in combination with an aggressive engagement with digital technologies, have allowed us to redefine the traditional linear protocols of the design process by instigating the shop drawings process into a shared platform, incorporating both the contractor's and architect's responsibilities proactively.

Paradigm Shifts and Intellectual Responses

Over the last century, building technologies have undergone significant transformations, which have given rise to paradigmatically different theoretical claims. Le Corbusier's five points of architecture, and particularly the free plan, the ribbon window, and the free facade, all point to a fundamental shift in being able to disengage structure from envelope, and by doing so, to liberate the organization of a building from its image. While Le Corbusier did not invent the reinforced concrete frame himself, his architectural conceptualization of it unleashed many intellectual projects to follow.[2] Much has been written on mass timber from a technical perspective—and yet nothing that positions its transformational aspects from a design point of view. In part, this essay aims to put forward some of the conceptual and theoretical preconditions of such work.

Consider the relationship between Le Corbusier's Villa Savoye, Robert Venturi's Lieb House, and OMA's Villa dall'Ava: as an element, the ribbon window undergoes significant transformation from the concrete frame to wood and subsequently to steel, but more importantly, each house reveals how its internal organizations are radically independent of each other, precisely because of what the separation of the structure and skin allows.

And while the images of early twentieth-century canons remained relatively consistent in their abstraction, Le Corbusier's five points gave way to an era when the iconography of facades established a substantial autonomy from the plans behind them, in great part because of the notion of the free facade, a freedom that even Le Corbusier did not venture to exercise. In contrast, the offspring of the "master" broadened their capacity to tap into historical models far and wide.

It is important to note that while many of the modernist canons from the 1920s to the 1960s radicalized spatial configurations, overturning nineteenth-century models, their relationship to environmental forces remained underaddressed. Lost was the thermal mass of load-bearing wall systems, but no ancillary approach toward insulation arose to compensate for its disappearance. For this reason, from today's perspective, the so-called industrial revolution did not recognize the environment with the intuition of its more antiquated predecessors.

In the latter half of the twentieth century, postmodernism offered even greater latitude to play with history, but its planning remained relatively untransformed. Rather than

A hip roof (left) and a mansard roof (right). As the ultimate defensive layer, roofs not only have to protect interiors, but need to look like they protect them. The evolution from simple shed, gable, and hip roofs to the mansard roof is particularly significant in demonstrating the stubborn role of representation in the formation of architectural thinking. The mansard, while mostly flat, needed to camouflage itself as a pitched roof, with its ulterior motive being the ultimate expansion of the top floor into a veritable piece of real estate: a fully-functional attic.

influencing their internal organizations, the construction systems that underpinned these buildings had a significant role in allowing varied iconographies to be tested on them, as overlays. Indeed, much of this generation of building was enveloped by Sheetrock and other laminar systems that were the result of late twentieth-century standardization: vapor barriers, sheathing, waterproofing membranes, plywood. From a labor perspective, what is significant about this laminar regime is that each layer is conventionally installed by a different trade, a factor that locks the architect into a conundrum. Indeed, architects are not so much free to use the sixteen divisions of construction as they are confined by them—victims of the budgets, schedules, and interfaces between each trade, all of which are locked in a bureaucratic embrace. This predicament, while challenging, is also the root of a distinct opportunity in the engagement of mass timber: how to overcome the laminar regime, eliminate reliance on redundant trades, and design with the idea of irreducibility in mind.

The Tectonic Image and the Emergence of the Rainscreen

The fidelity of correspondence between formal, material, and performative aspects is at the core of nineteenth-century buildings, but also applies to many of their twentieth-century equivalents. This has to do with the unique claim that tectonics relies on both facts and fictions: the idea that skins not only protect the building from the elements, but also illustrate it in their representation.

In a second chapter of this laminar history, we witness a more illuminating threshold, where spatial organization, material specification, and building technology performance finally become divorced from each other in the invention of the rainscreen system. Here, the outer sheathing of the building can maintain an indifferent relationship to its laminar infrastructure beneath. As a porous skin, it is finally free from the responsibilities and liabilities

Left: Titus Bernhard Architekten, House 11 × 11, Munich, 2012

Right: A log chalet in Switzerland

If the classic image of the log cabin is the result of stacked wood members at work, then the dovetail details of its corners are an indication of a language to which they are bound; the syntax is deeply implicated by its correspondence to technical duties and assembly protocols. In contrast, the rainscreen, while allowing for a similar monolithic identity, can only survive as a laminar system, whose particular assembly liberates the skin from its structure. This moral freedom is paired up with the introduction of architectural facility and ease; no longer burdened by any friction as such—from structure, assembly, waterproofing, etc.—the system is relegated to find other narratives for its *raison d'être*.

of performance, serving only to protect the waterproofing membrane from ultraviolet rays. Ironically, even with newly emergent monolithic systems such as CLT, this laminar infrastructure is a core requirement, which demonstrates, yet again, that the discipline of architecture might be driven by a commitment to the linguistic framework that serves its syntactic and semantic mission rather than to the structure that supports the building. Even with this newfound freedom, the building system is still entrapped by the laminar logic that characterizes so many buildings of the late twentieth century.

The Confluence of Figure and Field

Scaling up is one of the most challenging aspects of the mono-medium ethic, if only because building projects involve multiple constituencies, voices, and users. Building systems, in all their complexity, rarely allow for the kind of monocular focus on one medium possible in smaller projects or installations. Still, there are those unique moments where a single strategy can demonstrate its might. Naturally, the forces of urbanism can also affect the ways in which material propositions are deployed; and indeed they should, as it is the vitality of the city that brings relevance to the role of buildings. But if the material unit informs the configurational possibilities of a design, it is the result of thinking bottom-up, where the scale of bricks, stones, or logs reinforces the power of architectural organizations de facto. In contrast, the city has the converse power to inform the figures of architecture top-down. The negotiation between bottom-up and top-down thinking brings forward key analogies for material thinking.

As we embarked on the Melbourne School of Design (MSD) project, we discovered an urbanism on the University of Melbourne campus befitting a broader discussion relative to

Left: NADAAA, Melbourne School of Design (MSD), Melbourne, Australia, 2014. Conceived as a vertical studio space, the MSD atrium attempts to bring a field condition of spanning skylights into confluence with a suspended studio structure. In a tectonic inversion, the weight of the structure appears at the top, where massive laminated veneer lumber members span 22 meters (72 feet), requiring depths of 2 to 3 meters (approximately 6 feet, 6 inches, to 9 feet, 10 inches). As a coffered ceiling, the roof structure functions as a two-way slab, using the intermediate wood spanning members to give lateral stability; their geometries protect the interior from direct sunlight. What might appear as rhetorical distortions of the roof and perforations in the surface of the studio embody structure forces: the wood members atop are massive, thick, and solid, while at the bottom the wood members diminish to lean plywood planes reducing in weight, while suspended in tension.

Above: MSD floor slabs. The slabs were initially designed in concrete, which would have required added material formwork (and its corollary in labor). Instead, the formwork was reconceptualized as a CLT slab screwed in with steel bolts, wound with rebar, and topped with concrete, a combination that produces an optimal composite floor structure: a warm ceiling of wood, a resilient floor to work on, and no waste in formwork and labor.

architecture. With a deep and wide plot of land, our most economical strategy was the creation of an internal urban room in conversation with the urban rooms of the campus, conjuring in our minds precedents with powerful material triggers: Bramante's Tempietto, Louis Kahn's Yale Center for British Art, and Frank Gehry's DZ Bank, all of which share a spatial trope paired with an attitude toward material organization that is significant in the context of this essay. All are composed as urban rooms within which a totemic object has a rarefied role. The Tempietto draws on the varied fabric that surrounds it to establish its difference. Gehry's entrapped zoomorphic figure, however different in imagery, works in a similar way; Gehry designs his own backdrop, an uncharacteristically sober grid of windows that simulates urban conditions. In the Center for British Art, the placement of a staircase effectively produces its monumentality, further enhanced by a monolithic concrete drum. We also see how Kahn tried to incorporate the drum back into the tectonic logic of the building's concrete structural frame, to bring them into cohesion, building a direct rapport between the figure and its ground. While this interpretation is not supported by all details, it is an alibi that we adopted for the design of the MSD atrium, whose roof structure has an intentionally direct material relationship with the suspended studio within.

The project effects a particular transformation of the building's material units to build up the atrium. Structure and skin—timber members and plywood—work together in conspiring to eradicate the evident differences between the roof overhead and the monolith suspended below. The metamorphic transformation of wood is presented as seamless, blurring boundaries of structure and skin and imbuing all surfaces with functionality (structural, acoustic, or programmatic). But the sum effect of building this rapport is to produce what I will call a "tectonic grain": the ability of an assembly of parts to define a precise language, a syntax, and a lexicon that is legible. The grain is neither natural nor incontestable, but rather the artifice through which an architecture is developed, and in this instance it deals with the ability to read a deep structural system transforming incrementally onto the skin of a suspended studio, eventually becoming razor-thin as it levitates over the commons. While many architectures address the challenge of the figure, and many the field, few are able to address both at once: the tectonic grain enables a figure to emerge from the field itself.

The Tectonic Grain

As with geological strata, wood grain, or the flight pattern of a flock of birds, the tectonic grain involves a meaningful relationship between the part and whole of an edifice. Since the grain does not emerge from nature, the challenge is to build it up through exercises of patterning, aggregations, or assembly protocols of field conditions. It is also an ethic, artificial as it may be, that prescribes the limits of figuration as it relates to a rule set. The tectonic grain requires a catalytic detail as the basis for the development of an architecture. Here the detail is neither unique nor isolated, but rather the instrument through which an entire grammar may be unleashed. The grain thus defines the malleability of a proposition.

Consider the works of Agnes Martin and Brice Marden, artists whose canonical works are defined by a set of strict operations: striping for the former, and weaving for the latter. The patterns are discernible, yet Martin's are more readily accessible; Marden's require a deeper reading to draw out aperiodic conditions of recursion. Accordingly, even the most conventional of architectural assembly systems involve an innate grain, through which one may interpret variations. For instance, if one investigated the mortar-line dimension of a brick wall for

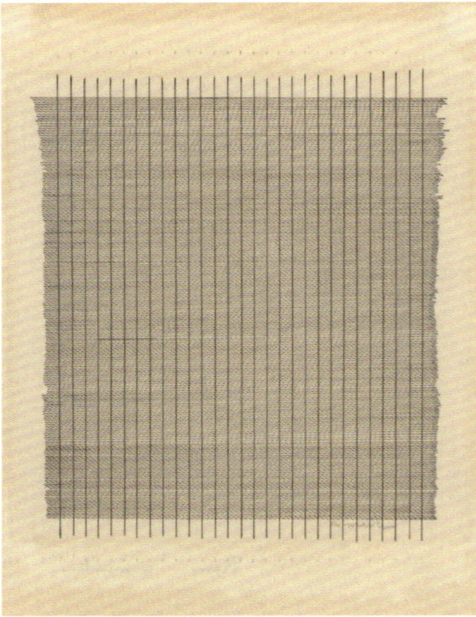  

From left: Agnes Martin, *Tremolo*, 1962. Brice Marden, *Couplet IV*, 1988–89. Office dA, Casa La Roca, Caracas, Venezuela, 1995.

its variability, one would come to the understanding that the running bond and Flemish bond, though different in appearance, are genetically identical. Casa La Roca is a demonstration of this principle, which also enables the figuration of the laterally stabilized curtain wall.[3]

The design of Casa La Roca was a direct response to Lewerentz. While his walls draw our eyes toward the mortar, we make the mortar into the protagonist by encoding in its genetic makeup the ability to expand and contract.

In some instances, the tectonic grain emerges from the manufacturing process itself and defines the limits of formal operations. Consider corrugated metal and its predisposition to bend on one axis while becoming even stronger on the other. The Zahedi House wall illustrates this tendency (see page 105), but also reveals the connection between the geometry and grain: that the corrugation is a manifestation of a ruled surface. Herein lies an important aspect of architectural representation. Where other forms of drawings may "illustrate" a phenomenon, the architectural representation is fabricated, and therefore has an innate relationship to its construction.

The idea of the tectonic grain is furthered in the Rock Creek House, where directionality is reinforced by stacked plywood running north–south, working between the masonry structural and wood skins to amplify a planimetric logic. This orientation reinforces the direction of the brick structural walls, but also achieves two key objectives for the house: the plywood's thinness allows light to pass from south to north, illuminating the interior, and its face-grain allows for the concealment of the home's private areas behind planar panels, conceived not as doors but abstract sliding walls. The thin, planar aesthetic of plywood is called on to achieve mass and solidity through stacking; butcher-block technology mediates between mass-timber strategies and thin millwork techniques. Working with digital technologies allowed for the incorporation of all infrastructure, from light switches to heat sensors, into the layout without undue added costs.

Left: NADAAA, Rock Creek House, Washington, DC, 2017. Stacked plywood reveals the end grain and face grain of plywood panels, porous on the north-south axis, while solid on the east-west.

Right: Office dA, Banq restaurant, Boston, 2008. Conceived as a flexible plan, the space is determined by its reflective ceiling plan: an undulating field of plywood fins, whose organization broadly follows the layout of structural, mechanical, and plumbing infrastructures overhead. Seen from the entry, the fins produce repetitive proscenia, creating the illusion of continuity; viewed laterally, the fins reveal their thinness and expose the infrastructure through the cracks. We used the I-beams overhead as a virtual ground from which we could suspend all sheets of plywood with geometric certainty. Puzzle connections between each 4-by-8-foot sheet ensure both technical and visual continuity between fins. The grain of the ceiling is a magnification of the plywood itself, and a vehicle to establish a meaningful relationship between the nature of a material—despite the fact that it is industrially conceived, or maybe precisely because of it—and the organization of the space.

Tectonic Hybridity

Behind the mono-material sensibility is an assumed ethic of purity, and the difficulties that underlie realizing it are taken up as badges of honor when overcome. Yet it is not uncommon that the assumed simplicity of single-minded decisions leads to complications. Thus, despite my own conceptual underpinnings, or maybe precisely because of them, the idea of hybridity has become an innate part of the tectonic riddles we face. For instance, in the context of mass timber construction, one might assume that an all-wood assembly would simplify deployment, not to mention enhance visual purity. But without the consideration of mechanical systems, such assumptions are immediately voided of value, since it is precisely these systems' incorporation that challenges the architectural agenda. If anything, most CLT structures that are supported by wood columns and beams also require at least one added foot of height per floor, making them difficult to resolve in buildings with strict height restrictions. Wood beams cannot be penetrated easily, so the systems must be channeled under the beams. In contrast, the hybrid steel-CLT combination internalizes this challenge as part of its equation, a priori, revealing that its alleged impurity is, in fact, more strategically conceptualized.

NADAAA, North Hall, Rhode Island School of Design, Providence, 2020

At the Rhode Island School of Design's North Hall—designed and completed in less than eighteen months—working with cross-laminated timber seemed to be a powerful way to produce consensus in response to the clients' desire that the building embody an ethic of sustainability. In part, the beauty of CLT systems is that they do not require added finishes; while the floor slabs would be covered to mitigate acoustic transmission, the ceilings could remain bare, exposing the grain of the members. The main predicament emerged from the lateral spans of the building, requiring structure, both columns and beams, framing a double-loaded corridor. Certainly, this could have been done in wood, tapping into laminated veneer lumber technologies, for example, but such an approach would lead to the problems outlined above. The use of steel facilitated both the penetrations and the depth of beam, allowing for an added floor to accommodate the program. As a hybrid system, steel and CLT better advanced the overall conceptual premise than timber alone.

The Critical Evacuation of Trades

In the Poché House, we discovered an opportunity to explore this hybridity in the organization of an entire building. The design responds to the diverse ways a house may be reformatted based on seasons, economies, and urgencies; in effect, it challenges the primacy of the detached single-family home while also working within its genre. It is thus a typological study of how a single device enables varied possibilities: here, a single staircase that winds around the periphery of a four-story structure, where three bedrooms and a living area with the same footprint are stacked. The arrangement of the stair on each floor distinguishes the rooms and allows for slightly different uses. Each bedroom is designed as an efficiency, including a

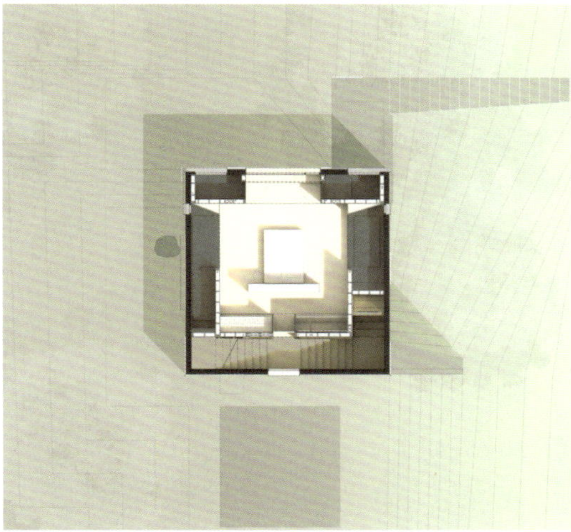

NADAAA, Poché House, plan and section, 2020

kitchenette, a double bed, closets, and a divided bathroom, with added space for bunk beds or ancillary bays in which seating can be situated in support of the room, all within the poché.

Every inch of space is programmed in the thick wall between the room and the external skin beyond the stair. The exterior wall is composed of prefabricated CLT panels; the inner wall is conceived of as a balloon frame to create space for the infrastructure of the house, including mechanical, electrical, and plumbing systems, as well as acoustic insulation. If the outer wall accommodates structural, environmental, and waterproofing necessities, it is also a load-bearing slab whose core is well-suited for other infrastructure; for this reason, the hollow wall of the interior is its twin sister, vacuous with reason, if only to hold concealed systems that are not commonly thought through in a synthetic way. By thinking of them together and organically, we are able to optimize lengths of ducts, the stacking of plumbing, and the efficiencies that are critical to a stick-framed house.

A Manifesto in Progress

To return momentarily to the mono-material ethic, there is a seductive allure to the idea that one might conceive a project made entirely of cross-laminated timber. First, CLT's industrially scaled process of assembly gives even small-scale projects the advantage of quick erection, optimal in both the kit of parts and the time dedicated to assembly. It can benefit from off-site and prefabrication technologies, allowing for lower tolerances, greater craft, and the short-circuiting of on-site complexities. Second, as a load-bearing panel, CLT offers its own innate thermal mass, which in combination with an insular layer can form a composite whose effective function becomes the integration of structural, environmental, and cladding systems.

NADAAA, Poché House, renderings of interior, 2020

Third, the sectional composition of CLT produces a seductive finish that, in its own manner, can be construed as complete upon erection. Fourth, the perpendicular cross-lamination of CLT's inner core is suggestive of other ways its particular section may be expressed, especially for structural adaptations where the depth of a panel is not required in a uniform fashion. Finally, all this can contribute to the elimination of extraneous labor and, consequently, unnecessary costs. Should this sound like a financial alibi, it is instead a form of intellectual value engineering, in service of exploring the irreducible aspects of an architecture released from excess. And yet I hope that the appeal to a more complex reading of tectonics, drawing from varied building systems, in both their technical and semantic persuasions, has been able to demonstrate that an approach that embraces the contradictions of layered systems may ultimately yield a more persuasive set of architectural opportunities. Lest this be interpreted as acquiescence, I suggest it is more an appeal to strategic thinking, a critical evaluation of hybrid systems, and a tactical approach toward contradictions and anomalies within construction narratives.

And indeed, despite all the appeals to rationality, it is maybe this complex interpretation of tectonics that enriches the argument posed by these construction systems. Whether used in pure or hybrid formations, these construction methods exhibit a consistent ambiguity between the facts of construction and the manner of their expression. The gap between those facts and the apparent narratives on the surfaces of these buildings is a testament to the core ambivalence that tectonics engenders: truth is not necessarily delivered top-down, but often rendered from the negotiation and mediation of contradictory parts; elements that in other narratives may appear marginal become the main plot, expanding our conception of truth in tectonics.

Ten Points on CLT Models and Public Performance

Yasmin Vobis

BASSWOOD

CLT appears to be the ultimate model-making material. Not only does it look like the familiar basswood sheets that have been a staple of architectural model-making for many decades, but its logic of assembly—from plane to three-dimensional form—is more or less the same. We prefabricate CLT in standard widths and cut out shapes using a CNC router following the same process as its model analogue: flat sheets of material are hand- or laser-cut and joined into more complex forms. Furthermore, CLT's prefabricated nature means that there is no messy casting and often no bolting, allowing the planar material to be applied very directly as structure. Unlike concrete, which transforms from a muddy, wet, formless pile into crisp geometric volumes on-site, CLT is ready-made.

FANTASY

Because of this easy affinity with model-making, that architecture made out of CLT looks like a model seems inevitable. This is particularly relevant given our contemporary context, when the rise of CLT in the United States has coincided with a disciplinary trend against digital rendering and complex form generation and a throwback to pre-digital design methods such as physical models and collage. Yet the fantasy of a clean correspondence between the model and the building quickly unravels once we consider the different pressures the building must address that the model cannot. To enact the sleight of hand from model to building requires an obsessive level of fidelity to the naive model, as well as allowing that naivete to challenge the way that buildings are typically put together.

GENERIC

Like all fantasies, this one has a dark side. When you ask an architecture student today what their project is made of, many of them will answer "CLT." This points to the fact that excitement around CLT as a more sustainable replacement for concrete and steel has pushed the material into mainstream architectural discussions. This frictionless acceptance by the design community is making CLT become about as generic and nonmaterial as concrete had been before it, a material that can "do it all," with the added bonuses of being "carbon negative," "biophilic," and "naturally warm." In this sense, CLT has become a benign stand-in for building materials in the early stages of design, loosely applied as a texture map to floors, walls, columns, and facades alike in a generic fashion. Of course, we know that mass timber has inherent constraints, but these rarely register. More often than not, we see projects that take the constructional logic of a concrete building and render it in wood. We are reminded of the moment when early Metabolists translated traditional timber construction into concrete, but here the translation is reversed.

ATECTONIC

Simple wooden models made early in the design process can embody a specific aesthetic, and can help us imagine their elaboration at a larger scale. Such models have an innocence, as they are not built like buildings. They are atectonic, emphasizing space. They suppress joinery; there are often no beams, no fasteners, and no connection plates. The glue that holds pieces together dries clear and all but disappears. Hierarchies between elements are flattened because the model is made quickly from standard sizes of material. The structure is the finish and works in mysterious ways. Flat-sheet elements, in their lightness, remain planar and span effortlessly. Slender columns do not buckle. There are no horizontal or live loads, meaning no shear walls or bracing (and in any case, the glue produces rigid moment connections). These models are often on the move, so there are no foundations to hold them down. Secondary framing is considered excess. Made from fresh basswood sheets, they do not suggest any eventual weathering, discoloration, or wear through use. Models such as these are characterized as much by what they leave out as what they contain.

BLOW-UP

These types of models are conventionally used for testing spatial concepts and to produce images. Squinting, or looking at thumbnails, one can peek inside to get an impression of the overall form and qualities of light and space. But these models turn into something else entirely when we blow them up with the ease of digital media: when we photograph them at the highest possible resolution and magnify them beyond our normal comfort level, yielding environments twenty-four, forty-eight, or ninety-six times as large as the original. We now feel that we can inhabit these spaces. Yet even though we have zoomed in, there is not more detail or another order of relationships that becomes legible. All of the sudden, we are confronted with the impression of a detail-less, structureless, immaterial world.

ARCHETYPAL

As shown above, these models have a dumb, stubborn specificity that can be interpreted in a literal way. By contrast, archetypal architectural models rely on idealization, suggesting ways of making architecture independent of dealing with its technical resolution. Their purely visual performance acts as a disciplinary prod to the profession. Open-ended and purposefully reduced to an essential set of relationships, they can nevertheless produce many more buildings than models that specify a particular solution to a particular situation. A famous example is the drawing of the Maison Dom-Ino. In this case, the image of the beamless, point-supported, concrete flat plate preceded—and ultimately motivated—its technical development, a problem that Robert Maillart and others would soon resolve from a different point of departure. Nonetheless, there is perhaps no other model that has been as generative, producing an unfathomable number of buildings and touching every aspect of architectural production from the mundane to the highly refined.

QUANTITATIVE

All of this is quite different from the way that quantitative disciplines (economics, oceanography, epidemiology, engineering, etc.) use models, which in these fields simulate and quantify performance and operate independently of the pure image. Just think of the action verbs used to describe models in the history of structural engineering: Frei Otto's dynamic models of minimum surfaces that *find* form; Robert Le Ricolais's tensegrity models that *resist* buckling; or Maillart's extra-large models weighted with sandbags and little gadgets that *measure* deflections. Or wind-tunnel tests, with their spaghetti of instruments that *sense* the pressures caused by wind loads. Or perhaps more common today, the digital models that *run* in RISA, SAP, and other programs used for structural analysis. In each case, the model is active and simulates the response of an idealized structure to applied forces. The engineer's model becomes an abstract performance, yet in order to do so, it relinquishes many of the more conventional aspects of visual representation.

DIALOGUE

Perhaps this is why the collaboration between different types of models can be so productive in the early days of a new building technology such as CLT. Each model brings to the table a different set of fantasies of the project: the spatial model and structural model, for example, and their inherent differences allow for a rich dialogue that pulls them out of their expected states. Each exerts pressure on the other, potentially upending initial assumptions. This is in contrast to building information modeling (BIM), which is fast becoming the standard for larger projects. The all-encompassing BIM model does not allow for a conversation to unfold between the different types of models by different members of the project team. The early and necessary focus on resolving problems in order to produce even just the first version of a shared model tends to bypass this back-and-forth in favor of standard resolutions. It does not allow for the fantasies embedded in the various models to produce friction.

PERFORMANCE

Going back to the blown-up wooden models, perhaps there is a middle ground between image on one hand and performance on the other. In their blown-up state, the absence of detail, structure, and material of these models makes room for other things. The emptiness and abstraction in the model shift the focus from the thing itself onto the imagined activities and subjectivities it makes possible. In that sense, there is a different sort of performance for these models beyond the unfamiliar visual and atectonic qualities they embody: social performance.

At a moment when discussions about CLT are polarized around either the image of the material on the one hand or its structural and environmental performance on the other, what is missing are projects that reach across these and start to rethink who this new material can address. Through CLT's expanded scale, reduced environmental impact, and unfamiliar materiality, we can begin to reimagine ways of working that depart from established historical frameworks and constructional conventions. This opens up new opportunities for an architecture in wood that—like steel and concrete before it—can both assemble and address new contemporary publics.

WRONG

"All models are wrong, but some are useful" is a common saying in statistics. It is precisely the wrongness of some models that makes them provocative in thinking about architecture and its construction, and gets us out of the mindset that there exists a right way to build. We have found that embracing the fantasies embedded in models helps us expand our idea of what is possible with this new industrial material—what it can become and who it can address, which we believe are urgent questions to ask at this moment of its rapid assimilation. Even though the use of CLT is quickly being codified, its cultural image is still in formation. What is required is an active reimagining of the material from every perspective. We need collaborators in this effort: engineers, artists, writers, ecologists, and more.

But in order to get everyone around the table, we need models.

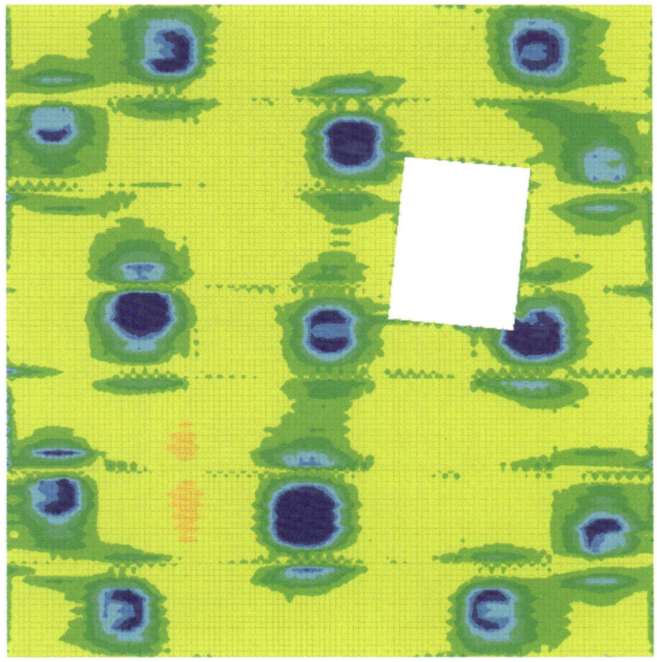

Ultramoderne, Chicago Horizon, Chicago, 2015

Top left: Chicago collage. Chicago Horizon relied on the idea of maximizing the size of the kiosk to combine the structural possibilities of CLT with the desire to open up its space to the city. The early models focused on a minimum set of ingredients to make this scalar shift possible: an oversized, thin wooden roof, thirteen columns, and a leisurely public imagined to inhabit it.

Top right: Structural model diagram. We collaborated with Brett Schneider at Guy Nordenson and Associates from the very beginning. Essential in this process were Brett's analytical models in conversation with our physical ones. Shown here is the out-of-plane shear in the direction up-down on the page.

Bottom: Model photograph, night view. We built a competition model out of thin plywood and basswood sticks to photograph. Elemental, it nevertheless crystallized a set of relationships that would challenge us through construction. The expression of the big roof as a single plane that would shift the focus to the activities below was imagined as a superlaminated plane of CLT. We realized only later that a two-way flat-plate structure had not yet been done in wood. Rather than resort to a conventional cladded frame, or introduce a set of beams, Brett became interested in the structural implications of the model and developed a method of tying together two layers of CLT with a large number of special screws to transfer shear and moment. The roof plate is therefore a hybrid structure, combining the strengths of CLT and steel to produce the thin 8-inch plate, which spans at times over 30 feet. The purist fantasy embedded in the model of an all-wood structure had to be actively constructed.

Interior photograph. The competition model afforded the image of a large, seamless roof plane. Our roof measured seven panels of CLT across, but the tight joints between them are obscured in the field of the laminations of the panels themselves.

Top: Column capital, under construction. The physical model had slots routed into the roof plane to receive the columns, in response to our early (wishful) thinking that the roof could be hoisted up on the columns, like at the New National Gallery in Berlin. In fact, how it ended up being built was with the roof hanging from the column capitals rather than sitting on them. Like the model, the columns disappear into the roof slab without further expression of the transfer of loads. The steel capitals are rendered invisible and present the image of an all-wood structure.

Bottom: Exterior photograph. The fantasies embedded in the wood model give the material an abstract quality that is removed from the traditional tectonics of working in timber and veers into less familiar territories. Naho Kubota's photographs of the project emphasize the CLT's abstractness, downplaying the textured appearance of the panels and any joints resulting from the construction process. Having requested to see the physical model photographs before photographing the pavilion herself, she understood well the potential slippage between the two.

Tower 05: Wood Grain Model
Plan: p.3 (right)
Elevation: p.10 (right)

Tower 06: Wood Grain Model
Plan: p.4 (left)
Elevation: p.12
Exploded Blanks: p.175
CLT Forecast: p.226

Tower 01: Wood Grain Model
Plan: p.1 (left)
Elevation: p.9 (right)
Blank Panels: pp.94–95
CLT Forecast: p.235

Tower 02: Wood Grain Model
Plan: p.1 (right)
Elevation: p.9 (left)
Exploded Blanks: p.173
CLT Forecast: p.237

Tower 10: Wood Grain Model
Plan: p.6 (right)
Elevation: p.14 (right)
Blank Panels: pp.96–97
CLT Forecast: p.234

Tower 08: Wood Grain Model
Plan: p.5
Elevation: p.13 (right)
Exploded Blanks: p.174
CLT Forecast: p.227

Tower 03: Wood Grain Model
Plan: p.2
Elevation: p.11
Exploded Blanks: p.176
CLT Forecast: p.236

Tower 09: Wood Grain Model
Plan: p. 6 (left)
Elevation: p. 16 (left)
Blank Panels: pp. 98–99
Structural Analysis: pp 202–5
CLT Forecast: p. 233

Tower 12: Wood Grain Model
Plan: p.7 (right)
Elevation: p.10 (left)
CLT Forecast: p.230

Tower 11: Wood Grain Model
Plan: p. 7 (left)
Elevation: p. 14 (left)
Blank Panels: pp. 92-93
Structural Analysis: pp. 206-9
CLT Forecast: p. 229

Tower 13: Wood Grain Model
Plan: p.8
Elevation: p.15
CLT Forecast: p.232

Tower 04: Wood Grain Model
Plan: p.3 (left)
Elevation: p.13 (left)
CLT Forecast: p.225

Tower 07: Wood Grain Model
Plan: p.4 (right)
Elevation: p.16 (right)
CLT Forecast: p.231

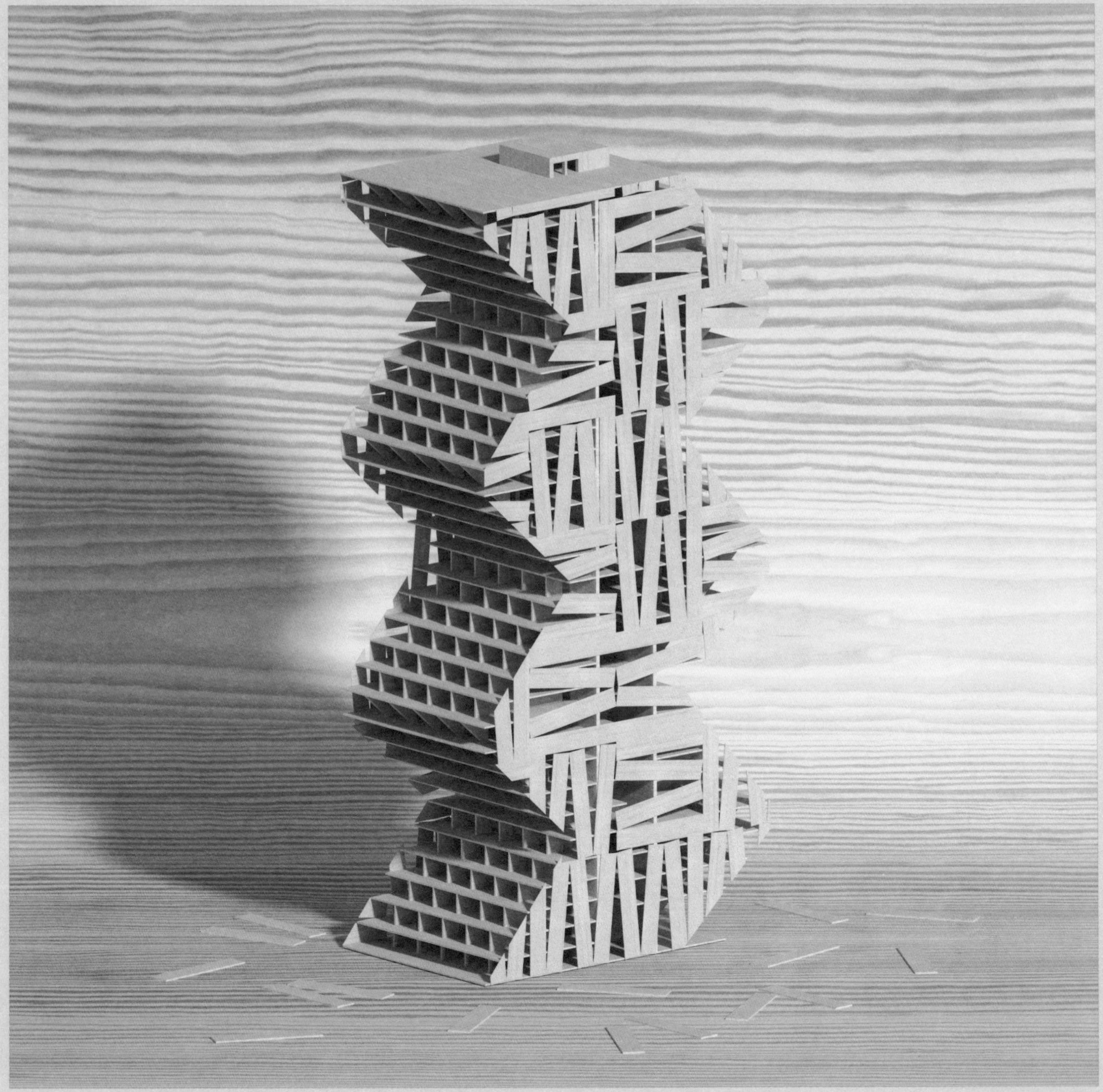

Constructing the Supergraphic: A Drawing of a Wall as Much as a Wall

Sam Jacob

There is something unbelievable about CLT. When we see the flatbed truck loaded with CLT panels arrive on-site, then the crane hoisting them into the air, it seems shockingly simple. Whole walls, whole building parts, dangling before being dropped into position. It has a surreal quality, more like what you'd find in a cartoon than on a typical construction site. Maybe it's like the paintings of tunnels that Wile E. Coyote makes in his attempts to catch Road Runner (except this time it works!). Or the cartoon saw that cuts perfect circles through a floor. Or the hole punched through a wall in the outline of the character that's just run through it. Like all of those cartoon-world examples, CLT performs in a way that flattens so much of the esoteric and arcane knowledge of the discipline and the profession of architecture.

It makes building look so *easy*. Easiness is an important and undervalued quality for a discipline that's been hooked on different strains of complexity for so long. The easiness—and speed—of CLT on-site is different. Radical, even.

Its blunt simplicity banishes so much of the fiddly detail of traditional forms of construction—think of all the complexity of one material meeting another in, say, Carlo Scarpa; or the endless cozifying embellishments of Arts and Crafts or Frank Lloyd Wright at his worst; or the bolted-togetherness of High Tech in its baroque, performative phase; or the juddering facetedness of decon and its descendants. CLT says no to all of this—even makes them impossible—through its own intrinsic engineered directness.

In part, this is because CLT acts as surface and structure simultaneously. This double function reconfigures traditional ideas of construction that often separate the two. Substantially different than the stacking of, say, a masonry wall, or the ponderous casting of concrete. Different, too, than frame and infill.

Sam Jacob Studio, Cartoon Museum, London, 2019.
A project where the world of flat 2D cartoons is made spatial. Qualities of the drawn world become part of the real world so that representation becomes architecture in an immediate and direct way. Some elements show architectural elements as flat 2D graphics, while others form layers that frame the space.

Constructional logics are more than practical. Historically, they have been imagined as sites of such profound issues as morality: the idea of "truth" in early modernist rhetoric; or, conversely, an apparent artificiality, as in the patent narration of applied "falsehood" in postmodern architecture. Think of how the component-based language of high tech was a way of imagining architecture as a technological object, a machine-like entity producing environments for habitation. Or how the craft intelligence and experience of the bricklayer's hand become embedded in the fabric of a wall. Or how the poured concrete of brutalism encodes not only the construction process—the residual markings of the rough-timber formwork it requires, for example—but also, one might argue, a postwar vision of social organization into monumental form. In all of these ways (and more), how we build is an expression of assumptions and values that range far wider than the problem of making a building.

The act of building—including material choices, construction techniques, and structural strategies, but not only—incorporates ideas about labor, about our relationship to resources and the environment, about all kinds of things that are often imagined to be external to architecture as a profession. In reality, architecture internalizes all these preconceptions.

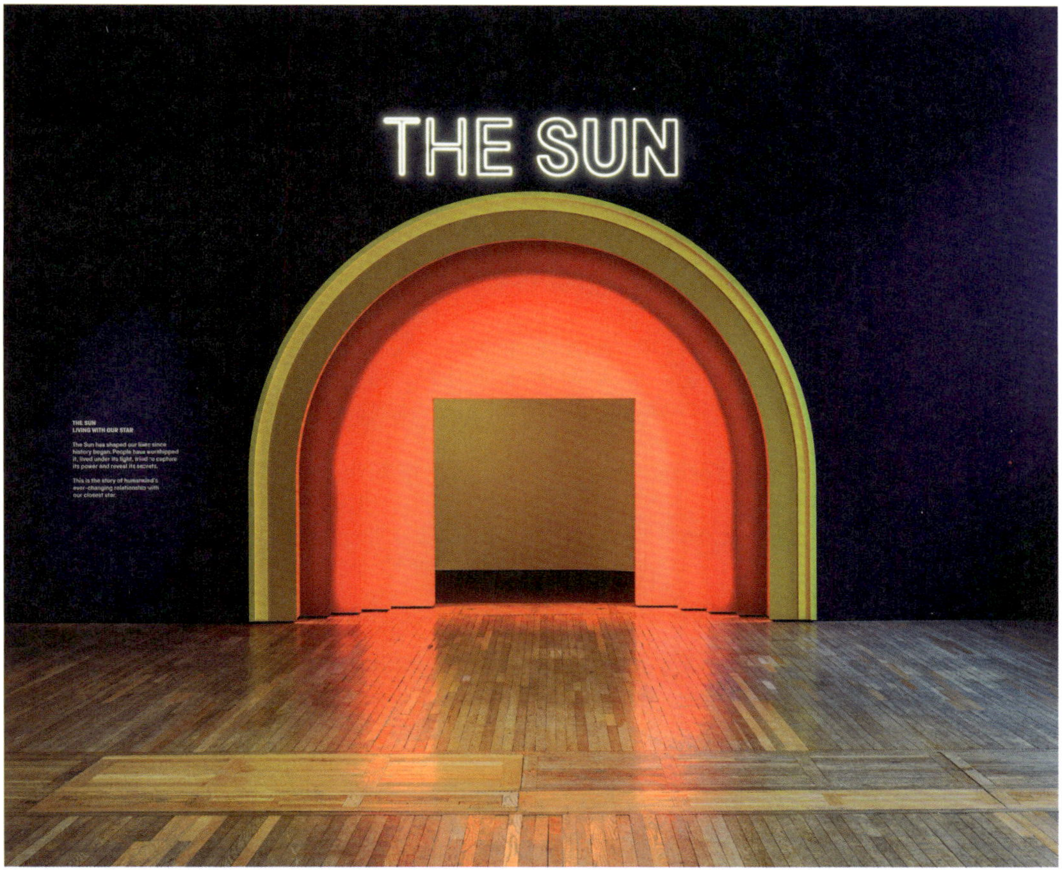

Sam Jacob Studio, The Sun, Science Museum, London, 2018. An arch forming the entrance to a display about the sun. Its form draws on architectural traditions of threshold, while its color scheme is derived from textbook diagrams cut through the sun. The effect merges both: it's spatial and graphic simultaneously, as if it were possible to walk through the surface of a drawing.

We should try to understand CLT from this angle, perhaps guided by Marshall McLuhan's media theory. Not to look outward, to imagine what we might do with CLT, but rather to consider it as a medium.

That means in CLT's "easiness" lurks something more difficult. Because in the space that's created by its simplicity, CLT asks us to confront a new set of questions. Cartoon worlds may seem abstracted and simplified, but they contain their own specific logics, physics, rules. These are worlds that exist on the space of the page.

Like paper, CLT originates with trees. Both are timber processed into a form with an overall evenness. Natural kinks and warps are smoothed out though slicing (CLT) or pulping (card). On one hand, we can be excited that—managed in the right way—CLT is a sustainable and renewable material, one that reduces embedded carbon and sidesteps energy-hungry processing and construction techniques. On the other hand, CLT's process of manufacture produces something qualitatively unlike other construction materials, something that challenges our assumptions about them altogether.

CLT shares something else with paper: it, too, feels like a medium, far more than almost any other building material. Perhaps that's because of its conceptual affinities with a page—just scaled up. Or that it seems like a real-life version of a sheet of card ready to be cut and assembled as a model. "Real" CLT construction is somehow inherently close to the model that represents it, usually thought of as a not-real thing.

It's worth remembering an early Bauhaus exercise where Johannes Itten would give students a piece of paper but ask them to think of the paper itself as an object: thin, yes, but three-dimensional. Students would work with the flatness of the page, but in space. Perhaps that, too, is part of what CLT is: a flat surface to be placed into space.

What if, as CLT seems to insist, the building is just another form of architectural representation that sits alongside the media that architects work with, like drawings and models?

That question may have something to do with CLT's quality of endless blankness. CLT panels evoke an abstract order not unlike the ISO paper-sizing system. And like sheets of A4, A3, A2, and so on, CLT presents us with big, blank surfaces of a particular format, surfaces that insist on flatness with the same primed quality of a page before the pen makes a mark. In the case of paper, that two-dimensional blankness is able and ready to accept content: text, drawing, or whatever else the author intends. With CLT, though, that blankness is ready to accept a different kind of content: architecture.

Working with CLT involves two key things. First is the act of cutting. The cut defines the holes for what will become windows or doors, or perhaps a roof line. The cut transforms the generic, blank format into the specifics of a project. The cut is the single act that gives scale, use, inflection, character. The act of architecture is performed through cutting, slicing, incisions, cropping, chopping. It's a revelation of profound clarity that these actions are, within the medium of CLT, the most significant ways of producing architecture.

Second is what produces the cut. Picture the CLT panel lying flat on a CNC bed, a spinning bit on a robotic arm describing lines and arcs. Cuts as smooth as the surface, working in another axis. Cuts are linear, like a pen traversing a page, or like a plotter scaled up. What's driving the CNC head is a drawing. The translation from drawing to building is (at least in comparison to traditional forms of building) almost instantaneous, almost parallel. Is the wall, CLT asks us, both a wall and a drawing of a wall at the same time?

Opposite: FAT, The Villa, Heerlijkheid Hoogvliet, Rotterdam, 2008. The simple rectilinear form of the building is wrapped in timber screens—sometimes layered, as a relief, and in other places pulled away from the facade to form a colonnade. The cutting of the timber is used to create a supergraphic frieze, a narrative, scenographic outer layer. Aspects of drawing are translated into cutting patterns so that a graphic language merges with the construction process and material quality of the building.

Sam Jacob Studio, Plank Scarf and Plank Tape, 2016. Part of a range of products produced by the studio. Both play with ideas of timber between expectation and reality, where the idea of a wooden plank is rendered in materials that behave in a completely different way. The scarf is a knitted plank that you can wrap around your body, the tape an adhesive layer that can be applied to any surface to render it as an idea (rather than a reality) of woodiness.

CLT is a form of representation as much as it is constructed, a drawing of a wall as much as a wall. The building is drawn at one-to-one scale directly into the material of the building through the act of cutting. The vector on the screen becomes the vector of the blade becomes the thing itself. Drawing becomes integral to the act of construction, rather than, as in traditional construction, a document to be translated into building. CLT is native to digital drawing, an output that is equal to outputs of the same information in whatever medium: pixels on a screen, ink on paper, cuts in wood. Each is a translation of the same digital information into different media.

Traditional modes of supergraphic design break down into constituent parts. The graphic element is obvious—visual and flat; perhaps something adjacent to information, perhaps pattern; the kind of thing that most often happens on a page. Modified by the prefix *super*, though, whatever the graphic element might normally be is transformed into something exceeding that state: something bigger or more powerful, but also placed over (superimposed), or replacing what preceded it (superseding). The graphic is applied, hosted by something else with which it has an antagonistic relationship (obliterating whatever the host might be). It's parasitical in the sense that it couldn't exist without the host, and potent in its effect, though somehow also flimsy and superficial. For those reasons (and the simple pleasures of being overwhelmed by the visual field of the graphic surface), the supergraphic has traditionally operated as a particular kind of decorative design technique. Supergraphics might bring building and graphic together, but even as they approach one another, they reinforce their difference. The built remains solid and structural, the representational cast in the role of two-dimensional surface.

CLT's form, flatness, and tooling reframe the relationship between drawing and building. Boundaries between traditional categories of representation and reality dissolve. Graphic, surface, and structure are not divided, but simultaneous. This is less a supergraphic than what we might call a *synagraphic* architecture, where the wall is the drawing and the drawing is the wall. We look from building (which, let's say, for now, means issues of structure, shelter, and spatial organization) to media (which could mean things like character, content, and meaning), and from media to building again, but with CLT, it might be impossible to say which is which.

Cut-Out

Nelson Byun

For the closing decade of his life, Henri Matisse was bed- and chairbound in his studio. Complications of cancer and anxiety from the Second World War had sapped his strength for good. Moreover, the act of painting had become a physical challenge. Recalling his friend Pierre-Auguste Renoir, who died happily with a paintbrush strapped to his bandaged hands, Matisse promised, "When my time came, I would not be a coward either."[1] In the early 1940s, he turned to sheets of colored paper and scissors as liberators from his troubles, and worked intensively toward a new form of art called découpage, or the cut-out. This medium provides a useful analogy to speculate on the architectural potential of the CLT blank.

Quoted in Hilary Spurling, *Matisse the Master: A Life of Henri Matisse, the Conquest of Colour, 1909–1954* (New York: Alfred A. Knopf, 2005), 465.

Matisse famously described the operation as "drawing with scissors," a process by which he was able to connect "line with color, contour with surface."[2] The works were cut from standard French artist-paper sheets painted by assistants with vivid green, blue, red, orange, and yellow gouache—a water-based and fast-drying opaque matte paint. Matisse used oversized scissors to carve out diverse shapes and motifs—including plants, animals, and figures—with ease and control. These were then arranged into spontaneous and boundless compositions that his assistants pinned directly to walls. The works were both small and large in scale, left singular or arranged into groupings, and continually reworked. Together, they covered the walls of Matisse's studio from floor to ceiling, corner to corner. Surrounded by the cut-outs, he was able to escape his confinement and enter different worlds, such as the "little garden" of *The Parakeet and the Mermaid*,[3] a piece that measures approximately 25 feet wide by 11 feet tall and includes as many as 150 cut-outs of leaves, fruits, and birds ranging from 6 to 30 inches in size.

Quoted in Karl Buchberg et al., "The Studio as Site and Subject," in *Henri Matisse: The Cut-Outs*, ed. Karl Buchberg et al. (New York: Museum of Modern Art, 2014), 12.

Quoted in Buchberg et al., 11.

Cutting into colored paper allowed "the contour of a shape and its internal area [to be] formed simultaneously,"[4] solving what Karl Buchberg, Nicholas Cullinan, Jodi Hauptman, and Nicholas Serota call the "tension between drawing and colour" for Matisse.[5] At the easel, he was first a draftsman, abstracting subject matters brilliantly into simple shapes and silhouettes with graceful lines on canvas. These paintings have the effect of "apparent simplicity,"

Quoted in Buchberg et al., 12.

Quoted in Buchberg et al., 12.

according to the artist; in truth, there were often a significant number of preparatory sketches behind them.[6] Later, in his transition to a colorist, Matisse applied forceful brushstrokes of vivid and non-naturalistic paints to his outline drawings to add dynamism in excess of a subject's reality. The style was famously described as the product of a *fauve*, or wild beast, by the critic Louis Vauxcelles in 1905. However, Matisse's use of color, which seems impulsive and even violent at first glance, was also the product of iterative study. Tonal and textural relationships were meticulously considered to achieve maximum visual intensity. For Matisse, drawing and color were separate phases of development in painting. It was not a fluid process, as each required periods of contemplation and technical refinement. In contrast, cutting lines into color was truly "simple" and "wild," as the fusion enabled his creative intuition to flow without pause between the two approaches. The technique also released the artist from the boundary of the canvas frame and the fixed attributes of paint; instead, expansive studio walls accommodated ever-shifting cut-outs with no apparent end. The cut-outs embody this sense of freedom.

See "Henri Matisse Drawings," accessed January 15, 2021, www.matissepaintings.org/drawings/.

Given CLT's inherent flatness and ability to be cut into, the blank is "colored paper" for architects, solving the tension between drawing and building. Like painting for Matisse, architecture has phases. Typically, a building is first designed through drawing, a process of figuring out and communicating how it is made. The level of detail an architect specifies often determines the resolution of original design intent in construction, where it can be altered or lost across individual layers of building assembly. Like Matisse's colored paper, CLT fuses multiple qualities together—structure, thermal insulation, fire protection, and finish are all embedded in the natural fibers of the wood panel. Using the CNC router as "scissors," which turn and rotate at the command of the architect's line, one can effortlessly cut diverse forms for wall, floor, and roof. A chainsaw in situ can do the same. This direct and personal definition of lines enables architects to design more freely, and in turn buildings can be more expressive in appearance.

Architects have long pursued the ability to connect drawing and building. To take one illustrative example: Frank Gehry has acknowledged that a kink in the curved staircase in his Vitra Design Museum, in Weil-am-Rhein, Germany, a structure of colliding volumes completed in 1989, is a flaw due to a misinterpretation of architectural drawings by the builder.

Thereafter, Gehry began working with advanced digital software used by the aerospace industry to engineer and fabricate complex forms, a decision that drove what is now known as parametric design and building information modeling. Knowing that the computer could engineer any form that his mind conceived, Gehry designs intuitively through hand sketches and models, cutting and crumpling scrap paper and cardboard and gluing and taping them together. These studies are eventually developed into three-dimensional digital models and drawings for the builder's reference. "If I knew where I was going, I wouldn't go there. So I rely on intuition. I guess my great model for that is Matisse, with the cut-outs," he explained in a lecture on his work process at the National Gallery of Art in Washington, DC.[7] One can read Matisse's fluid lines, casual cuts, and playful manipulation of surfaces in Gehry's dynamic building envelopes and spatial orchestrations of metal, glass, and stone. The computer allowed Gehry to bridge the gap between drawing and building. The blank can deepen this connection, as it shares traits with the materials architects commonly sketch on and make models with, creating an opportunity to articulate nuances of the individual mind, hand, and eye at the scale of a building.

Frank Gehry, "Working Process - Frank O. Gehry," lecture, National Gallery of Art, date unknown, Washington, DC, video recording, 30:51, https://www.youtube.com/watch?v=VXS475E2YEs.

Another discovery of Matisse's was what Hauptman calls the "positives and negatives, reversals and inverses, the organic relations between shapes, their generation of one from another" created in the process of cutting.[8] Once the cut-out is cut out, there is a "left-over," and both had equal value to the artist. This is especially clear in his book *Jazz*; one can play the game of visually piecing together shapes without ever knowing which the artist intended to use first. For instance, in the stencils titled *Lagoon*, algae motifs in vivid colors sometimes float above their cut counterparts, while others are separated on different pages. There is a sense of movement in the physical parting that contributes to the theme of voyage in the book.

Jodi Hauptman, "Inventing a New Operation," in *Henri Matisse: The Cut-Outs*, 19.

Unlike many other materials, the CLT blank has positive and negative forms that can both have a role in the design of a building. For example, when designing a facade, one can consider using left-overs to make another facade or surface. The strategy can lead to new visual readings where both positive and negative can be perceived; parts of the blank take turns as figure and ground. Another idea, inspired by Matisse, is to incorporate large-scale motifs and their reversals into the envelope of a building (or series of buildings). Bystanders can interact with and be immersed in architecture through a visual game of piecing positive

Henri Matisse in his studio,
Nice, France, 1952

and negative together. Furthermore, because nothing is wasted, the left-over maximizes timber's ability to sequester carbon. The entire CLT blank is up for grabs to explore new tectonics and aesthetics of building, in a material economy where "more is more" in mitigating the effects of climate change.

There is another significant resonance between the cut-out and the blank, a trait that indexes how they come to appear in the world. When Matisse's cut-outs left the studio, the pinholes from their mounting remained what Hauptman has described as "a tangible record of the labour required to make them and the myriad compositional paths not taken."[9] The CNC machine leaves similar pinholes on each CLT panel during manufacturing, which are later used on-site to hoist the panel into place via crane. Like the pinholes, these thoughts on the CLT blank are meant to point to a vastness of possibilities to leverage in the material's application. They start to suggest the material as a liberator, allowing architects to set aside qualms about communicating design for construction and to freely project drawn lines to define structure. When Gehry was building his home in Santa Monica and needed more light in a space, he picked up a hammer and knocked a hole in the wall. Now imagine Matisse's studio and the sound of scissors cutting.

9 Hauptman, 21.

Lauren Halsey

our hood
What if
WE
Sister Dreamer
Success

CRENSHAW
SQUARE
Michelle Lee Shirley
Omar Abrego
Steve Washington
Brendon Glenn
Kendrick Blackmon
Ezell Ford
Carnell Smell Jr.
Marquintan Sandlin
Kisha Michael
Diante Yarb
Latasha Harlins
Tamir Rice
Amia Tyrae
Michael Brown Jr.
Terence Crutcher
Autumn Johnson
Erica Garner
Eric Garner
Sandra Bland
Michael T. Slager
Lanard Jackson
Isaac Jones
Philando Castile
Tanisha Anderson
Janisha Fonville
Yvette Smith
Malissa Williams
Timothy Russell

Previous spreads: Lauren Halsey, *The Crenshaw District Hieroglyph Project (Prototype Architecture)*, 2018. Installation views, *Made in L.A.*, June 3–September 2, 2018, Hammer Museum, Los Angeles.

Above: Lauren Halsey, *The Liquor Bank*, 2019. Hand-carved gypsum on wood, 47 5/8 × 47 5/8 × 1 7/8 in.

Surface Tensions

Victoria Camblin

In January 2021, a Los Angeles news website published an article with the headline "Boarded up storefront becomes canvas for street artists." The piece described the descent of local artists on a downtown West Elm furniture store for a public installation seeking to turn "unsightly boarded up windows into works of art."[1] We can infer from its popularity in contemporary design that the plywood used to board up windows is not inherently "unsightly"; even if it were, much of the mid-century-inspired product typically on view in a West Elm storefront is made of something similarly engineered. Installed on the building's exterior, however, the material takes on an unbearable quality, compelling its treatment as a "canvas," a surface seeking content and coverage.

This hostility toward plywood may have to do with our general mistrust of "surface," which is commonly believed to conceal something, as an antagonist of realness and depth. "Beneath the surface" is where the truth of a thing lives; higher knowledge awaits those who penetrate it. The deceptive work of the surface can be intentional or naive, a mask worn on purpose, like a face-lift or a studio-set facade, or adopted organically, pathologically—an agent of survival, a means of protection, like a forced smile amid despair or an "under new management" sign on a business that is not. To invest in surface, in this view, is to withhold an undesirable reality, even to harbor malignancy.

The distinct quality of plywood's surface and its distinct qualities *as* a surface—its assertive *surfaceness*—endow it with particular potency as a sign. The meaning of its characteristic grain is not fixed but floats, independently of its aesthetic or use value, between interpretative contexts. Malleability is engineered into this particular product: "ply" comes from the French *plier*, "to fold" or "to bend," and the wood is characterized by a layering of both matter and meaning. On street-facing windows, the appearance of plywood carries negative significance. Its presence there indicates loss—someone or something has left the building—and expresses the shifting fortunes of an entire neighborhood or city. The more boarded-up windows there are in a particular locale, the worse the economic downturn, the higher up its impact within a chain of power, the crueler the change. Perhaps someone fears looting; perhaps the looting has already taken place. Whatever their purpose, these surfaces brought in to conceal an asset's contents, to hide the (dis)use of its interior, suggest more than they obscure, at once narrating something far greater than the history of a particular site and making a mystery out of its present and future. They say nothing while implying something—something to protect, to fix, to steal, to know—and with that promise of a hidden truth, they invite the pioneer.

Ten years prior to the West Elm intervention, Jennifer Bolande was commissioned to contribute to West of Rome's *Women in the City* series, another public art exhibition on the streets of Los Angeles. At the time, the Great Recession's effects on housing and unemployment were at their most severe, and it was common to see boarded-up storefronts across LA County. A piece of plywood functioned as a billboard for economic crisis—a sign Bolande subverted in a work called *Plywood Curtains*. The artist printed detailed, high-resolution images of plywood onto fabric, which was then pleated, outfitted with basic hardware, and installed as curtains in the windows of vacant storefronts. The plywood's distinctive grain was reproduced so faithfully as to provoke at least a double take: one sees a boarded-up window, then notes it as atypical. Are those skillfully bent ribbons of ultrathin plies, a feat of wood engineering à la Marcel Breuer or Frank Gehry? Is this a boarded-up mid-century modern-inspired furniture store?

Bolande's undulating trompe l'oeil effectively locates the power of plywood as a signifier in the nature of its surface. *Plywood Curtains* communicates "boarded-up windows" despite taking form as soft furnishings that inhabit the sphere of domestic life, functional and undisturbed. Curtains are drawn shut at night for privacy and open for light during the day—a normal cadence of revelation and concealment that puts us at ease. The surface of plywood is so laden with meaning and yet so context-contingent that its uncomfortable character—its relationship to the untrustworthy and changeable conditions of reality—can be conveyed through its material opposite, using only a faithful photograph.

Trompe l'oeil is a mode of painting that deceives the viewer by simulating a natural or a built environment in two dimensions. In Jacques Lacan's discussion of the artistic device, the moment when what was thought to be depth resolves itself into two-dimensional surface—like seeing close-ups of Bolande's installation that reveal its stitching and seams—is when longing occurs, when desire for something missing and unknown ignites. Painting or otherwise dwelling upon a surface conjures fantasy lost or unrealized; here, it has the visual texture of thwarted commercial enterprise or neighborhood flourishing. To make something real of such a surface, one must seek substance not beneath but within the grain.

Lauren Halsey's *The Crenshaw District Hieroglyph Project (Prototype Architecture)* reclaims surface as a place of historical document and of actualization by cutting into it. Exhibited in Los Angeles as part of the Hammer Museum's 2018 *Made in L.A.* biennial, the installation consists primarily of plywood and gypsum, a soft sulfate mineral widely used in ancient Egypt, where it served as mortar in the construction of the pyramids and as a plaster base for tomb paintings. This material, like plywood, is thus both surface and structure. Rather than compartmentalizing these two functions as mutually opposed, Halsey harnesses and reconciles their perceived duality. The result is both a usable structure and a system of signs.

Carved into each gypsum panel are hieroglyphic records of the Crenshaw area of South LA, where the artist grew up—an area, like those adorned by Bolande's *Plywood Curtains*, facing radical socioeconomic change. These cuts depict graffiti, local storefront signage, and scenes of residents' daily life in the neighborhood, alongside references to Egyptian iconography. Recognizable rectangular patterns mimic those of brick walls and sidewalk paving stones—representations of building materials oriented vertically and horizontally to create space, giving depth to a courtyard, elevation to a residential apartment block, and a third dimension to a surface of only two.

None of the exposed or represented surfaces in Halsey's temples convey "plywood." In fact, none of them convey "surface." Had plywood been used as a surface, or had its grain been depicted through incision, its viscerally recognizable appearance—its solicitation of projection and loss fantasies, its suggestion of tension and instability—might have compromised the artist's message of community vibrancy and agency, presence and possibility. That the material should nonetheless haunt the work's listed contents is an assertion of surface *as structure*, an integration of appearance and substance that escapes the plywood trap—without rejecting the material. Lurking in the construction of *The Crenshaw District Hieroglyph Project*, plywood is an invisible reference to why such a monument is necessary in the first place: to preserve and continue the creation of the spaces that, regarded as surface alone, it might serve to efface. A repossession of the unfolding story of South Central takes place by integrating the surface signs of its changing reality into the material foundations of a new one.

1 "Boarded Up Storefront Becomes Canvas for Street Artists," ABC7, January 12, 2021, https://abc7.com/covid-19-los-angeles-art-installation/6149320/.

Jennifer Bolande

Plywood Curtains, 2008–11. Photographically printed poplin fabric. *Plywood Curtains*, a site-specific art installation, first appeared in vacant store-front windows around Los Angeles following the recession of 2008.

Following spread, clockwise from top left: *Plywood Curtains*, 495 South Lake Boulevard, Pasadena; 5514 Wilshire Boulevard; 5514 Wilshire Boulevard; Pasadena Ford, East Colorado Boulevard

Above and opposite: Jennifer Bolande, *Mountain*, 2003–4. Birch plywood and pigment prints, 72 × 75 × 60 in.

Jennifer Bolande,
Smoke Screen #5, 2007.
Pigment prints on
plywood backed with steel,
96 × 48 × 2 3/4 in.

Tower 02: Exploded Blanks
Plan: p.1 (right)
Elevation: p.9 (left)
Wood Grain Model: pp.132-33
CLT Forecast: p.237

Tower 08: Exploded Blanks
Plan: p.5
Elevation: p.13 (right)
Wood Grain Model: p.135
CLT Forecast: p.227

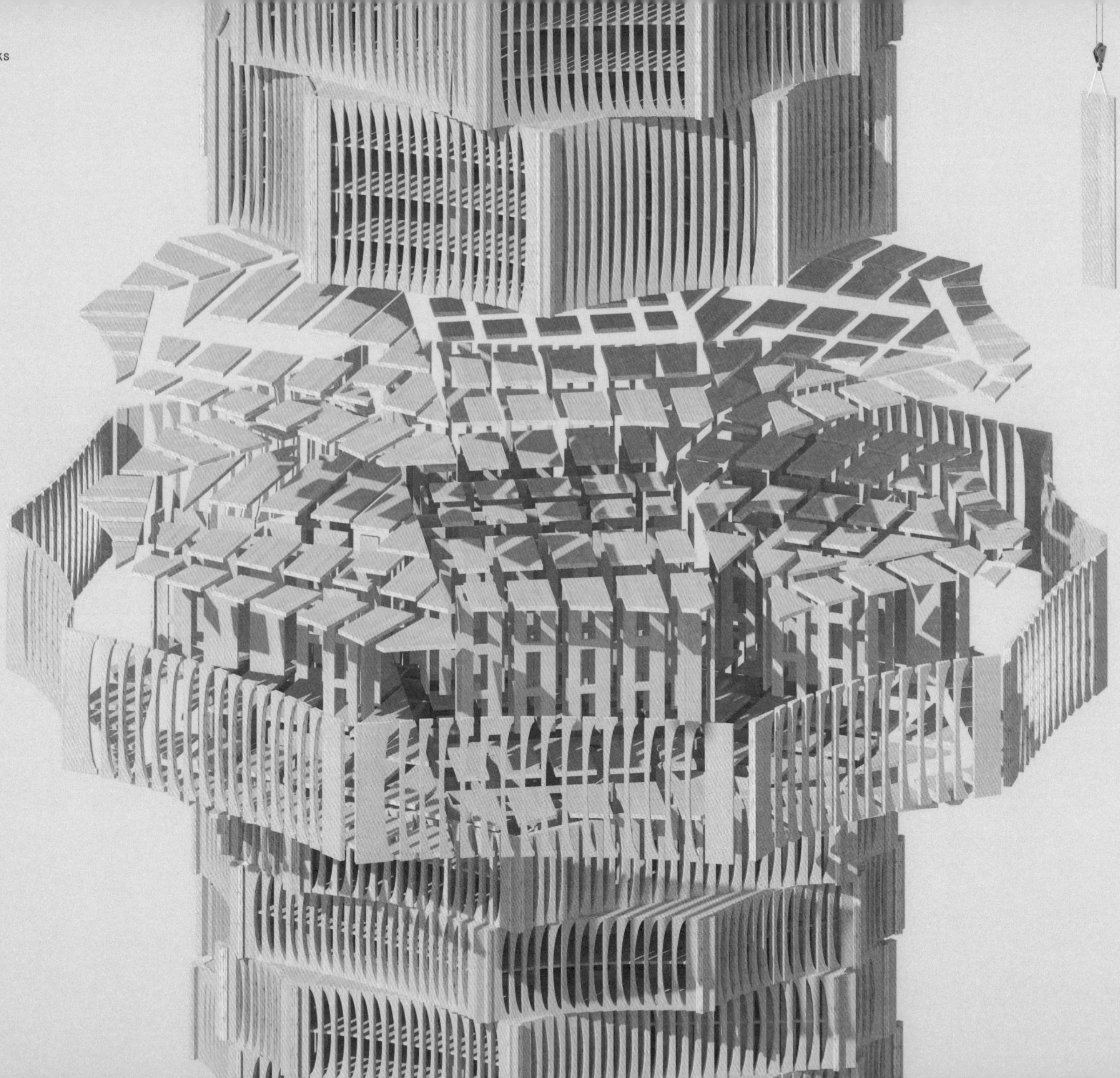

Tower 06: Exploded Blanks
Plan: p.4 (left)
Elevation: p.12
Wood Grain Model: p.130
CLT Forecast: p.226

Tower 03: Exploded Blanks
Plan: p.2
Elevation: p.11
Wood Grain Model: p.136
CLT Forecast: p.236

House 11: Exploded Blanks
Plan: p.43 (right)
Elevation: p.50 (bottom)
CLT Forecast: p.234

House 02: Exploded Blanks
Plan: p.37 (right)
Elevation: p.46 (top)
CLT Forecast: p.233

House 09: Exploded Blanks
Plan: p.42
Elevation: p.49
Structural Analysis: p.201
CLT Forecast: p.225

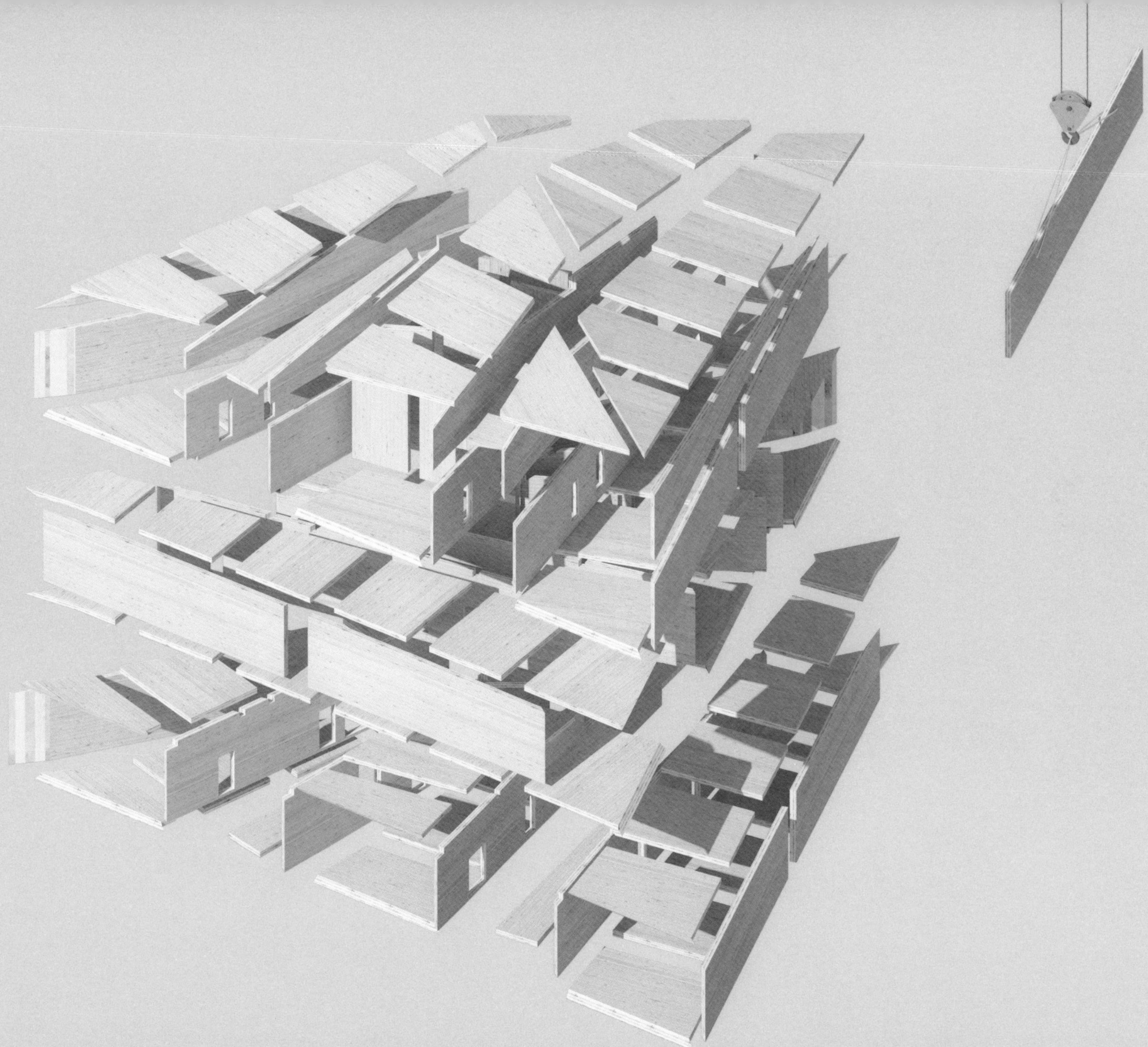

House 08: Exploded Blanks
Plan: p.41
Elevation: p.47 (bottom)
CLT Forecast: p. 229

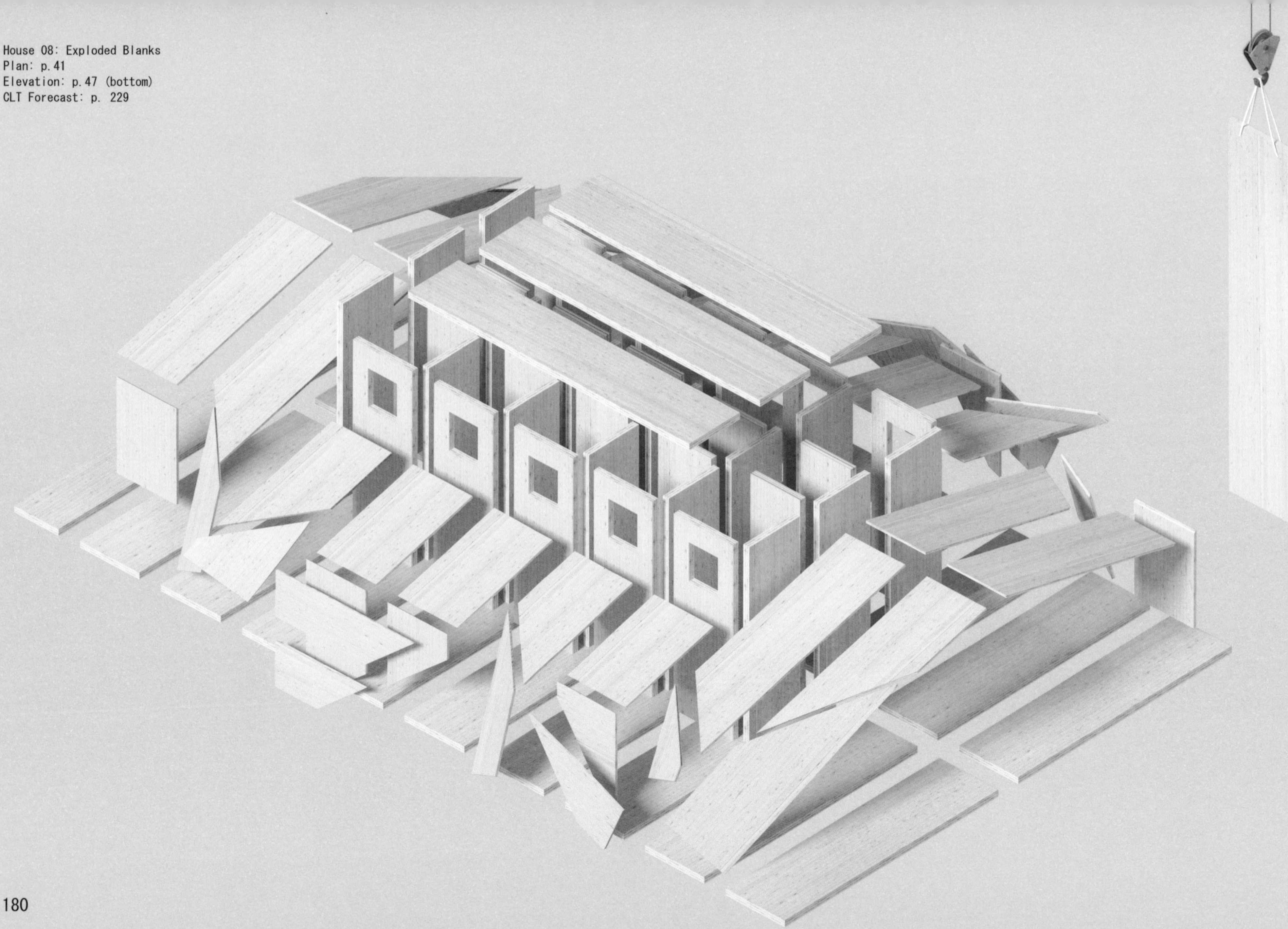

Switcheroo, Blanks Everywhere

Jennifer Bonner

A post by Big Freedia from the early days of Instagram has stuck with me. In the video, she's driving a car, singing, "We in New Orleans—ice everywhere, ice everywhere. Ice everywhere, ice everywhere. Ice everywhere, sleet everywhere." With this part weather report, part lyrical invention, she announced the road conditions on a January evening—New Orleans had iced over. Her fan base, in tears from laughter, was all-in on her witty remix: she had cleverly swapped out lyrics from her song "Azz Everywhere."

1 Bounce music is high tempo, frequently 90 to 110 beats per minute.

Known for advancing the genre of bounce music,[1] Big Freedia creates hooks that are addictive and infinitely long. Here, her up-tempo cadence places emphasis on "everywhere," which I would argue both makes her improvisation catchier and, even more, promotes an all-encompassing *vibe*. "Everywhere" means everywhere, literally. In culture, vibe is a primary way of broadening ideas and popularizing aesthetics. Big Freedia's use of the repetitive chant is artistically consistent and convincing. It also sets up an "everywhere" construction that is extremely easy to apply to repetitive themes emerging in other contexts, including in contemporary architecture, and notably around materiality—wood everywhere, wood everywhere. Wood everywhere, wood everywhere.

For architects looking to mine lessons from Freedia, a closer consideration of vibe might be a way to absorb contemporary culture back into the field. Architectural critics at the end of the last century also asked questions around vibe, but through the lens of the city. This essay shifts the discussion on vibe away from, say, Michael Sorkin's reading of Amsterdam's neighborhood charm, found in "small increments" like bricks, pavers, and window panes,[2] toward the vibe on our digital screens. And #crosslaminatedtimber definitely has a vibe:[3] highly polished architectural photography of softly lit domestic and commercial spaces; zoomed-in details that boast tectonic connections; construction shots that make visual both human labor and the handiwork of the crane on-site; photorealistic renderings of work-in-progress mid-rise towers texture-mapped with CLT wood grain. Trend pieces, like

2 Michael Sorkin, "Notes on Vibe" (1998), in *Some Assembly Required* (Minneapolis: University of Minnesota Press, 2001), 70.

3 As of December 18, 2020, #crosslaminatedtimber appears in more than 16,300 Instagram posts.

Left: Mavis Pusey pictured in front of her painting *Within Manhattan*, ca. 1970

Right: Mavis Pusey, *Dissolution of X*, ca. 1970

"Seven Wooden Kitchens That Offer a Different Take on Timber" (*Dezeen*) and "Mass Timber Going Mainstream" (AIA), or race-to-first stories, such as "Milwaukee Is On Track to House World's Tallest Timber Skyscraper" (NPR) and "Zaha Hadid Architects Wins Approval for World's First All-Timber Stadium" (*Dezeen*), not only point to mass timber's everywhereness, but add journalistic reinforcement and a competitive undertone to an emerging sensibility. At the crux is the aesthetics of CLT's vibe, chock-full of texture maps, wood grain, and the kinds of blankness we've attempted to explore in this book.

Another significant takeaway from Big Freedia's post is the technique of exchangeability. In her case, to swap out lyrics from an older song in order to create a new take, one that has both immediacy and currency (even if pithy, at fifteen seconds), reveals an inventive method. Although architects are well-versed in propping up architecture with exemplars of other architecture, we are now at a critical impasse—the canon is under scrutiny.[4] Freedia's rapid-fire switcheroo suggests a way to rethink precedents through interchangeability: replace something with something else, see what effects that swap produces, and repeat. Such experiments with vibe cede the scholarly to the casual, and hint at an architecture filled with more humor and a disciplinary history made more malleable.

Petitions to remove Philip Johnson's name from institutional spaces are only the latest example of the field's much wider reckoning with its own role in perpetuating systemic racism.

With a limited range of useful built examples of the blank to call on, this essay looks at a series of artworks and buildings that are not constructed out of mass timber in order to

Jennifer Bonner / MALL, Four Over None, 2020. A load-bearing structural facade for a housing development challenges the orientation of CLT blanks in a visual exchange with Pusey's work.

challenge the way we think about CLT. More specifically, the exercise that follows productively misreads the original art or architecture as and through CLT blanks.[5] Reimagining a work or a building as newly constructed out of dozens of blanks is a different method than studying a precedent. The exchange momentarily opens up conceptual avenues for an innovative wood product that is otherwise stuck in narratives of environmental do-goodism.

5 See the introduction to this book for a lengthier description of the CLT blank. For the purposes of this argument, the blank is an industrial, off-the-shelf material measuring 9 feet by 50 feet.

To begin this study, which is primarily a search for works that are amenable to a visual exchange with the blank, a first inclination is to turn to artists well-versed in abstraction. The geometric forms in the art of Mavis Pusey are a near-perfect aesthetic match for the proportions of a raw, off-the-shelf CLT blank. Pusey's work presents, in her words, "geometrical forms in a variety of geometrical configurations ... based on buildings around the Manhattan area"; she was "inspired by the energy and the beat of the construction and demolition of these buildings."[6] Measuring 73 inches wide by 96 inches high, the painting *Within Manhattan*, completed circa 1970, is almost building-scale itself. Arrangements of rectangles redact a scene of other rectangular blocks beyond. Those blocks, reminiscent of shutters and generic industrial facades, create a kind of nine-part-grid backdrop upon which we might read a series of scattered blanks. Foregrounded at the top of the geometric pile are long, slender board-like shapes in white and a pale tan color reminiscent of wood. In other works, namely her lithographs, Pusey exaggerates these rectilinear forms further by adding texture—wood grain

6 Quoted in "The Artwork of Mavis Pusey," accessed December 18, 2020, http://www.mavispusey.com.

Left: Richard Serra, *Blank*, 1978

Right: Richard Serra, *Equal Size, Unequal Weight*, 1988. In this work, Serra's paintstick canvases are the same size as a CLT blank.

and speckles of black paint that architects might associate with material hatches. If Pusey looks at construction and abstracts it, might architects look at her abstraction and construct with it? Pusey was almost certainly painting boards of lumber; if we are on board with the visual switch, the blank becomes a compositional readymade, ready to challenge a load-bearing structural facade.

While Pusey's work overtly represents wood grain with color and pattern, a series of paintings by Richard Serra a decade later unequivocally steers us to his anonymous surface. In *Blank* (1978), Serra staples two wall coverings made of black paintstick on canvas directly to opposite gallery walls. His "blank" attempts to deal with "the entirety of the room,"[7] similarly to the way the CLT blank becomes anonymous surfaces in domestic and commercial interiors, a backdrop against which daily activities play out. Anchored to the floor (as paintings rarely are) in adjacent corners, the canvases appear to be walls themselves—oddly more like a wall than the actual wall.[8] Doubling the imagery of blankness by mirroring the canvases allows the viewer to recognize Serra's blank is inherently different from the blankness of the gallery. *Blank*'s canvases each measure 120 ¼ inches square, although a photograph of the original installation makes the canvases appear longer horizontally, because of the camera angle. Here, the trade or exchange between Serra's blank and the CLT blank is suggestive of the potentiality for horizontality of a room or space. In architectural practice and the building industry, there are currently dozens of built examples of mass timber buildings where the identifiable CLT panel is revealed in the floor plate, sequestered to the ceiling of an office space, for example. Serra's *Blank* encourages us to imagine the blank as a load-bearing wall system. Another work, *Equal Size, Unequal Weight* (1988), stretches this idea of a pair of walls even further, to a scale that's eerily even more perfectly blank-like, 9 feet, 6 inches, by 60 feet. Like a thick,

7 Quoted in Gary Garrels, "An Interview with Richard Serra (2010)," in Richard Serra et al., *Richard Serra, Drawing: A Retrospective* (Houston: Menil Collection, 2011), 75.

8 "I try to keep [my surfaces] as anonymous as possible, so that they don't call attention to themselves." Quoted in Serra et al., 33.

Top: Yoann Bourgeois, *He Who Falls (Celui qui tombe)*, 2016

Bottom: Jennifer Bonner / MALL, architect, and AKT II, structural engineer, Haus Gables, Atlanta, 2018. An on-site construction cam captures CLT panel number four (of eighty-seven) being installed with a 40-ton crane.

matte, monochrome layer of black paintstick, a mono-material wood blank becomes an ordering device, collapsing the structural with the spatiality of architecture.[9] Serra's seventies and eighties blanks direct built-in repetition toward room-making, suggesting today's blank can do the same.

This image of a levitating blank is also easily attainable with CLT. With the addition of several blanks rotated at ninety degrees below, architecture can achieve a floating blank that is also part of a load-bearing stack.

Transitioning from works of abstraction to works of performance, we might consider the French artist Yoann Bourgeois, who productively destabilizes not the vertical planes of Pusey's canvases, but the ground plane. Likened to merry-go-rounds or overscaled swings, his constructs are theater stages in motion—thickened planar surfaces akin to a seven-ply blank.

Think an entire theater floor spinning and swaying, with several actors running around in dizzying circles, climbing, and scaling large wooden masses. In *He Who Falls (Celui qui tombe)* (2016), Bourgeois creates an almost perfectly square horizontal plane made of what looks like wood framing sheathed in monochromatic plywood. Levitating approximately four feet off the stage below and supported by wire cables attached to the four corners, Bourgeois's stage begins to sway, left to right, right to left. Actors' bodies engage the wood surface by holding onto it, slipping under it, and jumping on top of it. The audience senses Bourgeois's stage is precariously heavy and cumbersome, and the actors' interaction with the swinging pendulum underscores the riskiness of the performance. Big, heavy plane swinging—watch your head and get out of the way!

We often think of the CLT blank as a prefabricated material ready to be placed on-site—nothing more than a basic floor panel. Efficiency is also an important aspect for CLT construction, which is usually touted as cost-effective, with less labor on-site and for shorter periods of time. Yet CLT might offer even more conceptual payoff than the simple idea of erecting a house in ten days. A fruitful swap between Bourgeois's work and the blank grants attention to the performance of the blank being installed. To illustrate this point, imagine the theater's ceiling gantry system now poses as a 40-ton crane at a job site. In this theatrical event, operator and install crew swing blanks into place, outlined by the architect's erection sequence plan. A neat stack of blanks sits adjacent to the construction site as horizontal sheet materials, ready to be picked up by the crane and installed vertically in situ as perimeter walls. The process is fast, and mesmerizing to watch, as 1,400 pounds of engineered wood (in this case, one blank with one square window cut-out) floats seamlessly into place. A camera captures the blank's movement between the horizontal stack and the vertical wall. Here, the blank is less merry-go-round, more earring, dangling from straps above. The stills from construction videos are analogous to Geraldine Aresteanu's images of Bourgeois's performance. Each documents and destabilizes the horizontality of a stage and the verticality of a wall, respectively, highlighting the possibility of more oblique encounters for the blank in future CLT projects. The act of installation for blanks has yet to be fully conceptualized; it's merely a means and method for the construction process, open for interpretation.

Top: Diller + Scofidio, Kinney Plywood House, Westchester County, New York, 1981

Bottom: Jennifer Bonner / MALL, Four Over None, 2020. Two elevations made of blanks didactically scale up the Kinney Plywood House to multi-family housing.

We can also identify two works of architecture that might be willing to participate in extending this parlor game beyond art: a house made out of plywood and a wood-clad theater. Long before the development of CLT, innovations in engineered wood led to plywood, a sheet material we can think of as the thinner and more lightweight precursor to the thicker and heavier blank. Both laminated into thicknesses of three, five, seven, nine, and thirteen layers and stacked on top of one another in alternating directions, plywood and CLT operate under similar logics.[10] For the purposes of this argument, the plywood sheet is an industrialized, off-the-shelf material standardized at the optimal size of 4 feet by 8 feet. Traditionally used as sheathing, plywood is one of two primary wood components in a typical Type V construction and central to the creation of a structural diaphragm. Rarely visible on

For more on plywood, see Erin Putalik's essay in this book.

the interior or exterior of buildings, the proportions of plywood often disappear, sandwiched within the overall wall assembly. By contrast, Diller + Scofidio's *Kinney Plywood House* (1981) experiments with plywood's objectness, most notably in the house's exterior image.

This early project by Diller + Scofidio looks just like it sounds—approximately fifty-seven sheets of plywood wrap a house in its entirety, akin to a material texture map by one of today's render engines. Most plywood sheets are tiled horizontally, indicating the primary ordering system, while the two short elevations allow the vertical rotation of several sheets, announcing a gabled figure. Operating under the constraints of a small budget, the architects precut the plywood with dimensions for stock windows and stained the material gray.[11] We can almost imagine a subcontractor single-handedly rotating each lightweight and easy-to-manage panel into place before nailing it onto its wood frame. Diller + Scofidio's repetitive square cut openings are centered between two sheets. The cuts are not always used as windows; some are filled back in with plywood and or left intentionally blank. Overall, the emphasis is on blankness. We see the architects' insistence to build out the window frame even though the actual window has gone missing. Their dogmatic frame accentuates qualities of the sheet and the inherently blank image it produces.

11 "Kinney Plywood House," Diller Scofidio + Renfro, accessed December 18, 2020, https://dsrny.com/project/plywood-house.

To play out our now-familiar sleight of hand, replacing the 4-by-8 plywood sheet with the CLT blank suggests the possibility for an automatic rescaling—plywood house becomes CLT housing. It is exactly in this projection from house to housing that architecture leverages technological advancements toward expanding concerns of typology. On the long elevation, four rows of plywood sheets measuring 32 feet in length become four rows of CLT blanks measuring 200 feet in length. Turning a two-story single-family house into a four-story multifamily housing block, this rapid material switcheroo has major consequences in terms of scale, but not many visual repercussions. The shift toward the construction of a block obviously creates a massive volume compared to the volume of a house, but without time lost during construction: the time it takes to stack sixteen blanks rivals that of installing sixteen pieces of plywood.

But the initial hunch to simply scale up materials is too simple, even reactionary; a longer look hints at even more fascinating contributions at play. Diller + Scofidio fully exploit the piece of plywood as an object while engaging a notion of blankness simultaneously. Architects take note, this is the thesis at stake: architecture's new industrial blank has the

Aldo Rossi, Il Teatro del Mondo, elevation, 1979

possibility to be graphic and elevational, structural and load-bearing, while also positioning blankness, heavily influencing the imaging of architecture.

And then there is the Teatro del Mondo, a project that for several decades has conjured up many ideas for architecture. It has been studied, photographed, analyzed, exhibited, redrawn, dismantled, rebuilt, referenced, and reimagined from every possible angle. This temporary floating theater, designed by Aldo Rossi for the 1979 Venice Biennale, was constructed out of two materials, tubular steel and wood cladding, to produce an inside-outside effect for its audience. With a squint of the eyes, a snap of Big Freedia's fingers, the real building (in photograph) flickers and a mental image of the theater as CLT blanks dominates all preceding discourse. Simply put, Rossi would have loved CLT. His larger body of work on planar elevations, vertical striping, color blocking, figural shapes, flatness, and punch openings is ripe to be considered anew, freshly constructed out of a pile of blanks. In the Teatro del Mundo, tubular steel is no longer necessary; the 82-foot-tall theater could have been built from one and a half blanks alone. Additionally, in the frontal elevation of the project, the two adjoining stair cores, acting as appendages to the center volume, look to be the exact proportions of a single blank. Switching out the theater's boarded-up aesthetic to a series of blanks cleverly combines cladding and structure while artfully imitating the original. No cladding is necessary for a temporary installation—the blanks can be left exposed momentarily. The architect's only specification to the manufacturer would be to orientate the boards vertically to match Rossi's boards on the outermost layers of the panels: a spec made easy by CLT's versatile cross-laminations—vertical-horizontal-vertical-horizontal-vertical—for a five-ply panel.

A quick recount of the essay's five switcheroos: (1) a board for a blank; (2) a canvas for a blank; (3) a stage for a blank; (4) a plywood sheet for a blank; and (5) a blank facade for a blank. Or was it (1) redaction for a blank; (2) anonymous surfaces for a blank; (3) a merry-go-round for a blank; (4) tiles for a blank; and (5) stair cores for a blank? The swaps between examples of art and architecture and the blank outlined here are meant to infect the everywhereness of CLT in the field—to disrupt a nostalgic view of materiality in exchange for an infinitely long discourse on blanks, with ample room for discovery by future architects, artists, and engineers. The aspiration is to consider the blank as an architectural element—an object, and a decidedly commercial one—resisting the tendency to think of it merely as a material. There is something too earnest, too pious, about architecture's past relationship to materiality. This view centers architectural thought on CLT in the romantic interiors of northern European #timber houses in foggy green forests. The methodology outlined here is decidedly American. You might call it a new vibe: Blanks everywhere, blanks everywhere. Blanks everywhere, blanks everywhere.

Blank Characters: Elisions in Artistic Practice and Domestic Spaces

Sean Canty

> Space has a double nature: indeed, space can be occupied or not, filled with matter or empty. Space filled with matter (i.e., a *volume* or, in phenomenological terms, an *obstacle*) can be measured by means of a system of coordinated architectural elements, or *order*. Unoccupied space is *void*, and within that void actions and gestures can take place. Architecture can consequently be defined as the production of the void by means of order (by positioning and decorating obstacles to human movement).
>
> —Pier Paolo Tamburelli, "Space; Or, Bramante's Problem"

Blank Primitives / Blank Primes

Architecture starts with many blanks: blank pages, blanks screens, blank material, blank sites. But these blanks are never entirely neutral. Scale, size, structural stability, aesthetic value, and technical frameworks imbue them with potential. One category of blanks that is intrinsic to the discipline (and discourse) of architecture is geometry. The geometric blank, rooted in Euclidean geometry, is typically an easily recognized unit of form: cylinder, cube, rectangular prism, sphere, pyramid, cone. Conceptually, as solids, they are filled. As surfaces, they harbor and contain empty space. Like a tectonic unit of construction, the geometric blank carries a set of relationships: one of measurement and one of perception. These relationships govern the intrinsic quality of each blank while also anticipating its relationship to other geometric figures. As such, the geometric blank privileges a particular aesthetic legibility by means of abstraction and transformation. Abstraction reduces complexity in favor of clarity, precision, and shape. Although blank, these geometries are not without character.

Left: Ellsworth Kelly, *Tablet #41 [Five Sketches]*, 1954-55

Right: Ellsworth Kelly, *Tablet #138 [Three Sketches]*, 1960s

Blank Shapes

Ellsworth Kelly's *Tablet 1948–1973* works with blankness through a process that is both artistic and archival. Through the re-presentation of an oeuvre of sketches on scraps of paper, Kelly imitates (in the most genuine manner) the domestic scrapbook. Instead of a collection of family photographs, however, *Tablet* depicts familiar Kellyesque figures, sketched in pencil or pen, alongside found material: sheets from scratch pads, newspaper clippings, flyers and brochures, and envelopes and letters from friends.[1] The set of drawings illuminates Kelly's process of rehearsing form and composition with geometric blanks. Roughly 15½ by 21 inches in size, each sheet rarely adheres to a uniform layout to present its specific group of sketches. Because of the inconsistency of the compositions, swaths of blankness lie between each sketch. In *Tablet #27*, Kelly assembles sketches of round figures set within rectangles whose schematic contours approximate circularity or squareness. These approximations are very present in the work, despite their blankness.

1 See Carter Ratcliff, "Diary of an Elisionist: Ellsworth Kelly's *Tablet 1948-1973*," *Art on Paper* 6, no. 6 (July-August 2002): 30-35.

Kelly's irregular forms hint at the personal. The distinct shapes and use of color can be read, as Carter Ratcliff outlines in the essay "Diary of an Elisionist," as a counterargument to the geometric universality of the modernist tradition. Kelly foregrounds the contingency of form and, as a result, its associated personal meanings.[2] Throughout the constellation of works in this series, Kelly's drawings on found scraps seem to negate or leave out the content already present in the material. They can also be read as an aggregation of Kelly's gestures with the spatial relationships that are inherited within the found items. The implication of geometric blanks in Kelly's drawings is one method to draw attention to their adjacencies and, in turn, to implicate the familial relationships within each sheet. Spending time with *Tablet*,

2 Ratcliff, 32.

one might read these blanks as oscillating between a conjoining of multiple things and an omission. Linguistically, this oscillation mirrors the effect of an elision, where the omission of letters in two words creates a distinct meaning and measure in the resulting contraction. Within Kelly's aesthetic language, these elisions are a means of elaboration that offer readers multiple ways of engaging with his relative shapes.[3]

Ratcliff, 37.

Blank Stages

If Kelly's *Tablet* can be analogized as a form of scrapbooking, another artist redirects our attention to the elisions embedded within the curatorial space of museums and galleries. Céline Condorelli's ongoing project *Support Structures* reorients our attention to the spatial supports that enable particular modes of display. This is most evident in her use of curtains, which establish and preside over visibility: rising and falling, hiding and revealing, excluding and including.[4] As a preexisting spatial support, a curtain shapes both the production and reception of what is shown on a stage (such as an exhibition). This allows the curtain to be perceived as neutral—a natural, immediate, and universal unit in its relationship to the stage.[5]

See Andrea Lissoni, ed., *Céline Condorelli: Bau Bau* (Milan: Mousse Publishing, 2017).

Lissoni.

By extension, Condorelli's ongoing work with curtains explores the duality of support and display. As she explains, "Curtains are in constant movement and their form is never fixed—they respond and give presence to what passes unseen. Strangely immaterial, they have no form until they are hung, they entirely depend on a support structure to give them shape."[6]

Quoted in Lissoni, 24.

In exhibitions like *Curtain Show* and works like *All Our Tomorrows*, Condorelli leverages the curtain as a partition that alters the existing conditions of the gallery space. One is privy to the process by which the curtains function; the relationships that guide the gestures and conditions of the curtains can be examined. In the essay "How Things Appear: Céline Condorelli's Counter Display," Marco Scotini likens this to the experience of watching a marionette: "The Marionette entails a condition of being in time and space that always openly declares its mechanism of appearance, its propensity for transformation, the elements that limit or encourage it, the forms of its iteration and of its variability, its capacity to form different configurations and adapt to different contexts."[7]

Marco Scotini, "How Things Appear: Céline Condorelli's Counter Display," in Lissoni, 12.

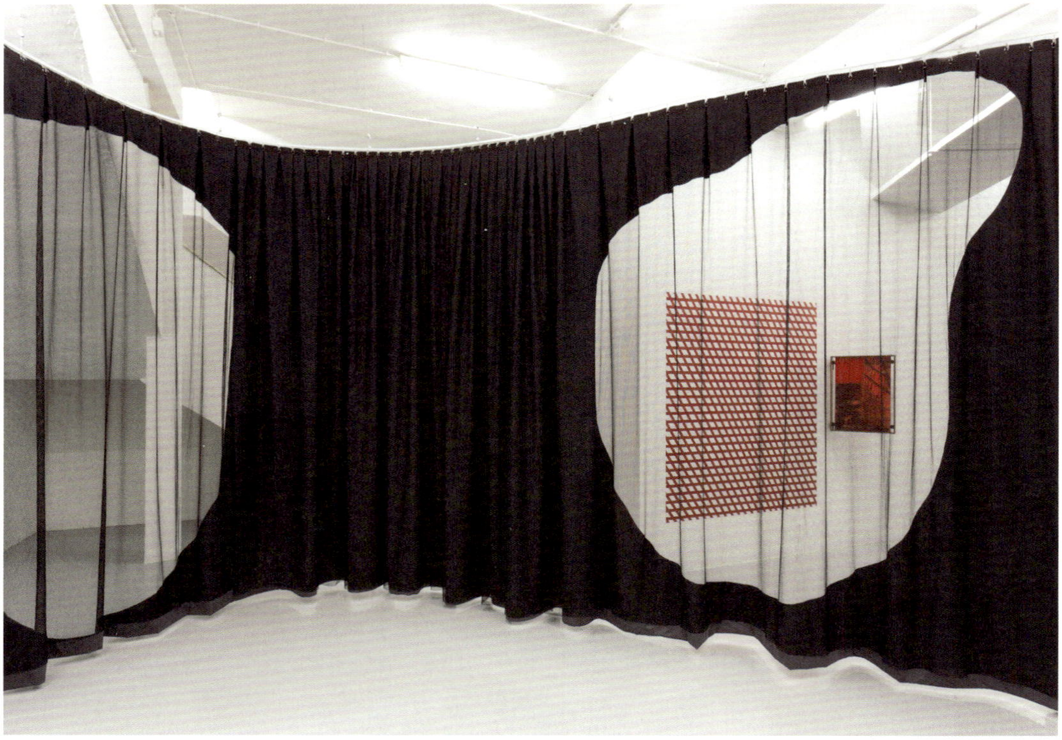

Céline Condorelli, *All Our Tomorrows*, 2016

Strategies of elision situate Condorelli's curtains (much like Kelly's paintings) between the graphic and the spatial. In *All Our Tomorrows*, round acrylic ovoids are cut away from a black scrim curtain. The curtain moves on a curved track: a parallel gesture that echoes the ovoid shape in elevation. In plan, the curtain traces an ever-changing void within the space of the gallery. This resulting amorphous void waits for content to fill it, either through occupation by a person or through optics and framing. In these pieces, the blank stage is constantly remade through the curtain's movement along its track. The mechanism that moves the curtain into its resulting adjacencies is foregrounded through its relationship to blankness.

Pictorial Blanks

Blankness can't really exist—at least not for too long. Its emptiness is made present and sustained by some extrinsic actor. The artist Lucio Fontana's *Concetto Spaziale* (Spatial Concepts) do just this. Crafting the blankness of a canvas through figural slits, cuts, and holes, Fontana imbues a surface with both depth and character by means of constructing voids. In these pieces, the canvas has been emptied and denied all additive content. What is left is simply to subtract. The series literally figures the surface of the canvas to construct space by means of erasure, breakage, and tearing. Fontana retunes and transgresses the pictorial tradition in which three-dimensional space is represented on a two-dimensional surface. Instead, the technical support of the canvas undergoes a process of literal transformation to construct and configure spatial depth. Painting the back side of these canvases black also attenuates and heightens the effect of depth within the space of the void. Unlike the tradition of stereotomy (the science and craft of subtracting stone solids), Fontana's techniques speak to our contemporary condition of the tectonic, an architecture of surfaces layered up in order to frame and construct space. Additive and subtractive methods are conflated. Such material deformation (and its spatial effects) draws attention to the characteristics of its edges. At moments of negation, the canvas curls, folds, peels inward, dissipating into the void, constructing a threshold, an interior on the back side we cannot access. The cut lines produce subtly curved surfaces, framing holes or slithers of space just beyond, gesturing toward both roundness and inscrutability by way of a pictorial blank.

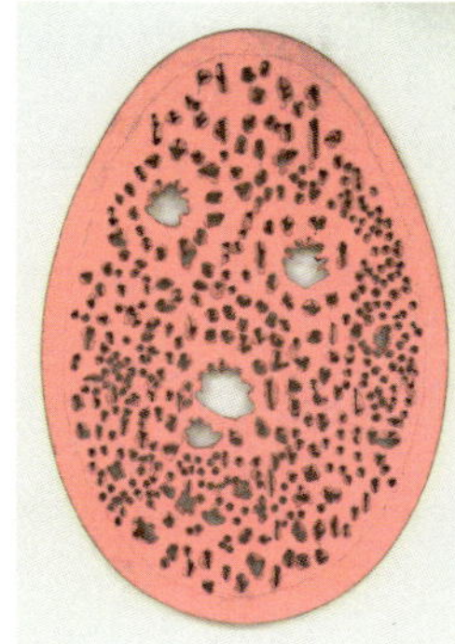

Lucio Fontana, *Spatial Concept, The End of God (Concetto Spaziale, La Fine di Dio)*, 1963

Blank Containers

Kazuyo Sejima and Ryue Nishizawa of SANAA develop blankness as an aesthetic experience, staging life in a different way. Their structures for the village of Inujima, in rural Japan, draw upon material refraction, reflection, and spatial inflection through curvature to legislate moments of distortion and pause. A series of hybrid gallery/house structures commingle the everyday spaces of the village with bespoke architectural interventions. Each intervention blends tradition and abstraction through structures that are meant to display and frame both art and site.

As Eve Blau explains in her essay "Curating Architecture with Architecture," these structures deploy an architecture that not only curates art, but stages the condition by which production is possible.[8] Blau quotes Sejima's description of SANAA's approach: "Each of the buildings that will be used for exhibitions has been designed to blend in with the surrounding landscape, and is made of wood, acrylic, aluminum, and stone. Art will become one with the local scenery, as previously existing residences and new structures become exhibition spaces and a new landscape emerges. A new museum will be realized and that museum will also create a new environment."[9] The reconstitution of empty structures and the addition of new ones actively identify blank spaces within the village. The existing character of these blank spaces is altered by introducing new containers for the experience of viewing and inhabiting art.

[8] Eve Blau, "Curating Architecture with Architecture," *Log*, no. 20 (2010): 18.

[9] Quoted in Blau, 24.

One such structure, the Nakanotani Gazebo, is situated on a small hill. It has a shallow and irregular aluminum dome that sits atop thin aluminum columns set into an elliptical slab. The dome's polished surface reflects the surrounding environment, people, vegetation, and paths of movement—a reflecting pool of context, making the surface conceptually blank, because it's always filled. "Curating, in Sejima's hands," Blau writes, quoting Sejima again, "plays on the 'ambivalence between something and nothing ... the floating identity of materials and space,' in interventions that subtly inflect and transform time and space around them."[10] In the context of Inujima, the gazebo is one instance where context and surface collapse to elide one's perception of the village and its surroundings. These spatial elisions oscillate between a perceived omission and addition, using the blank surface to articulate something specific within the experience of Inujima.

10 Blau, 28.

Blank Middle

This sampling of blank types moves from flatness and the conceptual to the consequences that blankness exerts on both the artistic and architectural artifact through the aesthetic experience of viewing art. Each of the examples above asks what can still be present in the effect of blankness. Alternatively, they show us how absences foreground other things. Blankness equally draws our attention to what's missing, misplaced, or forgotten. To consider blankness as a disciplinary endeavor opens up an opportunity to speculate and think through alternative engagements with the canon of architecture. In particular, we might use blankness to reconsider the discipline's conceptual and technical support structures, from questions of representation to particular types within architectural production.

My studio work and research reshapes spaces of domesticity and their subsequent rituals to fill in gaps in the American housing stock. The absent—or blank—middle in housing encompasses a lack of housing that meets the growing demand for walkable urban (or suburban) living and the need for choices at different price points.[11] Both factors are a response to shifts in household demographics, which are complicated by the growing gap between the need for affordable housing and dwindling supply. As the nature of households continues to change, housing stock could adapt to reflect a wider spectrum of types that can accommodate diverse subjects and their unique household structures. These new types could address

11 See, for example, Daniel G. Parolek, *Missing Middle Housing: Thinking Big and Building Small to Respond to Today's Housing Crisis* (Washington, DC: Island Press, 2020).

Studio Sean Canty, Janus House, 2018

American society's ongoing departure from the single-family home and its prioritization of the white nuclear family. In this context, the blank middle's effects are twofold: it articulates the absence of needed housing types within the existing stock, while also gesturing toward types that have absent centers, including donuts, courtyards, dogtrots, and the like.

Blank Rooms

Responding to these typological blanks, my work leverages the use of geometric blanks, which are conjoined and transformed in dialogue with existing housing types. Three projects extend this particular thinking of blankness at the architectural scale: the Janus House, the Concord House, and the Round House. The resulting elisions are orchestrated for both viewing and occupation. These works attempt to challenge stable housing types in the way they use conceptually absent spatial centers. Each project shapes dueling readings: a calibrated balance between the vernacular and abstract, the centralized and the axial, the individual and collective, finding new ways to be closely together and apart.

The Janus House is a one-and-a-half-story duplex residence. The house arrives at its composition by merging key traits of two recognizable housing types in a single volume: the axiality of a dogtrot house and the centrality of a courtyard house. Brought together, they enable a mixture of organizational gestures in plan between center and edge. Interior rooms are arranged linearly, radially, or with a blend of these two dominant orders. The house similarly oscillates through a family of geometries: material vernacular, figural perimeter, and

Above and opposite: Studio Sean Canty, Round House, 2020

constant center. In this house, transparency is exchanged for material gloss and sheen on the exterior facade. The interior courtyard is glazed and porous, dematerializing the boundary between house one and house two, where both become one—an idea of shared occupation.

Although each residence has the same footprint, subtle distinctions imbue the plans with functional specificity, speaking to a diverse range of households. One residence includes a mezzanine study that gives the space an airy, loft-like feeling. The other house foregoes this solitary space for a second bed- and bathroom as well as a dining area. Between the residences, diagonal sightlines allow visibility between the shared living areas. These sightlines create a visual experience of commonality across the distinct living areas, which remain separate but not quite private.

The triplex is the starting point for the Concord House. From the exterior, the three residences appear to be combined within the container of a single-family home. The house's gabled silhouette references the New England farmstead type, yet departs from its expression in elevation. The Concord House draws its name from both its location and its formal and programmatic concordance—between disparate geometries and disparate subjects. The house is situated on a corner lot whose property lines are not parallel. An interior commons for the three residences introduces a degree of connection and separation at the center of the house.

Programmatically, the commons is a blank room. Geometrically, the commons takes the form of a circle containing a series of nested centers within. Access to the second-level

residences is inscribed through an off-axis circle, and a circular stair connecting both levels of the commons articulates a third center. Entrances to each wing are placed tangentially to the circular commons. The three residences share formal and organizational logics, but vary in scale. A two-story residence is situated in one wing and connected with an internal stair. The other wing houses a larger, self-contained apartment on the ground floor. The upper level is split between a third, smaller apartment and the remainder of the two-story residence.

At the roof, the commons is articulated through a gabled figure. This figure tucks into the roof in two distinct ways, creating a connection to the exterior. Moving around the house's exterior makes visible the conjunction of the axial and centralized figures that make up the overall volume of the house. The front facade subtly bends and contorts the convex exterior, while the elevation along the back produces a concave corner.

Tectonic Blanks

While attentive to questions of form and social formations, each of these houses also leverages the tectonic blanks of wood-frame construction and mass timber. The Janus House and the Concord House both deploy a combination of wood-frame construction and prefabricated structural cassettes. The Round House leverages the CLT blank, along with a renewed interest in structural cassettes, to speculate on the formal and spatial potential of roundness and domesticity. This application of tectonic blanks also addresses a formal gap in residential types, a blank of my personal interest, of curvature as a spatial alternative to the orthogonal and the flat.

Two residences are merged into one house in the Round House. The house is defined by two horizontal planes: the roof and the ground. This is also a metaphor for the logic of assembly, where the house's walls are sandwiched between the ground plane and the stressed skin of the roof. The roof is a defining element of the house's form, while the interior spatial division is kept relatively simple. This house, like the other two houses in this essay, considers the role of stressed skins in enabling curvature through traditional building practices, alongside balloon framing and CLT blanks. The roof is slightly oversized, to provide a generous porch around the exterior of the building. The wraparound porch also provides a level of privacy that is distinct from that in the shared central courtyard. Familiar levels of privacy between exterior and interior are inverted. Inside, the building has rotational symmetry around a central courtyard. The public and private spaces of the two residences alternate in plan. The fenestration in both the courtyard and on the exterior of the building plays with the expansiveness of views in both orientations of the project, contrasting the panorama with the picture window.

Intentional Blanks

From the artistic to the domestic, blankness creates space for newness and invention, reframing something existing by elision and the clearing of space for unexpected encounters. Blanks aren't really blanks; they are articulations of potential, invisibility present, both something and nothing. The CLT blank as a new tectonic entity offers new models of space and efficiencies of construction, as well as a renewed aesthetic value for wood.

One of the most salient roles of the architect is that of a master "elisionist," articulating the space of the void for human occupation and social encounters. Precisely what architects do is the shaping of existing voids and the construction of new ones, "the production of the form of non-being by means of the production of the form of being," as Pier Paolo Tamburelli writes in the essay "Space; Or, Bramante's Problem."[12] This paradox between something blank that yet has form—or gives form—is at the heart of the architect's craft. Tamburelli reminds us that the void "*has a form*, and so architecture, in its material evidence, forces us to imagine a different definition of 'void', one that allows it to receive a form and yet at the same time still contain infinite possibilities. . . . Such a definition allows architecture to be thought of as a between order and void."[13] Blankness as a conceptual practice privileges architecture's capacity to engage the blanks of our discipline, the blanks of form, and the blanks of space altogether.

12 Pier Paolo Tamburelli, "Space: Or, Bramante's Problem," *San Rocco* 11, *Happy Birthday, Bramante!* (2015): 112.

13 Tamburelli, 112.

House 09: Structural Analysis
Plan: p. 42
Elevation: p. 49
Exploded Blanks: p. 179
CLT Forecast: p. 225

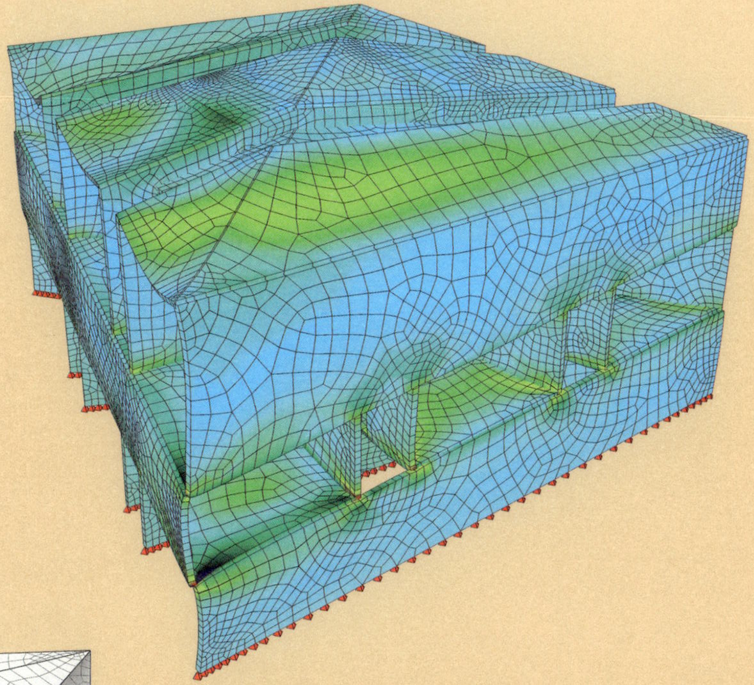

Tower 09: Structural Analysis
Plan: p.6 (left)
Elevation: p.16 (left)
Blank Panels: pp.98-99
Wood Grain Model: p.137
Structural Analysis: pp.202-5
CLT Forecast: p.233

Tower 09: Structural Analysis
Plan: p. 6 (left)
Elevation: p. 16 (left)
Blank Panels: pp. 98–99
Wood Grain Model: p. 137
Structural Analysis: pp. 202–5
CLT Forecast: p. 233

Tower 11: Structural Analysis
Plan: p. 7 (left)
Elevation: p. 14 (left)
Blank Panels: pp. 92–93
Wood Grain Model: p. 140
Structural Analysis: pp. 206–9
CLT Forecast: p. 229

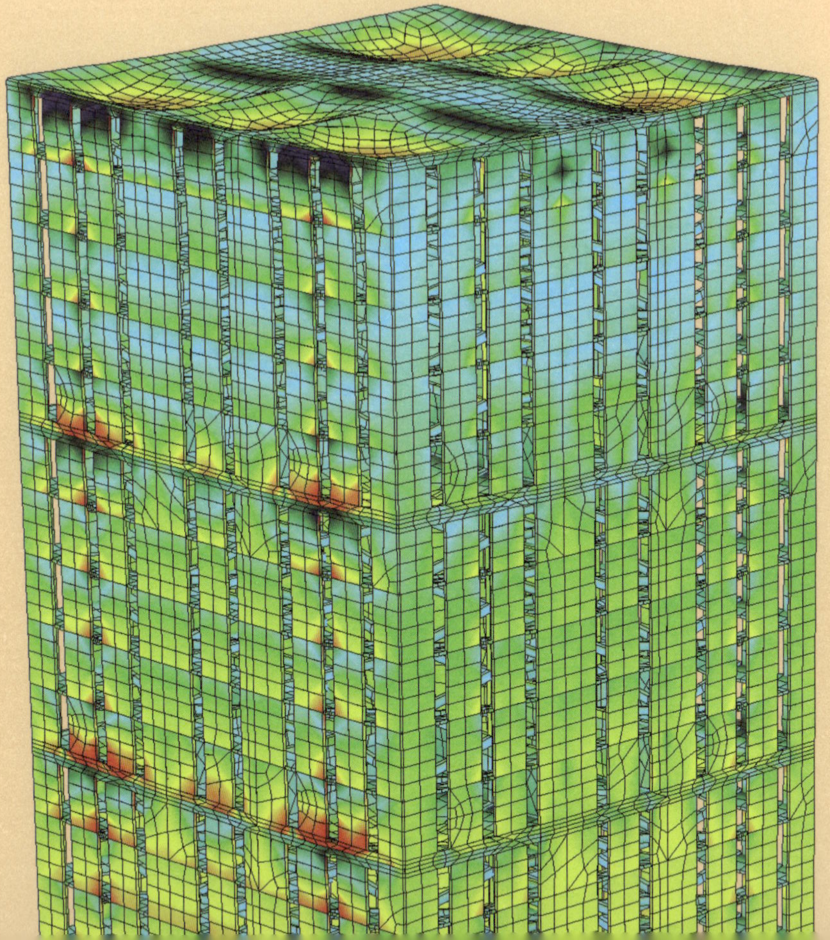

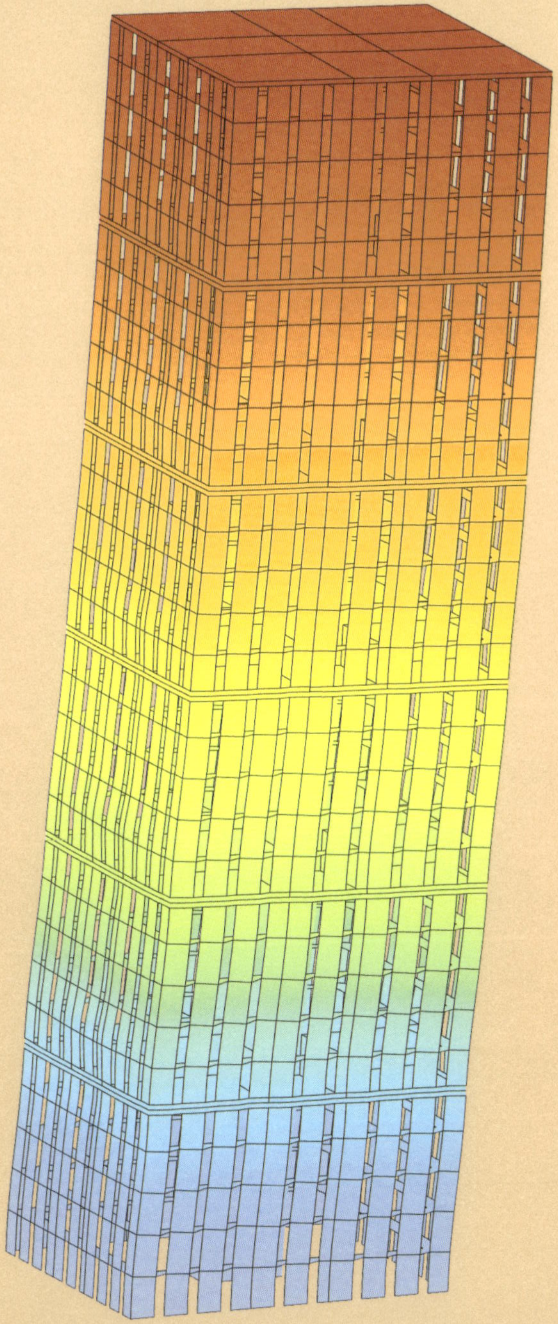

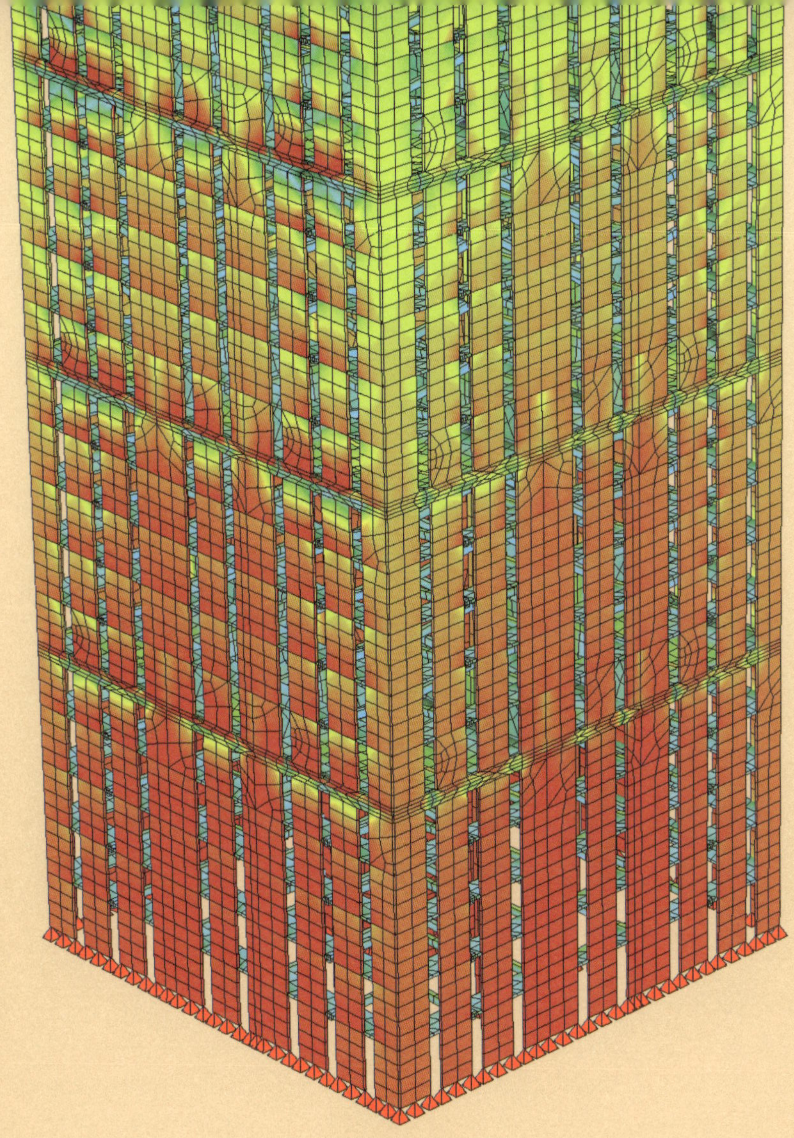

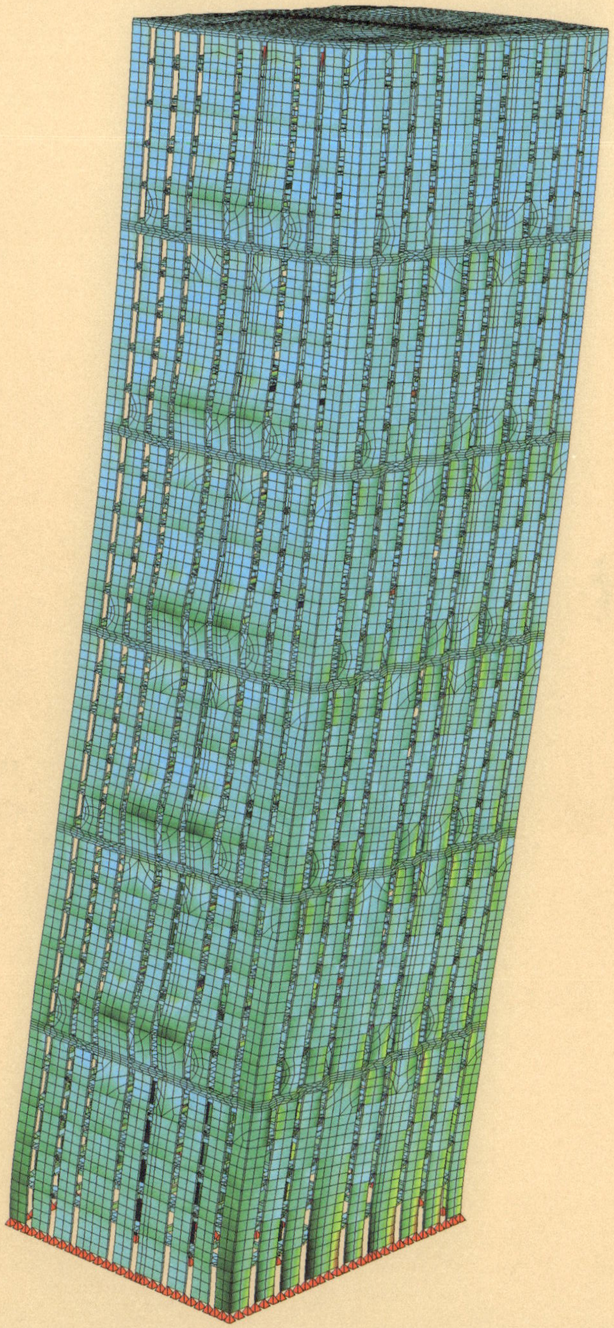

Tower 11: Structural Analysis
Plan: p. 7 (left)
Elevation: p. 14 (left)
Blank Panels: pp. 92–93
Wood Grain Model: p. 140
Structural Analysis: pp. 206–9
CLT Forecast: p. 229

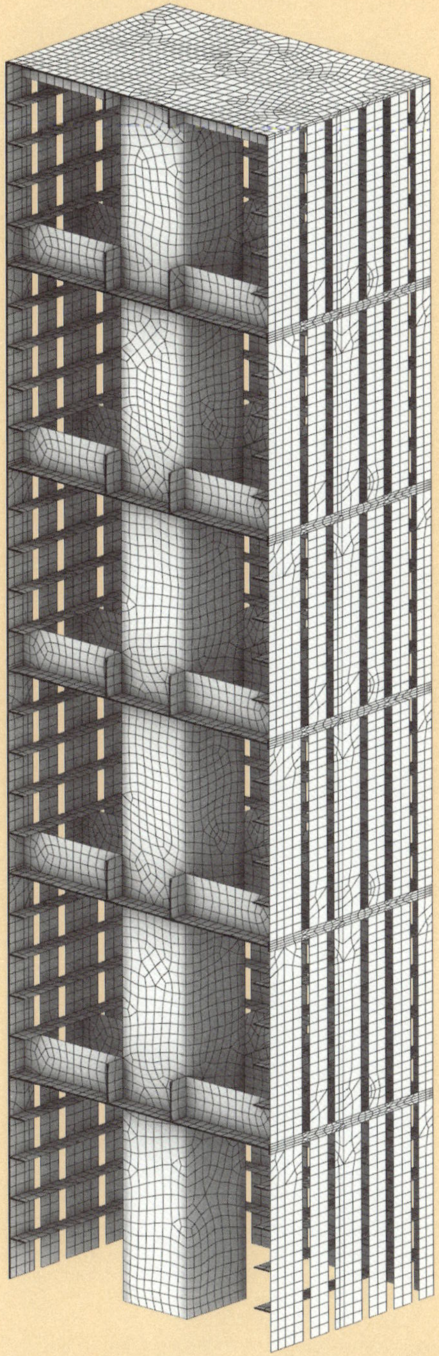

House 01: Structural Analysis
Plan: p. 37 (left)
Elevation: p. 52
Blank Panels: pp. 85, 100
Structural Analysis: pp. 210–12
CLT Forecast: p. 237

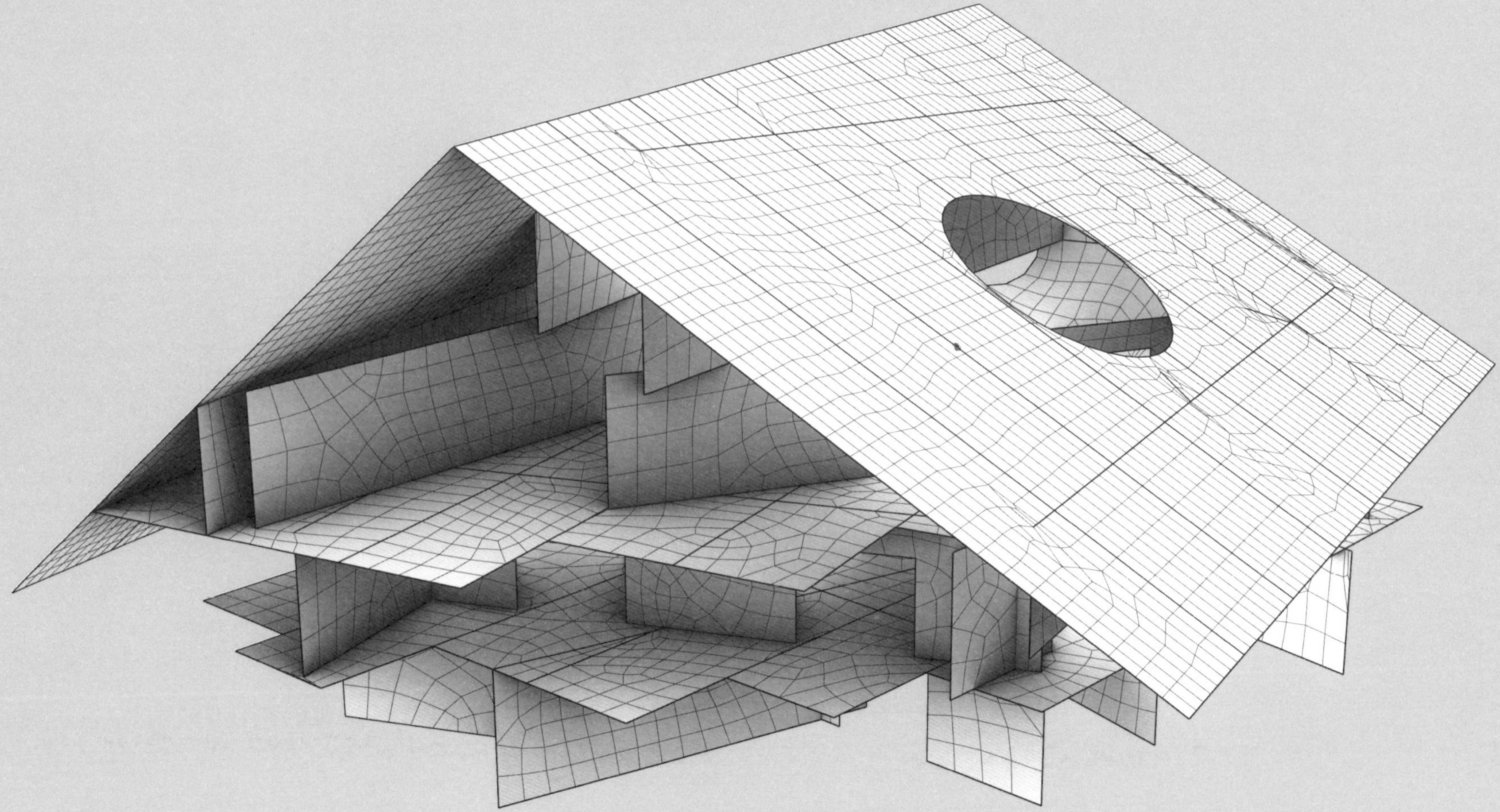

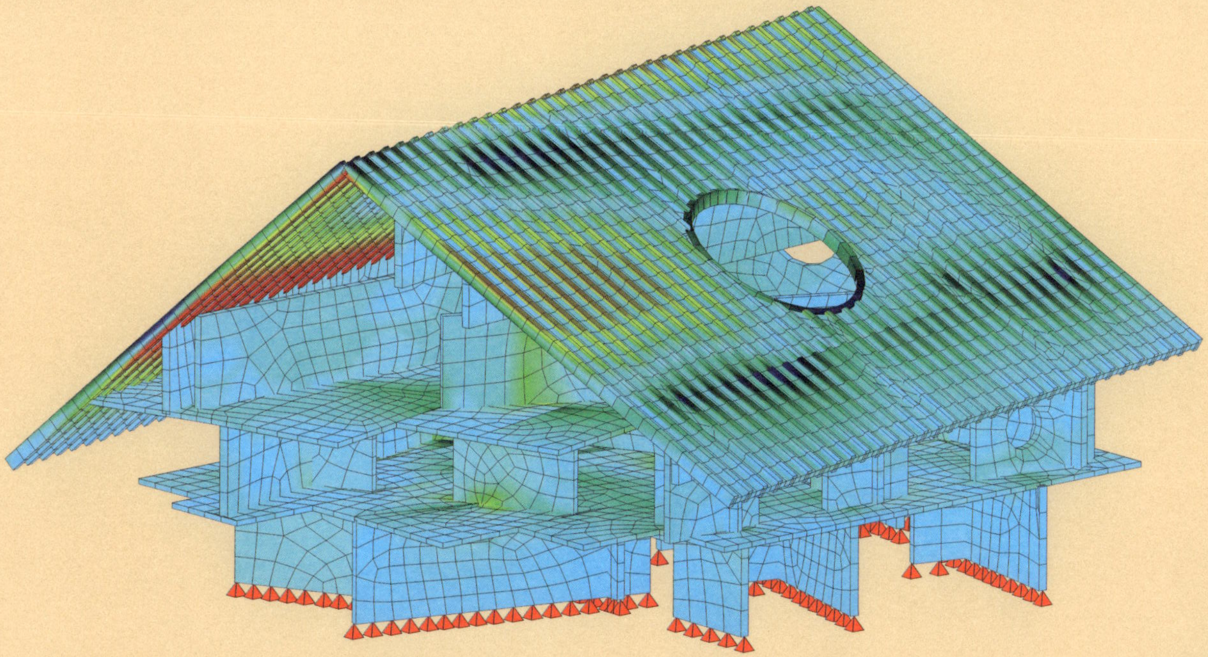

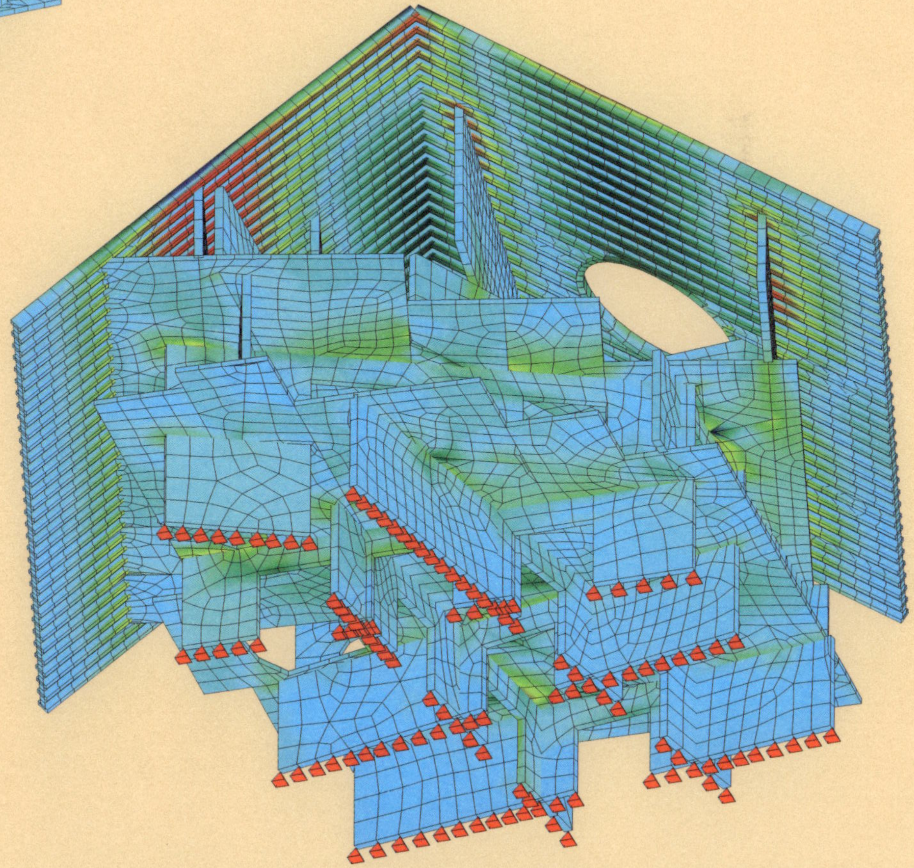

House 01: Structural Analysis
Plan: p.37 (left)
Elevation: p.52
Blank Panels: pp.85,100
Structural Analysis: pp.210-12
CLT Forecast: p.237

Dialogues of Material

Hanif Kara

1. The Problem of Relevance

It is not a straightforward task to set up a critical examination of a construction material, particularly without relying on built precedents. In gathering material for this book, Jennifer Bonner and I set out with a model of inquiry that aimed to be both personal and penetrating, with a distinct point of view, as a means of generating methods and immediate, practical knowledge that could align the design and use of cross-laminated timber with a much-needed agenda for the practices of architecture and engineering. We recognize that the urgency of producing this dialogue around CLT risks the possibility of it becoming outdated, incomplete, or contradictory.[1]

1 For example, we do not dive deeply into the roles of history and ecology, and we chose to leave out important questions about fire resistance and sustainable forestry. These latter considerations are the subjects of scientific research and socioecological politics currently progressing at a global level and would require a broader study.

The dominant materials story of mass timber is multifaceted but stands in resonant contrast to the established dialogues of concrete and steel, both now and in the past. Taking fast-growing juvenile softwood species as its raw material, mass timber has triggered a "guilt-free" renaissance in research and development supported by scientists, industrialists, and governments. CLT's capacity for carbon absorption, coupled with increased precision in off-site manufacture and fewer additional on-site trades, results in environmental benefits and more rapid construction.

In this book, we hoped to swerve and speculate on these narrative threads, and in so doing draw out various assumptions behind them. Driving our urgency is that, in my view, much of the dialogue in architecture, engineering, and construction on the subject of CLT preserves a common status quo, seducing by exaggerated or false metrics and labels, while acting as a delivery device for mass consumption rather than a critical discussion of design propositions. Neologisms like "timber is the new concrete" or "timber will replace steel" might have gained currency, and are surely well-intended, but ultimately are not helpful.

At the same time, we cannot also entirely ignore the moral, climate-driven argument for CLT. Modernists' advocacy of reinforced concrete was validated by its formal possibilities,

Thomas Heatherwick Architects and AKT II, structural engineer, Maggie's Yorkshire, Leeds, 2020

Left: A mix of mass timber types as natural material, filled with plants to encourage healing and inspire visitors

Center: Crawling structural glulam ribs incline, taper, and curve, demonstrating the potential to sculpt form

Right: Ribs fuse smoothly into ceiling, a deliberate use of an engineering detail by the architect to show the isostatic force lines but hide the connection

riding on an ethos of austerity and efficiency; the advocacy of wood construction—even before considering CLT—is validated by the climate crisis above all. This argument carries with it a reaction *against* reinforced concrete, both as a matter of embodied energy and because it is the material most involved with the consumption that has eaten up the planet. CLT construction finds itself in the opposite position as concrete: trying to discover its formal qualities, apparently disdaining millennia of traditions in wood construction.

My aim in this essay is to present an argument for mass timber by tracing and challenging some discursive tropes of the discipline of structural engineering relative to those of architecture. I assert that when new materials are introduced to the built environment, initial reactions often oscillate between overenthusiastic engagements and skepticism, resulting in a naive acceptance or biased rejection of the material by both engineers and architects.

The narratives that develop out of such a condition can be fraught with peril. On the one hand, they are hijacked and suppressed by the ubiquitous control and efficiency of "market conditions," which are largely interested in the short term. On the other hand, they can be subject to the ambitions of designers of the time, who often have limited knowledge. Small groups of "experts" can be overwhelmed by and protective of newness that facilitates a false artistic legitimacy and unshared expertise. It is important to understand what these reactions might have presupposed, not only to critique the extent to which varying claims on a material like mass timber are justified, but also before adding our own assertions that can (and must) start from a practical standpoint, taking certain things for granted in order to operate.

2. The Interdisciplinarity of Inquiry, Industrialization, and Title Traps

As a practicing engineer involved in education, I feel a responsibility to bring the kind of dialogue hopefully generated by this book to the mainstream of practice—to unfold a new set of questions of what we can contribute and what is needed. Among engineers, design seems to be understood as a back-and-forth, or even a contest, between freedom and constraints. Freedom is mostly conceived as "form" (usually meaning shape), a notion that attracts conceptual elaboration, and both the market and academia value originality of form. Constraints vary and include both necessity (e.g., obeying the laws of statics) and responsibility (sustainability, budget, accommodation). Of these, the nondisciplinary profession of structural engineering, which includes the vast majority of practitioners, is usually understood to pertain to constraints, following the customary division of Western culture between the arts and humanities and the sciences. This, however, limits engineering to its knowledge, when in fact engineers are much more adroit than architects at reading the complexities of construction—from a client's demeanor, to resources and the management of trades, to structural technique, to intelligent adaptation, and so on. Leonardo Bruni, in the fifteenth century, recognized that the capacity to see what was common among differences could be compared to metaphor. Metaphor was the highest mode of expression of the rhetorician and the poet, and since Aristotle has been known as a gift, unable to be taught.

Similarly, practical wisdom cannot be rendered as a receipt. One must be practiced in order to practice well. I would take it one step further: in my case, long-term academic engagements have also pushed me to recalibrate what I practice in the profession within the discipline, in order to advance both. The work that engages the subject of this book is one such example.

Like all professions, structural engineers struggle to remain "fit for purpose" when they fail to counter criticism from the industry, clients, and other professions. We continue to be overwhelmed by a shallow prescriptivism that is paralyzing experimentation and research in design. Engineers have allowed the marginalization of their work, partly because they tend to regard design as a "cost, not an investment."

More particularly, from the lens of a practicing engineer, the use of mass timber in buildings is sometimes surrounded by the "wrong" figures, who are powerless, risk-averse

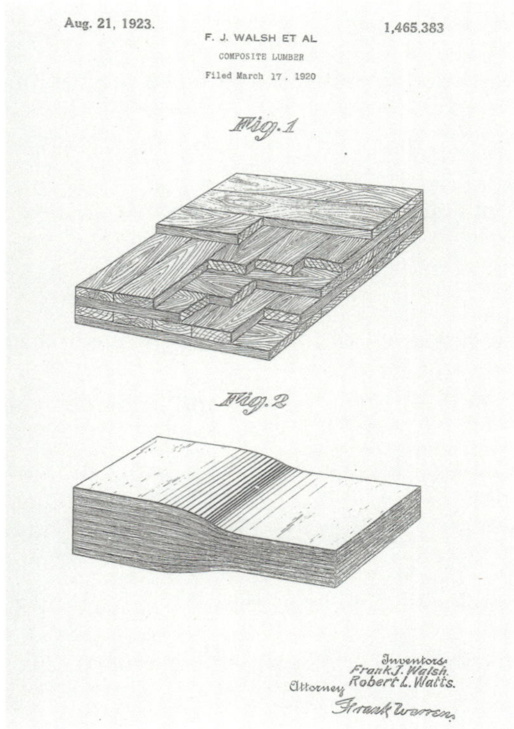

Left: Caruso St John Architects, Art Gallery Walsall competition, timber block concept model, 1995. Seeing this made me wonder for the first time why the seductive mass timber model could not simply be the real building.

Right: F. J. Walsh et al., United States patent for composite lumber, 1923

"service providers" surrendering to the triumphs of the industrialized systems on which CLT depends as a product. One motivating factor is to see if by getting closer to the material, we can regain some ground.

For the past two decades, I have been interested in reviving the roles of the architect and engineer through and from the roots of science that is rational, global, and evolutionary, so they can find their place in the modern supply chain of the built environment. I have also built bridges between practice and education, advancing the role of the structural engineer not only in the discipline of engineering, but also in constructing integrated narratives about design that prepare students to appreciate the complexity and culture that define professional practice. Interrogating enterprises shared by both disciplines has enabled me to identify commonalities in scholarship and practice in areas as varied as technology, procurement, creative and innovative approaches to design, the representation of work, and the production of buildings.

Although these commonalities with architecture might not include the advanced calculations and complex methods of analysis that figure in my work, I recognize a shared substantive desire to survive within the market. I am fortunate to have supported the work of several pioneers in architecture, allowing me to witness the means by which successful heterogeneous outcomes can be reached. Within the general world of construction and the specific subject of a relatively new material, I write from a position of direct experience, and only partly as a scholar.

ACME, architect, and AKT II, structural engineer, Hunsett Mill, Norfolk, United Kingdom, 2006–9

Top left and bottom right: A smooth and carved exterior with windows carefully cut in CLT to maximize light do not comply with tectonic constraints

Top right: Planes of blank walls are assembled vertically at speed, though each wall is a different shape

Bottom left: CLT enables the stereotomic interior

Mass timber as a material and the questions it raises fit into that ongoing trajectory and offer new avenues of exploration. I have learned that when we look at the same thing over and over, we uncover more about it until it confirms itself and the potential for dynamic dialogue increases. Equally, when we fix a given problem or element and seek a variety of ways of viewing it, both architects and engineers can benefit from our inherent similarities, differences, and starting points, as well as the risks we each assume. In my own work, I have been encouraged by colleagues not to stray into the fickleness of age-old battles in architecture between those who demand autonomy and those who insist on integration and interdisciplinarity in all its forms. But I have not been free of the insatiable obsession with the "new" that requires a parallel position that aligns, exploits, and is shaped by expansive processes of networks, including the market economy, infrastructure, and communications.

Working with Jennifer Bonner as a practitioner and educator on questions around CLT came with its own riches and identity, both anticipated and revealed over time. Our attempts to seek deeper knowledge in the academic context were not only opportunistic—they were meant to encourage a fast-paced slippage into experimentation. We believe that experimentation has presented the possibility of generating a new kind of coherent practice and pedagogy. We understood the making of this book as a project about the inquiry itself, rather than a record, guidebook, manual, or look book filled with a staccato progression of unlinked ideas.

3. Stereotomic or Tectonic Unit: The Blank, Two Structural Planes, and Post-Trabeation

Our starting point for considering CLT is less reflective and more speculative, both relative to our current moment and for a future we can rationally envisage over the next twenty-five years. How, then, can we explore the design of cross-laminated timber? We have to take some shortcuts; we cannot rehearse the history of architectural discourse connected to materials to reach answers. Though relevant, that history is already well-covered.

To generate a productive and meaningful exchange of greater complexity and utility, Jennifer and I selected the CLT blank as the basis of our conceptualization. The blank also becomes a trap that has to be justified at many levels. Comparison and our own experience led us to the blank as a "root unit" of structure that can be applied and generalized to represent characteristics unique to CLT, but it cannot make structure alone. The blank then takes on the role of the irreducible structural element and essence of form in CLT. It can be aggregated, serialized, and distorted (to a point) to give form to architecture without dominating the coherence of the whole. This historical process of selection and articulation that gives form to all types is analogous to the role of reinforced concrete in Le Corbusier's Maison Dom-Ino.

Still, I am cautious not to privilege form over material in all cases, as this would make CLT invisible and risks a discussion limited to techniques of form-making. In my practice, I have been engaged in the timely development of an array of tools designed to revolutionize established norms and processes. These tools have transformed practice through the use of computation to facilitate self-generating democratic parameters that create form. Founding a practice and simultaneously starting to teach at the Architectural Association in 1996 meant I was complicit in what some described as a "neo-functionalist" approach, characterized by compelling new uses and novel forms. Programs were dissolved into non-Cartesian grids and

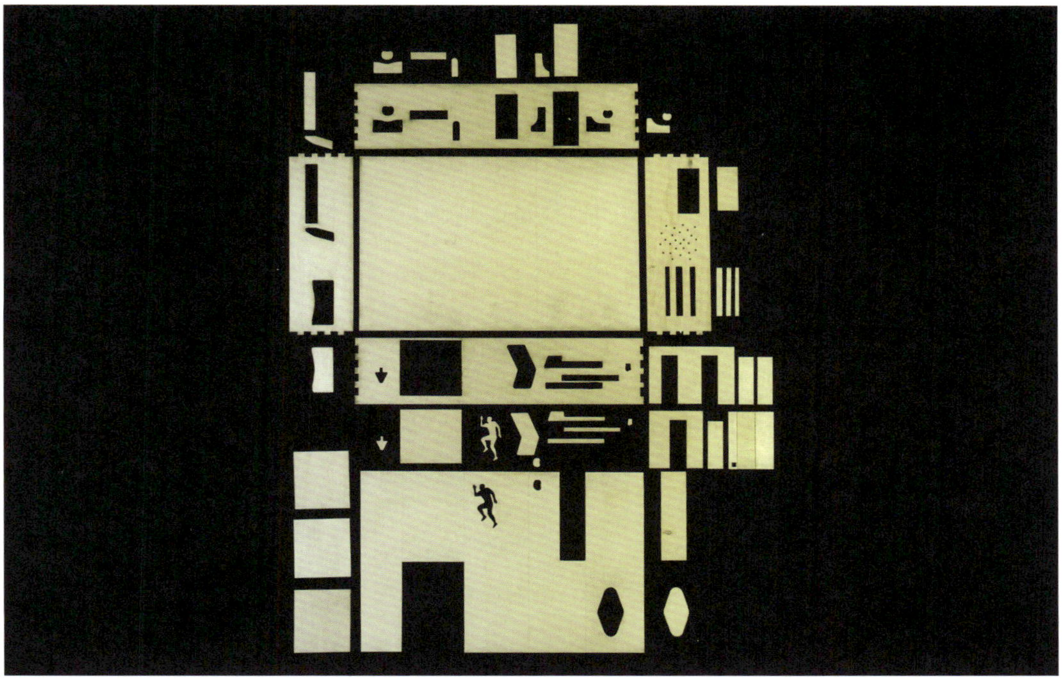

dRMM, Naked House, Flatpack Housing, 2006. An influential project for early CLT enthusiasts, and an origin point for the now-commonplace concept of a flat-pack home that can be built anywhere.

forms made new demands on construction. This allowed engineers like me to respond by expanding our own discipline to parallel that of architecture.

But I am also probably the last of a generation that recognizes the grand narratives of the modernist and postmodernist conditions, which on the one hand erase history, but on the other rely on the symbiosis between tradition and innovation. Recognizing the power in the physical act of making something, the digital turn and its success in constructing "the smooth" undoubtedly distanced us from this symbiosis, to a point where the flatness of a much larger structural element became almost forgotten conceptually. Today, we see that "flat" surfaces were ignored and excluded in that phase of our work, certainly by one group of architects. Architecture that deals with traditions of use and the history of construction, with all its ambiguity and claims to ethics, now needs to be reincorporated. In this respect, CLT is a new material borne out of contemporary means of production and new technology with the potential to advance a different sort of architecture.[2]

At the same time, mass timber doesn't completely preclude this type of smoothness, as in the sculpting of Maggie's Yorkshire, where the forms required mixing different types of timber.

Structurally, we recognize that the crossing, laminations, and origins of the timber of CLT are all variables that currently depend on the processes of manufacture. There are and will be opportunities to design new variations—for example, diagonal laminations that combine different species of laminate, and so on. We have not atomized our ideas to that level of detail. As we mention in the introduction, our conceptual stand-in for CLT is a blank of approximately 9 by 50 feet—in effect, our version of a brick. (This generalization relies on the

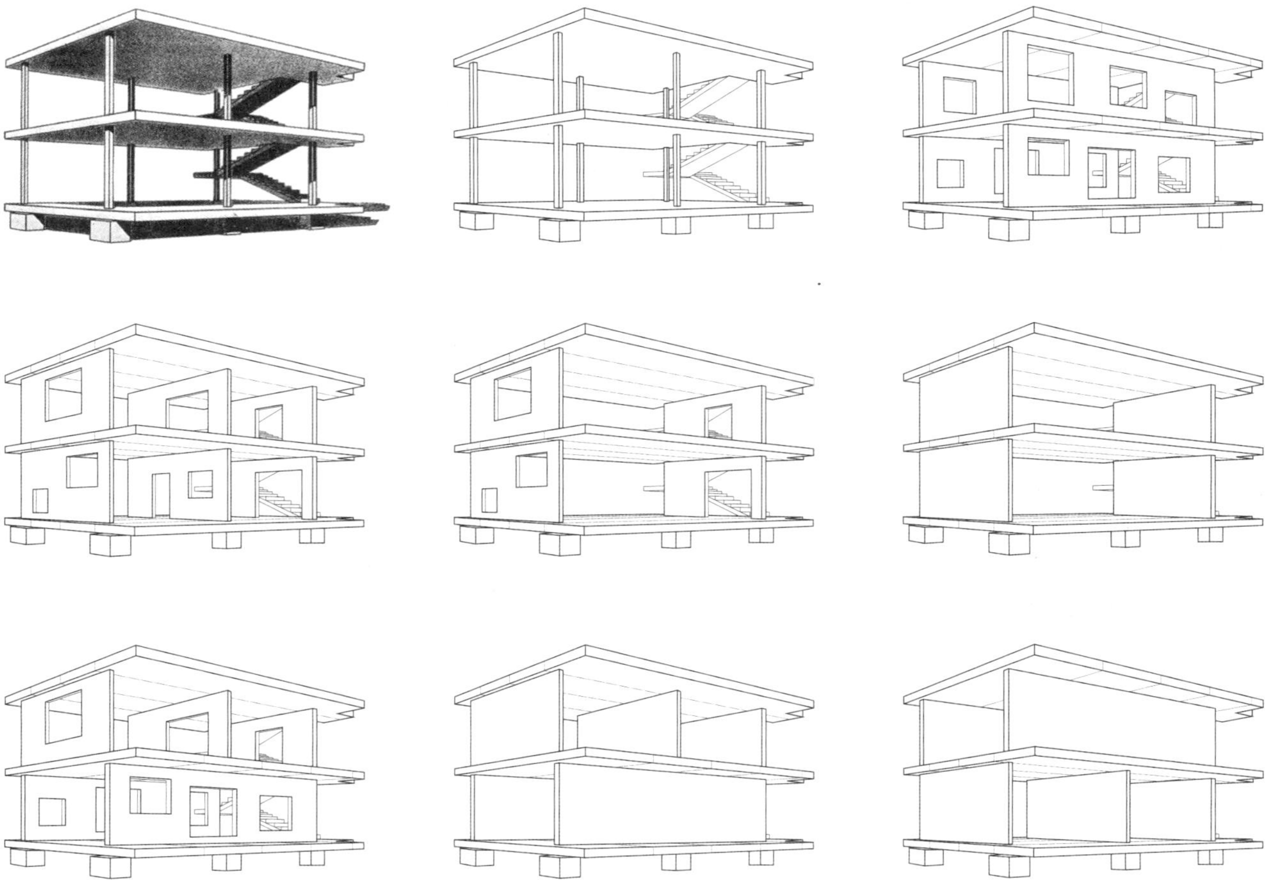

Le Corbusier's Maison Dom-Ino recast by the author, 2020. Structural planes offer a more robust structure for stacking than columns.

largest dimensional size already being manufactured, with latent checks and balances, including what can be handled, transported and easily assembled.) Rather than the variables of its creation, what has attracted my attention most about CLT is its "part-to-part" connections, which become both more interesting and more critical than those of other existing materials.

Take Maison Dom-Ino as a test case. Replacing columns with load-bearing CLT walls, and the floor with CLT supported in the same way, means that the design of the interior is now influenced by the wall, without beams under the slab. Corners also become important, not only from the inside, but also in defining the outside: to make row houses when lined next to each other, or towers when stacked up. Here, timber serves as structural support, enclosure, and architecture.

The traditions of wood were built around carpentry, for the most part (and elements of this craft continue to appear in the work of Kengo Kuma, among others). Carpentry isn't prominent in architecture schools, however, and we chose the CLT panel for our inquiry because it is an industrial product, with implications both for the trades involved—like much of contemporary architecture, a CLT building is more assembled than crafted—and for jointing techniques, of which the least attractive is the metal clip.

This brings us to tectonics, which in its narrow sense is the act of assembling materials used in construction—here, the specific internal logic of CLT. Its making, transportation, and assembly all figure in to a discussion of CLT's tectonics. In a broader cultural context, which relies on a longer gestation period, any account of tectonics has to transcend the mere mechanical to include societal and aesthetic implications. In the case of CLT, these implications are just beginning to become clear and cannot be fetishized.

This is also where the brick analogy falls apart, as positioning blanks is tectonically not the same as stacking bricks. To achieve stability, at least two vertical planes must be connected by a lateral plane to create a unit that both supports a vertical load (floor or roof) and transfers it to the vertical planes (walls). This results in a surface structural system in which loads are transferred uniformly. Vertical CLT planes, which need no surface infill to resist wind loading, can act as external elevations. This is radically different from conventional trabeated structures, which rely on beams with lintels spanning to posts, creating a skeleton that must be infilled.

The reduced unit of construction is now two vertical planes with a horizontal plane supported by or on these. The scope, structural capacity, and performance of this unit is bound up with the way vertical and horizontal planes connect and are assembled to form the structural module. For the engineer this makes a fundamental "statically determinate" system, where the walls resist lateral loads in simple terms. For the architect it offers new design opportunities.

Finite element engineering tools can and do examine the forensic scale, but engineers are unable to manipulate the material itself. Timber has no capacity to yield or crack, which makes it very different from concrete and steel—so the engineer must trust their instinct in using the material and rely less on advanced analysis and computation, bringing them closer to the architect once again.

How CLT connects also points to the possibility of the material enabling a stereotomic approach to construction. CLT can be a wall (a load-bearing plane) and a floor (a horizontal plane); it is also a dry system (unlike reinforced concrete, which is wet and dry). For these reasons, CLT lends itself to the notion of anatomy associated with stereotomic construction,

Rogers Stirk Harbour + Partners, architect, and AKT II, structural engineer, Highpoint, London, under construction, 2017. Assembly of a tower is typically repetitive, unlike for a house.

as it relies much less on the articulation of joints, especially in towers, necessary in tectonic approaches. In other words, we can pile the blanks and read a mass of material (particularly inside), carve voids in the form (as at Jennifer's Haus Gables), take corners away, and add windows almost where we want with less disruption to flow of loads (another difference from concrete, weight aside). CLT thus offers a way for the structural engineer to design means, methods, and materiality; this idea is clearly indebted to the work of Kenneth Frampton, and dates back to Gottfried Semper and Karl Bötticher, though all were talking only about bricks. Bricks in a ceiling are only decorative unless vaulted or arched, unlike flat CLT blanks. Along these lines, CLT helps us reimagine the role of being in a particular place in how we build, a question that is crucial to reexamine, and has a consequential impact on architectural tectonics.

In its possible openings toward stereotomics/atectonics, along with its carbon benefits and lightness, we might even claim that CLT ushers out many aspects of modernism.

4. Structural Determinism: The Tower and the House

In his book *The Tower and the Bridge*, David Billington makes a compelling case for the art of structural engineer:

> Technology is frequently equated only with machines, those objects that save labor, multiply power, and increase mobility. In reality, machines are only one half of technology, the dynamic half, and structures are the other.[3]

3 David P. Billington, *The Tower and the Bridge: The New Art of Structural Engineering* (Princeton, NJ: Princeton University Press, 1985), 3.

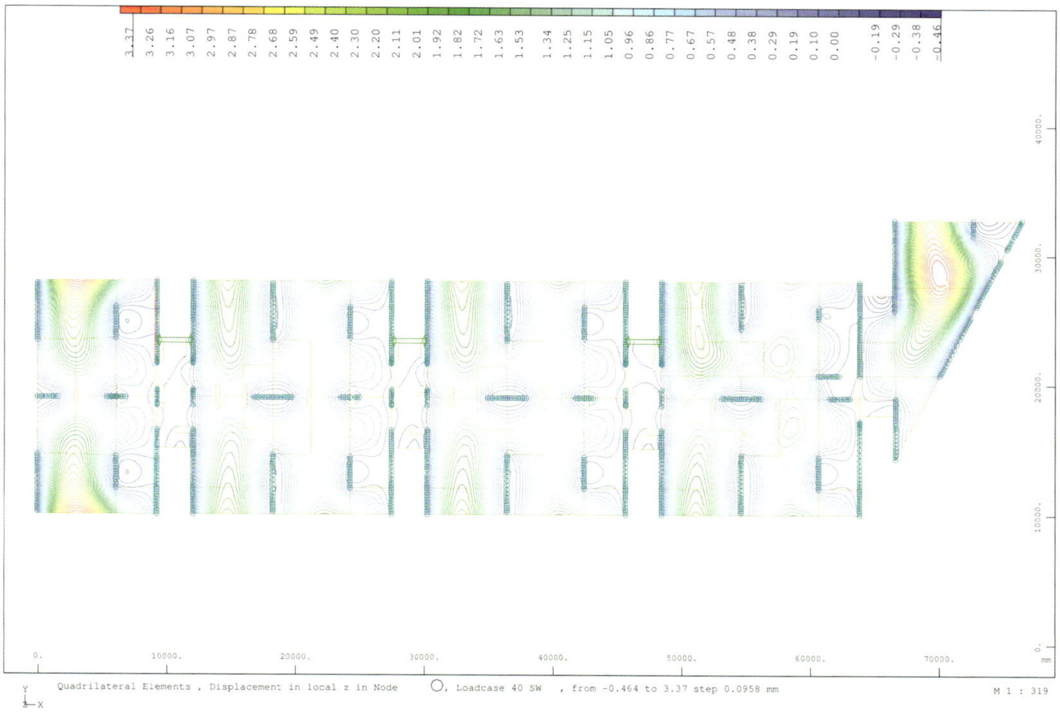

Highpoint structural analysis, 2017. Beyond Nervian isostatic lines.

While I was partly convinced by this in my early career, the success of my practice over the last twenty years has increasingly distanced me from this premise, and therefore this essay resists defining structures as an autonomous art form.

Billington also asserts that "some engineers have consciously practiced this art," which to him "is parallel to and fully independent from architecture."[4] For me, this approach stands on flimsy foundations, and I find it limiting. It gives credence to the idea of an elite structural engineer while denying recognition of the much broader scope of the field of structural engineering. Today, a more open definition of what a structural engineer is and does serves architecture and the community better and underscores the work presented here.

Billington, 4.

Engineering is neither an art nor independent. Rather, it is contingent on the starting point of the architect and supports that endeavor without relying on "aesthetic ideals of structure"—minimum material, minimum cost, and engineering elegance. Those who follow the objectives and ideals of the "structural art" movement must be applauded for the limited number of sculptural bridges, long-span roofs, aqueducts and so on they have realized, but my interest is in buildings that are inhabited, with floors and walls. Visual and aesthetic judgement is crucial here—unlike for purist structural engineers, who pursue scientific optimization at all costs. For me, the shift to designing with computers has created a need for substance—touch, feel, and texture—and we must examine this aspect, too, if we are to use CLT responsibly.

Perhaps my interpretation of what we do is closer to that of Walter Gropius, who characterized an architect as “a coordinating organizer, whose business is to resolve all formal, technical, sociological, and commercial problems.”[5] Quoted in Billington, 7. I take comfort in this characterization and serve the “technical” through the promise of engineering—transformation through new tools, new uses of old materials, new materials and the processes they bring, and deliberately resisting notions of “structural art” or technological or structural determinism.

This approach has brought me to investigating the boundaries of structural engineering research by testing the CLT blank at two scales (which offer a counter to Billington’s two types): a large house, one of the most common types in North America, and a CLT high-rise tower. These illustrative applications allow us to deal with two scales of making and building with CLT, but also address a range of architectural issues. Structurally, the house is far less complex than the tower, and allows a scenographic approach. But I would argue that the architect has to deal with more design issues in the house compared with the tower, which requires the architect to rely more on structural engineering, which begins to limit their freedom. Both architects and engineers can begin to apply the principles we have explored in other building types between these two extremes.

The speculations shared in these pages accept that change and development take time—which we do not necessarily have, in the case of CLT—and demand many perspectives that are interdependent. Cross-disciplinary dialogue between educators, practitioners, and the industry must be more rigorous and imaginative if mass timber’s full promise is to be realized. Engineers and technologists will need to grasp the mediation of the aesthetics of the blank as presented here, which as well as its size and resistance to malleability or workability has to do with color, smoothness, roughness, hardness, softness, lightness, heaviness—qualities ascribed to sight and touch. Through this book, we have attempted to make a guileless but willful step toward moving this project forward.

Everyone Has a "Good Side," and So Does CLT

Edward Han Myo Oo

In 2013, Mariah Carey participated in an E! interview with fellow *American Idol* judges Randy Jackson and Nicki Minaj and the show's host, Ryan Seacrest. A recording shows all four standing in a row, opposite the interviewer, with the left halves of their faces toward the camera.

Or this would have been the normal thing to do. Instead, Mariah angles herself conspicuously away from the interviewer, her colleagues, and the camera. A YouTube commenter rightly asks, "What is Mariah doing?! LOL." Why, even while answering questions, does she awkwardly turn her head the other way? Another comment on the thread seems to provide an answer: "If youre [sic] a true mariah carey fan you know she jas [sic] a good side (the right side of her face)."[1]

Let's face it—this isn't true of just Mariah. And as its imagery proliferates on social media, even architecture isn't spared. Like Bruno Latour writes in his foreword to John May's *Signal. Image. Architecture.*, "The message from the Cloud is clear: 'Thou shall get only *images*.'"[2]

Just Google image-search "cross-laminated timber"; the results suggest CLT has a "good side" too—angled so its edge grain is visible, its constituent parts legible. Unlike other laminated timber, where the wood is all oriented in the same direction, CLT's edge condition is aesthetically distinctive. In photographing a CLT panel, you find yourself angling the camera just enough for this edge to register, but not so much that you lose its "blank" side. This is in contrast to the frontal legibility of most architectural materials: concrete, terrazzo, tile, metal, cork, OSB, even gyp board. Not CLT. Call it a diva. Head-on, you see only the blank surface. With only the edge grain, you forgo a sense of the whole. Neither view alone does it. Cue rotation.

The rotation makes another point: CLT is thick. And although it's tempting to exploit CNC technology's promise of perfectly mitered, razor-sharp edges and a minimal, monolithic look, it's a shame not to let CLT reveal this quality. Might butt joints be more fitting? If "the joint is the beginning of ornament," as Louis Kahn wrote, then is CLT's edge something to foreground and celebrate, rather than hide?[3]

Further channeling Kahn, if one were to talk to CLT, what would CLT say it wants to be? How can a CLT tower signal that it is made of CLT? Can a cross-laminated material produce architecture that is also cross-laminated? Or *looks* cross-laminated? Like Mariah in the clip, can it stand out and announce itself, putting its best side forward?

Imagine a CLT tower that looks like a tall CLT chunk, with the exterior facade panels alternating in direction from floor to floor to produce an aesthetic of cross-lamination. The massing is rotated 45 degrees so this aesthetic reads from the street.

In studio, rotations in massing are qualified or post-rationalized as the result of site boundaries, programmatic considerations, or a formal game. But is our academic training so deep-seated that looking good is not reason enough?

1 "'American Idol' Judges Sound Off," E! Entertainment, January 10, 2013, 2:42, https://youtu.be/mOMGursiUnQ.

2 Bruno Latour, foreword to John May, *Signal. Image. Architecture.* (New York: Columbia Books on Architecture and the City, 2019), 16.

3 Louis Kahn, "Silence and Light: Louis I. Kahn at ETH Zurich," in Heinz Ronner, *Louis I. Kahn: Complete Work 1935–1974*, rev. ed. (1987; repr., Basel: Birkhäuser, 1994), 9.

Labor Not Wasted, Money Not Lost, Material Not Ruined

Daniel Garcia

Ornament is a touchy subject in architecture. Adolf Loos articulated his opinion on the decoration of "useful objects" in his 1910 essay "Ornament and Crime," where he not only reveals his unabashed racism and elitism, but argues that the production of ornament—not culturally derived—is labor wasted, money lost, and material ruined. Loos puts forward the tattoos of the modern criminal as a disciplinary analogue to ornament: the degenerate marks of an unevolved culture.

Of course, this manifesto was misinterpreted by a number of ideological purists and spawned decades of naked architecture. While Loos's essay comes across as a dogmatic renunciation of stylistic expression, it turns out that his principles were much more nuanced. His exteriors were neutral, but his interiors were dripping with expressive materiality. Still, his "Principles of Cladding" makes clear that he is no proponent of counterfeiting.

One could argue that the differences between cladding and ornament are questionable to begin with. What happens when material ambiguity and technological innovation blur distinctions between the two even further? CLT has the potential to challenge Loos's thesis; it is a completely engineered material, it is simultaneously structure and finished surface, and its language of forms rely almost entirely on digitality and computer-controlled manufacture. Not only does the manufacturing process invite an unencumbered and virtually limitless approach to engraving and perforation, but there is no argument to be made about wasted labor or material when the work conducted is automated and the material used is rapidly renewable. From this point of view, the promise of CLT's blankness is the invitation to engrave into all of its exposed surfaces. Sure, it's a wood wall, or ceiling, or floor, but the process through which it is manufactured and assembled renders it almost entirely open to new interpretations.

Jeffrey Kipnis puts forward cosmetics as a counterpoint to ornament in his 1997 essay "The Cunning of Cosmetics."[1] While ornaments attach as discrete entities to the body, he argues, cosmetics are indiscreet and relate only to the skin as subtle "erotic camouflage"; the two are in different taxonomic classes. But this analogy presupposes that the use of cosmetics is restrained and inconspicuous. Surely a drag queen's use of cosmetics offers a more extreme juxtaposition to skin than what Kipnis suggests.

What character, then, should this new kind of ornament assume? Perhaps the problem with both Loos's and Kipnis's arguments is their reliance on or basis in material purity. If we consider CLT to be almost entirely synthetic, and we regard digital engraving and cutting to make up its language of forms, then we could ostensibly project any image onto its surface with no regard for purity, because there is none to begin with.

1 Jeffrey Kipnis, "The Cunning of Cosmetics," *El Croquis* 84, *Herzog & de Meuron, 1993–1997* (1997): 22–28.

Log to Plank to Log

Anna Kaertner

Built on "open" land and often without expertise, the log cabin has long been a symbol of self-reliance and humble beginnings. Although most American single-family homes rely on balloon-frame construction to produce their volumes and figures, the log cabin still carries a certain cultural cachet, an "authentic" American identity. To this day, numerous companies, like Hiawatha Log Homes of Munising, Michigan, produce log homes. These homes are constructed using logs that have been precision milled to have identical radii. The joints are CNC-routed to fit—no chainsaws required. And of course, Lincoln Logs—a toy designed in 1916 by John Lloyd Wright, Frank's son—provides the same kit of parts as a company like Hiawatha, at a dollhouse scale.

The image of the log cabin is inseparable from its rudimentary construction: logs stacked and joined at the corners. The log itself needed little modification to become viable for building. Its size and round profile allowed one or two people to manage the material without any heavy or expensive equipment, like a sawmill. In fact, a simple cabin required only two metal tools: an ax, and a froe for the shingles or roof boards.[1] Corner joints were repetitive and did not require nails. Logs could be rolled to the site and up a jig. The log's geometry and scale are what enabled such a practical building technique.

CLT entirely transforms the log. The laminated layers produce a scaleless material. A 9-by-50-foot plank does not produce different material effects from a 9-by-50-inch sample. CLT also presents no consistent character; it is a literal blank sheet.

Though the material may be anonymous, the relationship between its planks is not. In some ways, the construction of a house in CLT resembles that of a log cabin: both rely on solid pieces of timber to come together like a puzzle.

CLT could easily form a gabled roof, with sheets secured to vertical walls in some way (long nails, folded steel plates). But plan geometries could make this impractical for large flat sheets. Instead, the roof might be conceived as a set of consecutive terracing beams generating a gable profile. Each CLT wall receives a notch to help carry the load. The profiles could be controlled and cut with the same CNC technology that Haiwatha uses to produce perfectly round logs. There is one important limitation: the CNC machine works with round bits, making square edges impossible. The unintentional result is a rounded and more efficient profile, a CLT log.

In this sense, the log is re-produced by the limitations of the machine, and the relationship between the parts—walls and roof—to each other. Visually, it might register as an homage to the American log cabin. Because CLT does not come round, the log may seem fake or ornamental—yet it is just as related to its construction process as the cabin's dovetail joints.

1 Alex W. Bealer and John O. Ellis, *The Log Cabin: Homes of the North American Wilderness*, 1st ed. (Barre, MA: Barre Publishers, 1978), 15.

American Wood

Hiroshi Kaneko

Metaphors are a productive source for architectural imagination. As the gap between intent and finished product shrinks—as metaphor and architecture draw closer—there is a proportionate diminution of possibilities for architecture to inspire, question, and provoke.

Engineered wood is a new technology to incorporate into our work as architects. Wood has been marginalized as a product of luxury and detail, or as a symbol of suburban domestic architecture. Since its introduction in the early 1990s, in Germany and Austria, CLT has spurred little architectural innovation. Its engineered properties, like fire resistance, structural performance, and malleability, have given architecture made with CLT intrinsic properties of thickness, exposed wood, and visual mass, but these are design results, not design drivers. The image of CLT has remained European, standing in for vernacular traditions and contemporary sensibilities.

For American architecture, this is a good thing. Given CLT's lack of saturation in our markets and in minds, we can aspire to craft architectural metaphors with the material that embody our current and idealized democracy, the America we wish to see.

Let's consider one everyday metaphor for CLT, paper, before even this is churned under in our rapid cultural production. Paper as an object offers little for the architect. It is the operations we can commit to with paper that begin to inform possibilities. Cutting, folding, propping, drawing on, and shaping with: these operations are among the many activities offered to us as children to teach us about symmetry, composition, transformation, and anticipation.

Paper is a material that offers us a process of working free of a burdensome conscience, able to be put in the blue bin if a snip is aberrant or snips too much. It invites itself into our homes without question, like masks made at school or paper snowflakes pinned to our refrigerator doors. Blanks can take on the plasticity of their schoolhouse predecessors, ready to be snipped free of corners or punched through for windows and doors.

These are operations that start with gravity in mind; with material properties but also unencumbered imaginations; underneath our fingers; in your neighborhood. It is an architecture crudely taped and glued together, drips of Elmer's glue slowly drying clear. It is the color of construction paper, of markers, crayons, and pencils. It is not perfect, nor does it need to be. It resists total digitization but suggests many possible digitizations.

The possibility of an architecture folded around paper extends beyond aesthetics. Paper invites the scrawl, the sketch, the unintended crease. The printed word can be taken as sacred, but more often it is the site of highlights, cross-outs and additions, and doodles that emerge out of boredom or the inability for text to capture a thought. The blank notebook can absorb ruffled pages, smudges, smears, and tears. I don't point to these irregularities out of nostalgia or an absurd invocation of wabi-sabi. These erraticisms, rather, contain larger hints of an architecture that assumes the malleability and workable nature of paper. Cutting, folding, creasing, sketching, painting, imprinting, taping, and gluing all point to binary oppositions in contemporary American architecture:[1] value placed in on-site malleability, sustained personal relationships with the building trades, and aspirations for diverse design offices that start with optimism, in the unforeseen milieu of the successive generations who are now crafting with their hands in elementary school.

1 In the essay "A Note on Race and Architecture," Cornel West discusses binary oppositions as avenues forward in architectural criticism that move beyond the sentimentalized histories of the Western world. In *Keeping Faith: Philosophy and Race in America* (New York: Routledge, 1993), 45–54.

Afterlife

Anna Goga

Since its early development in the 1990s, cross-laminated timber has become a product of computer-controlled mass-production technology. The CLT blank manifested itself as a digital tool, an act of erasure, which symbolically condenses all existing architectural elements into one. This reductionism and conceptual denial of what came before speaks to our current moment. In the 2019 essay "Architecture in the Age of Hyperobjects," Peter Trummer explains that architectural elements have started to address world-scale problems. For instance, he notes that instead of simply framing a view, a window has become a climate-control tool with implications for global warming. Similarly, the CLT blank, bringing together the best qualities of wood and panels, has become a magic-pill universal module, an autonomous hyperobject that promises a solution for many problems the construction industry faces today.

A construction material captures the culture of the time it comes into being, but it also constructs its own ideology. Technological, political, and social contexts have always challenged and distorted the meaning of the materials we use. Once upon a time, the prefabricated concrete panel appeared as a product of technological progress and the political climate of its moment. Interestingly enough, the panel also absorbed everyday culture and became a symbol. Prefabricated concrete panels floating freely in space seemed to defy gravity. The CLT blank, a new species in the panel family, inherited and improved on this choreographic nature. Its lightness and assembly create a performance of synchronized machines, cranes, and workers, moving together in the same rhythm, building a hyperarchitecture. CLT has exceeded its function as a universal structural element and has started to develop a symbological afterlife penetrating contemporary lifestyle and ideology.

We are just starting to observe CLT's conceptual transition far beyond its initial purpose, as it transforms the way we build our reality. One could argue that the hypercustomization of contemporary culture triggered the appearance of the CLT blank. In turn, it is starting to become a modest symbol unfolding new meanings. Its full cultural manifestation is yet to come.

Massive Architecture

Peeraya Suphasidh

Classical architecture has always been associated with its massive architectural elements: the columns, entablature, and domes repeated throughout Western architectural history. Monumental stone buildings in public spaces manifested a civilization's technical advance and prosperity. Centuries after completion, many of these stone structures still stand.

The industrial revolution advanced manufacturing capacity at an unprecedented pace. Steel-frame construction allowed modern buildings to leap in height. The structural strength of steel is compressed into a much smaller volume than that of wood or stone, minimizing the ratio of space to structure and leading to a more flexible use of space. The aesthetics of the readymade, of repeatability and standardization, were widely and quickly adopted. The lightness of the industrial era supplanted the heaviness of classical monuments; solid stone gave way to frames and finishes, some mimicking the old, but never with quite the same massive quality.

Despite all its benefits, industrialization has now exhausted the resources of the earth. The United Nations Environment Program estimates that buildings and construction are responsible for 39 percent of energy-related carbon dioxide emissions annually.[1] Perhaps the contemporary climate crisis will shape how we manifest our future monuments.

Constructing one cubic meter of concrete releases 152 kilograms of carbon dioxide, while the same volume in wood stores approximately one ton. The material quality of wood, its massive volume, lends itself to what I perceive as the shared agenda of our time. The more massive we build with timber, the more CO_2 will be sequestered, and thus the more chance we have to sustain our livelihood. Redundancy in material as a means of CO_2 sequestration may become a way to signify prosperity for future civilizations.

1 Diana Budds, "How Do Buildings Contribute to Climate Change?," *Curbed*, September 19, 2019, https://archive.curbed.com/2019/9/19/20874234/buildings-carbon-emissions-climate-change.

The Power of CLT as Its Own Graphic

Ian Grohsgal

The 860–880 Lake Shore Drive apartments (1949–51) were the first of many towers in which Ludwig Mies van der Rohe used standardized steel I-beams as both structure and ornament. Though he wouldn't admit it, the I-beams placed between windows are a purely graphical presentation of Mies's preferred material. The steel's decorative and structural functions were kept separate—the structural steel does not serve a graphic purpose, and vice versa.

At the National Assembly Building in Dhaka, Bangladesh (1962–82), Louis Kahn used the structural qualities of concrete to support brick's ability to create voids in basic shapes (circles, squares, triangles). The structure was too large for the brick to support itself; concrete showcases brick's graphic potential.

Mies and Kahn separated graphics and structure because they had to. The basic units of steel and brick can be changed only through an additive process—it would be almost impossible for a single I-beam or brick to both support and decorate projects at such large scales. With the development of the CLT blank and CNC technologies, creating graphics out of a structural material is subtractive and can happen much more readily.

In marketing, *resonance* refers to the relationship that a consumer has with a product. A high level of resonance indicates a strong psychological bond. Oatly, a company that creates milk from oats, has experienced intense growth and high measures of resonance in recent years. Like CLT, oat milk resurrects a resource that has been around for centuries in a newly sustainable manner.

Oatly rose above the hype of other dairy alternatives through four facets of brand positioning: the company consistently highlights the health benefits of oat milk; it reduced the product's carbon footprint to a mere 25 percent of dairy milk's footprint; it placed Oatly in artisanal coffee shops, an environment where it could connect with coffee-loving and sustainability-minded consumers; and it used graphic design to create a perception of the company as honest and friendly.[1]

Like Oatly, CLT has the opportunity to generate resonance through its combination of sustainability and graphics. Leveraging its appeal as an efficient and green structure, CLT can simultaneously create a distinctive graphic presence that forges positive associations for present and future inhabitants, in turn increasing demand for the product.

CLT buildings are billboards for CLT. Building graphically with CLT will create a virtuous cycle, drawing in more developers, increasing CLT's availability, and improving the overall experience for consumers of architecture.

1 Elaine Weng, "How Oatly Became the Trendiest Plant Milk on the Market," Lab Brand, November 28, 2018, http://www.labbrand.com/brandsource/going-deeper-than-the-buzz-how-oatly-became-the-trendiest-plant-milk.

The New Stereotomic Standard

Alejandro Saldarriaga

A tectonic process puts elements together to build a whole. A stereotomic process involves the act of removal, of creating through voids. A common consensus is that steel and "traditional" wood construction are tectonic by nature, and that stone and concrete construction are stereotomic. I argue that the true value of cross-laminated timber lies in its stereotomic qualities, even though it is a prefabricated industrial module.

In the late nineteenth and early twentieth centuries, steel lent itself to an architectural style that highlighted the industrial qualities and assemblage of the material. In contrast, by the mid-twentieth century, reinforced concrete had prompted designers to pursue a variety of expressive possibilities, including seamless, self-supporting surfaces and volumes. Because of its flexibility, reinforced concrete is the material that is most used for construction globally.

We are living in a moment when collective synergy has led to the creation of a new architectural material. While CLT has been positioned as a way to alleviate climate change and revolutionize the construction industry, how this material will affect *design* is still unclear. Many architects have speculated on whether CLT will lead to an innovative architectural style, as steel did in the modernist era. The root of these speculations lies in the notion that CLT, as a prefabricated module, is categorically a tectonic material, and that the architecture it renders should clearly emphasize the assemblage of the modules. But what if this assumption is faulty?

Like concrete, CLT has already been proven to be a self-structural module that can create uniform surfaces. But it is still lacking in terms of equivalent varieties of formal expression. If CLT demonstrates its ability to enable new and multiple approaches to generating form, it also has the potential to revolutionize architecture by providing an alternative to reinforced concrete. It is essential for architects to question the modularity behind CLT and find new expressive possibilities for the panel, making it the new stereotomic standard and supplanting reinforced concrete worldwide.

CLT Subtractive Architecture

Benson Chien

A house is the eventual result of joining together thousands of 2-by-4 sticks, the typical Type V construction building block. Erecting thousands of steel beams eventually leaves us with a contemporary tower. Architectural construction has widely been an additive endeavor. CLT's fundamental building block is 9 feet by 50 feet, a significant increase in scale over the steel beam and 2-by-4. With a building block the scale of a wall, creating space becomes an exercise in subtraction, rather than addition.

Subtractive architecture is akin to a Renaissance sculptor finding a masterpiece within a block of marble. This rare and outdated approach to architecture starts with a mass and carves out spaces. Stepwells in India, dug out of the ground, date back to 600 CE. The Loess Plateau, in China, is home to cliff dwellings, where communities have subtracted their homes out of the cliffside. Contemporary architecture conceptually alludes to a type of subtraction by creating spaces that appear carved out. Steven Holl's Hunters Point Library in Queens, New York, might look like a solid mass with swaths cut out, but the reality of its construction is still additive.

CLT offers an opportunity for subtraction ingrained in the construction process. The assemblage of blanks creates a mass resembling the outline of the building—the individual unit is no longer legible. The blanks act structurally and spatially, stacked, rotated, sloped, and intersected to create the structural backbone from which the architect freely subtracts, even across blanks. As a rule of thumb, as long as no more than 40 percent of the CLT is subtracted, the structure should still be viable.

The subtraction complexifies as CLT pieces layer together. Beyond the stock three-ply, five-ply, and seven-ply sheets, blanks can laminate to each other. Different subtractions into the blanks layered onto one another create a spatial composition of overlapping shapes. The thickness of CLT requires architects to view the CLT less as two-dimensional sheet and more as poché.

The earnestness of CLT's subtractive architecture demands that we equally consider what has been subtracted. If we carve out 40 percent of each blank, we must repurpose it appropriately. Conceptually, by subtracting and adding simultaneously, it would be possible to build a zero-waste building. Otherwise, the CLT negative can quickly transform into furniture, wood chips, even art.

Awkward Nesting

Aryan Khalighy

In 2010, Andrew Zago coined a new term for an emerging vein of architectural aesthetics: the awkward, which for him lies between "neo-traditional authenticity" and "easy-expertise." The awkward acknowledges the limits of control. Instead, it produces uncertain and unpredictable results by perverting fine-tuned skills to define new and unsettling territories of aesthetics and social relations. "The awkward stands in peculiar relation to the correct," he explains.[1]

There is consensus in the critique of digital architecture as a self-justified "style" devoid of cultural sensitivity. However, it is difficult to disregard the possibilities that digital technology has made available to design, and impossible to undo its effects. As an alternative to the positivism of early parametric architecture, where computational tools were directed toward efficiencies based on objective reality, both architecture and art practice have begun to employ digital tools to construct new realities based on creative imagination. There is no "correct" way of using digital tools, and there are unlimited territories that technology enables us to explore.

The Spanish architect Antonio Gaudí, who has been called an early protagonist of parametric design,[2] used hanging chain models to optimize arch shapes. More than a search for efficiencies, though, Gaudí's experiments were exceptional in the way an analog technique allowed him to explore complex novel forms and spatial consequences. He was simulating a dynamic process of form-making, where instead of a final fixed shape there are unlimited possibilities and constant flux.

A physics engine is a computer software that mimics physical reality by providing approximate simulations. In a physics engine, real-world parameters—gravity, solid/fluid dynamics, and so on—can be enabled, disabled, enhanced, or diminished. The possibility of creating fake physics echoes what Jean Baudrillard elaborated as his third order of simulacra, where the representation of the real precedes the real itself and we lose the ability to distinguish between nature and artifice.

Architecture, too, has employed this computational tool to generate new forms. Instead of using animation to present the fixed and finished state of a work, however, the dynamic process of form-making could inspire the design of a building. Given its particular combination of rigidness and manipulability, mass timber is an appropriate material to advance this experimentation.

A computational tool might model a number of empty boxes falling and stacking under a simulated gravity, producing an irregular tower as a pile of nested forms. Rather than departing from a traditional type or indexing a historical event, here the design process starts with the imagination of a pseudo-physical operation and unconventional construction sequences. As with Gaudí's hanging chain tests, one can read these operations as productive of an image of architecture in constant flux.

Antoine Picon has described the status of architecture today as unstable: "The world of information is not the world of things. . . . Form is not about permanence, but about the manifestation of action."[3] The instability that Picon describes creates an unpredictability appropriate to our time. This is a promise made by an architecture that refrains from claiming a position of correctness. On the contrary, it is an attempt to sponsor multiple readings and spontaneous perceptions through dynamic imagery, where things are perceived and envisioned in multiple alternative possible scenarios.

1 Andrew Zago, "AWKWARD POSITION," *Perspecta*, no. 42 (2010): 205–18.

2 See, for example, Rafael Gómez-Moriana, "Gaudi's Hanging Chain Models: Parametric Design Avant La Lettre?," August 16, 2012, *Criticalista* (blog), https://criticalista.com/2012/08/16/gaudis-hanging-chain-models-parametric-design-avant-la-lettre/.

3 Antoine Picon, "Matter and Language in the Digital Age" (lecture, Southern California Institute of Architecture, Los Angeles, March 9, 2016).

What If? A Reframing of the Corner Problem

Calvin Boyd

The search for novel solutions to the wicked and ever-changing problem of architecture is an endeavor as old as the primitive hut. These solutions, no matter how temporary, are what drive the discipline and profession forward. For instance, the application of steel allowed architects to build taller, more efficiently, and for less money, a material-science and engineering feat that permanently changed the field. Not all solutions that induce progress are as obvious and tangible. Many are arguably more subtle, like John Hejduk's interrogation of the diamond plan—the architectural and representational consequences of rotating a square plan 45 degrees. Despite this diversity, most, if not all, meaningful contributions to architecture have been the result of a clear and precise framing of the issue at hand.

One such recurring issue is the "corner problem." The problem is both tectonic and geometric, in that it that involves material intersections as well as part-to-whole relationships. A well-known example of a resolution to the corner problem can be found in the interior courtyard of Bramante's Santa Maria Della Pace, where every corner is inhabited by two superimposed columns. Bramante's choice to fuse the columns, rather than double them, emphasized his preference for a cohesive whole over distinct parts. These preferences, however major or trivial, lead architects to remarkably different solutions. Still, even in architecture, there comes a time when asking the same question the same dozen or so ways eventually leads to tired answers. As for the corner problem today, at the root of almost all proffered solutions is a desire to make the corner disappear: to round it seamlessly, intuitively, without fanfare. The radical nature of the problem and previous solutions has been lost.

Thus, in the interest of propelling architecture forward, it is time to reframe the age-old corner problem, and what better way to do so than with a freshly minted material, CLT. CLT blanks are inherently prefabricated but also capable of significant customization via sawing and routing. CLT is neither massive nor paper-thin. It is not entirely stereotomic, nor wholly tectonic. CLT is a material that exists in the in-betweens, and this allows ample room to reconsider what we architects so often take for granted. CLT's ability to be three-dimensionally notched and slotted has more consequences than simply how the material joins together in plan. It also prompts us to ask, What is at stake when a traditionally planar problem becomes sectional?

The arrival of CLT has brought along with it substantial economic and environmental effects. But equally as interesting are the quirky and sly ways the material is helping architects resharpen their pencils, in a design sense. After all, is not the joy of architecture its capacity to continually contend with the question "what if?"

Deadpan CLT

Elif Erez

The CLT blank is funny. It is bulky and a bit awkward, almost too fat to be used as a sheet, too slim to be monolithic. As such, it lends itself almost too easily to a kind of absurdist architectural humor that plays on an ambiguity of scale. The result is comedic by virtue of this ambiguity, a kind of deadpan—a deliberately "expressionless, impassive" front that heightens a punchline[1]—that's fitting for something called the "blank."

The CLT blank is adept at pretending to be something it is absolutely not at the right scale to be with a comedic straightforwardness. Take shiplap, an ordinary residential rainscreen siding material. Rendered in CLT, shiplap becomes absurdly large, transforming from cladding to a structural member through its lapped joinery. One might call this re-scaling an act of "indifference," a term Michael Meredith uses to describe the disciplinary position of a group of young American architects, along with a sensibility shared by twentieth-century artists such as John Cage, Robert Rauschenberg, and Jasper Johns.[2] Meredith places indifference as a disciplinary aesthetic in opposition to one that "expresses problem-solving," which loudly proclaims to be innovative. Indifference "performs" a deliberate play with the banal, the generic, the ambiguous, the cheap and commonplace.[3] The key word here is *performs*. Just as the self-critical American artists of the fifties turned to the calculated indifference of readymades, collection, appropriation, and irony to push back against existing value systems, especially those of American corporate production, "indifferent" architecture can hardly be presumed to lack meaning or political engagement. The deadpan just emphasizes the punchline.

In the video work *Deadpan* (1997), the artist and filmmaker Steve McQueen stands stoically while the facade of the building behind him peels cleanly off, narrowly avoiding crushing him thanks to the lucky placement of a window opening. The work is an appropriation of a scene in Buster Keaton's *Steamboat Bill, Jr.* (1928). In both scenes, the deadpan effect makes the message even more powerful—amplifying the situational irony in Keaton's version, and doubling down on that irony to comment on the absence of Black bodies and Black identity in art in McQueen's, a feeling of oppression that does not need words to be communicated. The CLT blank can aspire to the sort of deadpan practiced by McQueen: to borrow and replicate existing techniques and forms with a straight face, all the while commenting on the very value systems and cultural norms that produced those conventional forms and techniques.

The CLT blank is therapy for melodramatic expressionists. Its therapeutic effect resides in the act of stepping back, in withholding commentary or proclamations, to allow the medium itself to speak. And the blank is a master of no-comment commentary.

1 Oxford English Dictionary online, s.v. "dead-pan," December 2020, accessed January 21, 2021.

2 Michael Meredith, "Indifference, Again," *Log*, no. 39 (Winter 2017): 75–79. His list of architects includes Jennifer Bonner / MALL; he cites the critic Moira Roth's use of the term in relation to these artists in a 1977 essay in *Artforum*.

3 Meredith, 75.

Material Abstraction™

Edgar Rodriguez

It is a regular day at a timber production facility in Bygdsiljum, Sweden. As our guide describes the wonders of Swedish forestry, a conveyor belt moves an endless line of spruce and pine logs in front of us. The computer screens in the room where we stand show timber sawing–optimization software working at full speed. We stare, mindlessly, as a new 3D model pops on the screens every two seconds. The people overseeing the operation explain that the software is assigning a unique saw pattern to each piece of wood. The guides usher us out of the control room; we enter the warehouse where the logs are being sawn.

Today, I understand this manufacturing progression in two somewhat contradictory ways. First, and most evidently, it is the extraction of value from a natural resource. (The software company claims it enables users to "get the maximum value from every log."[1]) But it is also a materialization of sequential stages of conceptual abstraction. To break this down:

1. Initially, wood logs possess inestimable physical and geometrical complexity. These particular material properties faithfully represent the reality of wood.

2. The logs are sawn into regular units, and consequently, some of their original material features are modified. Through an operation of geometrical correction, wood is reconceptualized as a mechanically predictable and dimensionally standard material—a first degree of abstraction.

3. With the calculated binding of lumber pieces together, the properties of wood become programmable. CLT's synthetic mechanical versatility is one of its better-known characteristics. The idealization of the material properties of wood represents a second degree of abstraction.

4. The virtual surfaces used in simulations of mass-timber buildings are a third degree of abstraction. These nonspatial entities are fundamentally a mathematical model of wood. Designers and engineers work with presentations of these data entities on computers to design and program the properties of mass timber.[2]

In this sense, engineered timber is ontologically post-material; it is an object with an entirely codified physicality that is more like a mathematical vector and less like a tree. This interpretation of mass timber reveals that its resemblance to the original material is purely visual, making its image (of wood) its only fundamental material property. Conceptually speaking, we could argue that this group of material technologies is a kind of full-scale architectural representational medium. As designers, we should appreciate the vagueness of this medium as an opportunity to contribute to the formation of a more horizontal cultural subjectivity.

To return to Sweden, we eventually walked the entirety of the production line. It was interesting to see how the poly-surfaces that we modeled in studio were a representation of a process, rather than of an object. The conveyor belt keeps moving, always forward.

1 MillExpert Log Optimizer, USNR, accessed December 6, 2020, https://m.usnr.com/en/product/logopt.

2 On the distinction between the concepts of representation and presentation in relation to contemporary architectural media, see John May, *Signal. Image. Architecture.* (New York: Columbia Books on Architecture and the City, 2019).

JENNIFER BOLANDE is an artist working primarily in photography and sculpture who has exhibited widely in the US and abroad since the late seventies. Her works are in the collections of the Centre Pompidou, Moderna Museet, MAMCO Genève, San Francisco Museum of Modern Art, Museum of Contemporary Art in Los Angeles, and Los Angeles County Museum of Art. She is professor of New Genres in the Department of Art at the University of California, Los Angeles.

JENNIFER BONNER is director of MALL and associate professor of architecture at the Harvard Graduate School of Design. She is the author of *A Guide to the Dirty South—Atlanta* and guest editor of a special issue of *ART PAPERS* on Los Angeles. Her design work, including Haus Gables, a single-family residence in Atlanta constructed of eighty-seven CLT panels, has been widely published and exhibited.

NELSON BYUN is the founder of -NESS Projects, an architectural design studio based in Cambridge, Massachusetts. He served as teaching associate in architecture at the Harvard Graduate School of Design from 2018 to 2020. He holds a Master of Architecture with distinction from Harvard, where he received the Department of Architecture Faculty Design Award and Kevin V. Kieran Prize, and a Bachelor of Architecture from Syracuse University.

VICTORIA CAMBLIN is a writer, editor, art historian, and curator of public programming. She is executive editor of 032c, a Berlin-based magazine, think tank, media brand, and fashion label. From 2013 to 2018, she was editor and artistic director of *ART PAPERS*. Her writing has appeared in *Artforum*, *Art in America*, British *GQ*, and *Texte zur Kunst*, in addition to a number of exhibition catalogs and artists' books, and she has organized and contributed to events and exhibitions in Europe, the Middle East, and the Southeast United States.

SEAN CANTY is the founder of Studio Sean Canty, a design practice that shapes environments by conjoining discrete geometries, materials, and architectural types. Inspired by the ordinary, the intimate, and the playful, the studio's work foregrounds collectivity in domestic and institutional spaces. Canty is assistant professor of architecture at the Harvard Graduate School of Design and founder of Office III (OIII), an experimental architectural collective.

COURTNEY COFFMAN is manager of lectures and publications at Princeton University's School of Architecture. She has served as a content and copy editor for various architectural publications. Her own writing explores the visual culture of contemporary architecture alongside alternative histories and popular taste.

LAUREN HALSEY is rethinking the possibilities of art, architecture, and community engagement. Inspired by Afrofuturism and funk, as well as the signs and symbols that populate her local environments, she produces both standalone artworks and site-specific projects, particularly in the South Central neighborhood of Los Angeles. Halsey founded Summaeverythang Community Center in 2020, and is currently in the process of developing a major public monument for construction in South Central, where her family has lived and worked for generations. She is a recipient of the Hammer Museum's Mohn Award and a Painter and Sculptors Grant from the Joan Mitchell Foundation in New York.

SAM JACOB is principal of Sam Jacob Studio, a London-based practice whose work spans scales and disciplines from urban design through architecture, design, art, and curatorial projects. He is clinical professor at the University of Illinois at Chicago School of Architecture and a columnist for *Art Review*. Previously, he was a founding director of FAT Architecture.

Professor HANIF KARA is cofounder and Design Director of AKT II, a design-led structural and civil engineering firm based in London, and professor in practice of architectural technology at the Harvard Graduate School of Design. Kara has gained international standing in the field of the built environment through practice, pioneering research, and education in interdisciplinary design.

JAYNE KELLEY is an editor and writer based in Chicago. She is visiting assistant professor at the University of Illinois at Chicago School of Architecture, where she manages events and publications, and was previously managing editor in the publications division at the Canadian Centre for Architecture. She is coeditor of *The Museum Is Not Enough* (Sternberg/CCA, 2019) and coauthor of *The Western Town* (Hatje Cantz, 2013).

CHRISTOPHER C. M. LEE is cofounder and principal of Serie Architects. He is the Arthur Rotch Design Critic in Architecture at the Harvard Graduate School of Design and a design advocate of the Mayor of London. He graduated with honors from the Architectural Association and received his PhD in architecture and urbanism from the Berlage Institute and Delft University of Technology.

ERIKA NAGINSKI is Robert P. Hubbard Professor of Architectural History and chair of the PhD program in architecture, landscape architecture, and urban planning at the Harvard Graduate School of Design. A Guggenheim Fellow, she has published essays and books on seventeenth- and eighteenth-century architectural practices, early modern aesthetics, the politics of public space, and the critical traditions of the design disciplines.

ERIN PUTALIK is assistant professor of architecture and architectural history at the University of Virginia School of Architecture. She recently completed her doctorate at the University of Pennsylvania, with a dissertation that examined the ways in which the conservation and cultivation of forests and the innovation of new wood-based building materials catalyzed a range of experimental building practices in the early twentieth century.

NADER TEHRANI is founding principal of NADAAA, a practice dedicated to the advancement of design innovation, interdisciplinary collaboration, and an intensive dialogue with the construction industry. He is also dean of the Irwin S. Chanin School of Architecture at The Cooper Union. For his contributions to architecture as an art, Tehrani received the 2020 Arnold W. Brunner Memorial Prize from the American Academy of Arts and Letters.

YASMIN VOBIS is assistant professor of architecture at the Harvard Graduate School of Design and cofounder of Ultramoderne, an architecture office based in Providence, Rhode Island. The office, which she leads with Aaron Forrest, is focused on the intersection of the discipline and the everyday. Ultramoderne is committed to creating architecture and public spaces that are at once modern, playful, and generous.

Image Credits

CLT project visualizations on beige pages by Anna Goga and Edgar Rodriguez.

23 Public domain. Image Bibliothèque nationale de France
29 Diagram by Jennifer Bonner, Hanif Kara, and Edgar Rodriguez
54 Public domain
55 Image courtesy of APA – The Engineered Wood Association
56 Public domain
57 Fair use
58 Image courtesy of USDA Forest Service, Forest Products Laboratory
60–61 Eleanor Raymond Collection. Frances Loeb Library, Graduate School of Design, Harvard University
62 William W. Wurster/Wurster, Bernardi & Emmons Collection, 1922–1974 (Collection Number 1976-2). Environmental Design Archives, UC Berkeley (Box 218, Folder 78)
63 Reproduced from *Arts & Architecture*, July 1945, with permission. © Travers Family Trust
66 Courtesy of Waugh Thistleton Architects
67 (left) © F.L.C. / ADAGP, Paris / Artists Rights Society (ARS), New York 2021; (right) Photo by Wikimedia Commons user 663highland, 2010. CC BY 2.5, https://creativecommons.org/licenses/by/2.5/deed.en
69 (top left) Graphite and color pencil on tracing paper, 23 3/4 × 15 in. Jeffrey P. Klein Purchase Fund, Barbara Pine Purchase Fund, and Frederieke Taylor Purchase Fund. Museum of Modern Art. © 2021 Frank Lloyd Wright Foundation. All rights reserved. Licensed by Artist Rights Society. Digital image © The Museum of Modern Art/Licensed by SCALA / Art Resource, NY; (top right) Plans originally printed in Wainwright Real Estate Company, *The Wainwright Building* (ca. 1891). Public domain; (bottom) Courtesy of William Zbaren
70 (left) Chicago History Museum, ICHi-001066; (right) Mies van der Rohe Archive Fund. Museum of Modern Art. © 2021 Artists Rights Society (ARS), New York / VG Bild-Kunst, Bonn. Digital image © The Museum of Modern Art/Licensed by SCALA / Art Resource, NY
72 Photos by Tim Soar. Courtesy of GROUPWORK / Amin Taha
74 (top) © LAN; (bottom) Courtesy of C.F. Møller Architects and Dinell Johansson
75 Courtesy of Serie Architects
78 (top left) © State Tretyakov Gallery, Moscow; (top right) Collection Stedelijk Museum Amsterdam; (bottom) Photo by Akiharu Ichikawa / Hypebeast
80 (left) Album released by Def Jam. Fair use; (right) Courtesy of Walker Art Center
81 HD video, single screen in architectural environment, 15:52. CC 4.0 Hito Steyerl. Image courtesy of the artist, Andrew Kreps Gallery, New York, and Esther Schipper, Berlin
83 (top left) Archival pigment print. © Jose Dávila. Courtesy of the artist and Sean Kelly, New York; (top right) Color photographs with acrylic paint, sheet 19 1/8 × 18 3/4 in, image 18 × 18 in. © John Baldessari 1996/2009. Courtesy of Estate of John Baldessari © 2021; (bottom) Photo by Timothy Hursley. Courtesy of Jennifer Bonner / MALL
84 (left) Courtesy of Jennifer Bonner; (right) Two black-and-white photographs with vinyl paint (one shown), overall dimensions 76 × 36 in. © John Baldessari 1988. Courtesy of Estate of John Baldessari © 2021
101 Public domain
103 (top left) Photo by Wikimedia Commons user MatthiasKabel, 2006. CC BY-SA 3.0, https://creativecommons.org/licenses/by-sa/3.0/deed.en; (top right) Photo by Wordpress user Tokyobling, https://tokyobling.wordpress.com/2015/02/17/goryo-shrine-and-kamakura-gongoro-kagemasa/; (bottom left) Photo by Chuck Choi. Courtesy of Maryann Thompson and Chuck Choi; (bottom right) Photo by Roland Halbe. Courtesy of Ensamble Studio and Roland Halbe
104 Photo by Wikimedia Commons user seier+seier, 2005. CC BY 2.0, https://creativecommons.org/licenses/by/2.0/deed.en
105 Photo of Voromuro by John Horner. All images courtesy of Nader Tehrani / NADAAA
106–7 Courtesy of Nader Tehrani / NADAAA
108 Diagram by NADAAA
110 (left) Public domain; (right) Photo by Wikimedia Commons user Epicjeff, 2013. CC BY-SA 3.0, https://creativecommons.org/licenses/by-sa/3.0/deed.en
111 (left) © Jens Weber and Orla Conolly; (right) Photo by Simon Broccard, 2019. CC BY-SA 4.0, https://creativecommons.org/licenses/by-sa/4.0/deed.en
112 Courtesy of Nader Tehrani / NADAAA. Atrium photo by Peter Bennetts
114 (left) Ink on paper, 10 × 11 in. The Riklis Collection of McCrory Corporation. Museum of Modern Art. © Agnes Martin Foundation, New York / Artists Rights Society (ARS), New York. Digital image © The Museum of Modern Art/Licensed by SCALA / Art Resource, NY; (center) Oil on linen, 9 ft × 60 in. Fractional and promised gift of Kathy and Richard S. Fuld, Jr. © 2021 Brice Marden / Artists Rights Society (ARS), New York. Digital image © The Museum of Modern Art/Licensed by SCALA / Art Resource, NY; (right) Courtesy of Nader Tehrani / NADAAA
115–18 Courtesy of Nader Tehrani / NADAAA. Banq photo by John Horner
125–28 Photos by Naho Kubota. Courtesy of Ultramoderne
146–50 Courtesy of Sam Jacob / Sam Jacob Studio
155 © Hélène ADANT / GAMMA RAPHO
158–62 Photos by Brian Forrest. Courtesy of Hammer Museum, Los Angeles, and David Kordansky Gallery, Los Angeles
163 Courtesy of the artist and David Kordansky Gallery, Los Angeles
167–72 Courtesy of Jennifer Bolande
182 (left) Mavis Pusey Archive; (right) Mavis Pusey / The Studio Museum in Harlem
183 Courtesy of Jennifer Bonner / MALL
184 (left) Courtesy of Collection Stedelijk Museum Amsterdam. © 2021 Richard Serra / Artists Rights Society (ARS), New York; (right) Foto by Christian Baur / Fotoarchiv Kunsthalle Basel. Courtesy of Kunsthalle Basel, 31.1. – 1.5.1988. © 2021 Richard Serra / Artists Rights Society (ARS), New York
185 (top) Photo © Géraldine Aresteanu; (bottom) Courtesy of Jennifer Bonner / MALL
187 (top) Photo by Ricardo Scofidio. Courtesy of Diller Scofidio + Renfro; (bottom) Courtesy of Jennifer Bonner / MALL
189 Courtesy of RIBA Collections
192 (left) Ink and collage on paper. 15 1/2 × 21 in. The Menil Collection, Houston, Anonymous gift in honor of James A. Elkins, Jr. © Ellsworth Kelly Foundation. Courtesy of Matthew Marks Gallery. Photo by Paul Hester; (right) Oil on paper, 15 1/2 × 21 in. The Menil Collection, Houston, Anonymous gift in honor of James A. Elkins, Jr. © Ellsworth Kelly Foundation. Courtesy of Matthew Marks Gallery. Photo by Paul Hester
194 Photo by Bruno Lopes. Courtesy of Céline Condorelli
195 Oil on canvas, 178 × 123 cm. © 2021 Artists Rights Society (ARS), New York / SIAE, Rome. Photo by Adam Rzepka. Photo © CNAC/MNAM, Dist. RMN-Grand Palais / Art Resource, NY
197–99 Courtesy of Studio Sean Canty
214 Photos by Hufton+Crow. Courtesy of Hanif Kara / AKT II
217 Photos by Cristobal Palma. Courtesy of Hanif Kara / AKT II
219 Courtesy of dRMM
220 Diagram by Hanif Kara
222–23 Images courtesy of Hanif Kara / AKT II

Acknowledgments

Hunkered down in our respective homes, Hanif in London and Jennifer in Portland, we conceived and completed this project during the COVID pandemic. We could not have realized the book without the generosity and support of our colleagues, which we will always cherish.

First, we would like to express our sincerest gratitude to each contributor. Their essays served as a constant source of inspiration and encouragement to us as coeditors. We are extremely appreciative of the time and care each author brought both to countless calls with us and to shaping a speculative discourse around CLT. With deepest admiration, we thank Nelson Byun, Victoria Camblin, Sean Canty, Courtney Coffman, Sam Jacob, Chris Lee, Erika Naginski, Erin Putalik, Nader Tehrani, and Yasmin Vobis.

Much of the motivation for this book originated in our studio Mass Timber and the Scandinavian Effect, co-taught at the Harvard Graduate School of Design in the spring of 2020. We are indebted to our fourteen students, who developed a fascinating range of projects and ideas—despite having to switch to an online format midway through the semester. After the studio ended, Anna Goga and Edgar Rodriguez spent the summer creating the visualizations found in the book, collectivizing the individual studio projects into precise, cohesive architectural speculations. Anna and Edgar's intellectual contribution was rigorous and infectious.

The studio would not have been feasible without the support of Dean Sarah Whiting, Chair Mark Lee, Professor Mohsen Mostafavi, and the Department of Architecture, for which we are grateful. The Sven Tyréns Trust was kind enough to sponsor our visit to Sweden and the Martinsons factory in Skellefteå. We are thankful to Lina Broström, Ricardo Candel, Karl Graah-Hagelbäck, Arabiya Issa, Marie Kauma, Ove Nilsson, Birgitta Olofsson, and Tina Wik for their support during the studio research trip.

We would like to thank Neil Donnelly and Siiri Tännler of Neil Donnelly Studio for their artful graphic design. It was a joy to watch them inventively embody and expand on our conceptual ambitions, enriching the book with another layer of meaning.

We would also like to acknowledge the careful reading of each text by our associate editor, Jayne Kelley, who went above and beyond to draw out and sharpen the book's overlapping themes. Additionally, a warm thank you to Elif Erez for securing many of the image rights and illustrations found throughout the book.

Finally, we would especially like to thank both of our families for their love, patience, and support throughout the making of the book: Shamsah, Imaan, Raabia, Volkan, and Rae.

Right: Skeleftea, Northern Sweden

Project Index